THE OTHER SIDE
OF REBELLION

THE OTHER SIDE OF REBELLION

*The Remarkable Story of
Charles Bremner and his Furs*

Margaret R. Stobie

NeWest Press

First edition

Canadian Cataloguing in Publication Data

Stobie, Margaret R.

The Other Side of Rebellion

ISBN 0-920897-10-X (bound). — ISBN 0-920897-08-8 (pbk.)

1. Bremner, Charles. 2. Fur traders - Saskatchewan - Biography. 3. Riel
Rebellion, 1885 - Biography. I. Title.
FC3217.1.B73S75 1986   971.05'4'0924   F1060.9.B73S75 1986
F1078.E8 1986

59,054

Credits

Cover Design: S.Colberg
Typesetting: K. Wilson
Printing and binding: Hignell Printers Ltd., Winnipeg

Financial Assistance

Alberta Culture
The Alberta Foundation for the Literary Arts
The Canada Council

NeWest Publishers Ltd.
Suite 204, 8631 - 109 Street
Edmonton, Alberta
Canada   T6G 1E8

To Bill

Contents

Acknowledgements

It gives me great pleasure to acknowledge the kindness of Mr. Charles Denney of Heritage House, Edmonton, who sent me a copy of the Bremner family chart, and also one of the lengthy obituary of Charles Bremner (apparently written by one of his daughters) that appeared in the *Saskatchewan Herald*, May 24, 1919.

I wish to record a valuable conversation with the late Mr. Joseph Sayer, then in his eighties—son of Henry Sayer, one of the three original Bresaylor settlers—when I visited him in his cottage-museum there, where he was surrounded by facts and artifacts of Bresaylor history. I had conversations also with Mr. Edgar Caplette of Battleford, grandson of Louis Caplette and Ellen Bremner Caplette, and with Mr. Roy McIntyre of California, grandson of Charles Bremner, who called on me while he was visiting in Winnipeg.

I am happy to acknowledge the customary promptness and courtesy of the Saskatchewan Archives in Regina, who sent me several important items: photocopies from the House of Commons *Debates and Sessional Papers of the Auditor-General's report for 1899-1900, pertaining to the compensation paid Bremner for his furs*; the obituary of P.G. Laurie from the Saskatchewan *Herald*, May 11, 1903; and also an address by his son, Major Richard Laurie, to the Battleford Board of Trade, Feb. 28, 1933, about his father's early days, which included his experience with Riel in 1870 in the Red River Settlement. It appeared in the North Battleford *News*, March 9, 1933.

I am also grateful to Professor Gerald Friesen of the History Department, University of Manitoba, author of *The Canadian Prairies, A History*, for offering to read my manuscript and for making valuable suggestions about it.

Then there is the wonderful system of inter-library loans, with its obliging librarians. I am particularly indebted to the librarians in charge of such loans in the Manitoba Legislative Library, the Winnipeg Centennial Library, and the Elizabeth Dafoe Library of the University of Manitoba.

Preface

The highway sign marks only a grey ghost town; but not even a town, just a huddle of buildings by the side of the road. Two witnesses to old pride rise above them: the wooden church, beside the railroad tracks, the weathered grain elevator.

A mile or so to the south, names on the headstones in the little cemetery record its origins—Spence, Inkster, Seller, Bremner, Sayer, Taylor—one of the outposts of the Red River Settlement hundreds of miles to the south and east. Beyond the cemetery, rolling, well-treed hills lead to the Battle River, and across the river is Poundmaker's reserve. Cut Knife Hill is not far off. Like many other ghostly places, Bresaylor had its moment of high drama, for this is land that people fought over, and Bresaylor was caught in the conflict.

Its story is one of ordinary people, who did not create great events, but who were swept up in them, buffeted by them, who survived them and fashioned their lives again. In its largest pattern, it is the story of settlers of the West. Their records are to be found in early newspapers, in court documents, in reports of parliamentary committees, in *Hansard's* verbatim pleas of M.P.'s for their constituents, in journals, and in diaries. They are the fabric of our social history.

In the particular setting of the North Saskatchewan Valley a hundred years ago, the story is of what happened to the sprinkling of settlers around Battleford and to the west, who found themselves in the midst of the uprising of the Indians in a hapless attempt to reclaim their homelands. Especially it is the story of Charles Bremner, settler, farmer, furtrader, who came to build, and who was nearly destroyed by the rebellion. Taken captive with his family and neighbors by Poundmaker's men, his home and herds demolished by the Indians, labelled a rebel and thrown in jail, his furs purloined by the army, he was left destitute. In a fifteen-year struggle for redress of wrongs, his story moved to Ottawa, where his affairs were taken out of his hands and made a political gambit, a subject of debate between the ailing Macdonald and the emerging Laurier, and of the inquiries of a Select Committee of Parliament. Thereafter, his affair became a copy-book example of "Justice delayed is justice denied."

Yet Bremner's story is more special than that, for in an odd way, he was a pivotal figure. He was involved in the triumph and fall of leaders on both sides, both the Cree chief, Poundmaker, and the commander of the Canadian militia, General Middleton. The story also has an air of inevitable progression about it. If Bremner had not been made captive, he would not have been labelled a rebel; if he had not been labelled a rebel, he would not have been thrown in jail; if he had not been thrown in jail, his furs would not have been stored with the Mounted Police; if his furs had not been so stored, General Middleton would not have confiscated them; if Middleton had not confiscated the furs, there would have been no Select Committee; if there had been no Select Committee, Middleton would not have left the army in disgrace.

The story is not the cliché of the arrogant Englishman diddling the innocent colonial. It is something more complex and much more interesting than that. It is evidence that someone quite unknown and far-off could yet command the attention of the country's government, however muddled, even self-serving, that attention might be. The Bremner story is part of the larger epic of the fledgling nation reaching out to comprehend its own immensity and probing within to discover its substance in people and in such high themes as justice and rights and loyalty.

Part One

THE CHANGING LAND

Chapter One

Seeking

The faint beginnings appeared in the fall of 1881, when the *Saskatchewan Herald* of Battleford noted that "Men from Headingley, Manitoba, have been looking over the district with a view to possibly settling here." Some weeks later, Frank Oliver picked up the note for the Edmonton *Bulletin* and used it as the nub of an editorial on squatters' rights. Settlers were welcome and precious creatures, each new one giving reason to urge the government once more to survey the land so that those who tilled it could get title to their labors.

Along the great length of the North Saskatchewan, there were three centers of population. At the western end was Edmonton, a village of about three hundred residents, built around the old Hudson's Bay Company's fort; north of it, another village of similar size, the Roman Catholic mission of St. Albert with bishop and cathedral; and a few miles east, the Mounted Police post at Fort Saskatchewan—the three communities totalling a population of something over 700 people. Two hundred and fifty miles down river was Battleford, the capital of the North-West Territories, with the government offices and the police headquarters on either bank of the Battle River, and between them the village on the river flats, together making up a population, according to the 1881 census, of 852. A couple of hundred miles still further east was Prince Albert. Begun as a Presbyterian mission in the late sixties by people from the Red River Settlement, it was now the largest centre in the Territories, with a population of about 1500. Otherwise, in the 500 miles from St. Albert to Prince Albert, a handful of missions and Company outposts made pinpricks in the wilderness.

Sixty or seventy miles from Prince Albert, however, on the South Saskatchewan, was a little group of embryo settlements of possibly two hundred people each—St. Laurent, Duck Lake, Batoche, the last two named after local landholders—of French half-breeds from the Red River, disappointed followers of Riel who had come north after the failure of the insurrection of 1870. Only twenty miles west of them, on the great bend of the north branch of the river, was Fort Carlton, the Company's headquarters for the Saskatchewan district,[1] and a stopping place on the trade route. The inhabitants of these four tiny places, because of their proximity to Prince Albert, were among the first in the whole vast area of the Territories to have voting rights.

There were stirrings in the Territories in 1881. In the spring the first election had been held. True, it was of only one member to the otherwise appointed Council, for the eastern part of the Saskatchewan district was the only region to fulfill the requirements of one thousand non-Indian adults in a one-thousand-square-mile area. Prince Albert, Fort Carlton, Duck Lake, St. Laurent, and Batoche were proclaimed the electoral district of Lorne, named after the Governor General, and they elected as their Council member Chief Factor Clarke of the Hudson's Bay Company's post at Fort Carlton. He won out over a merchant of Prince Albert.

Following the election, in August and September of 1881 the Governor General, Lord Lorne, the Queen's son-in-law, toured the Territories by horseback and buggy. It was a visit that created great excitement among the settlers, who plied him with petitions about land and wood and hay rights, but it was of much greater moment to the twenty thousand Indians, for here was a member of the very family of the Queen, with whom they had made their treaty. It was a reassuring token of her regard and concern for them. Poundmaker, who had recently been created a Cree chief,[2] had the honor of being Lord Lorne's guide from Battleford to the Blackfoot Crossing on the Bow River. A third group excited by the Governor General's exploration was that of prospective settlers. It emboldened them, as it was no doubt intended to do, to venture forth into the vast, empty prairie. If he could do it, so could they.

But the greatest impetus to development and settlement in 1881 was the resumption of the building of the Canadian Pacific, the trans-Canada railway. By October, it was operating as far as Brandon, over 130 miles west of Winnipeg. As a result, a real estate boom had begun which increased to a frenzy with the arrival in Winnipeg of William Van Horne at the end of the year to take charge of operations. It even sparked a bizarre episode of land-jumping in Edmonton, 900 miles away, and Frank Oliver became yet more vehement in urging the need for surveys and protective rights for squatters.

In the midst of the land boom, a group of well-to-do farmers of Headingley near Winnipeg—the Bremners, the Sayers, and the Taylors—decided to take advantage of the high market prices to sell their farms and explore the possibilities of resettling in the Saskatchewan country. Land there was plentiful, to be had almost for the asking, with unbounded space for the young people to branch out on their own—Charles Bremner's son Andrew, the eldest of the family, was twenty and needing his own land—and it offered an enticing combination of farm land, range land, and fur trading bush country. Furthermore, from all accounts, the Red River people who had gone north were doing well.

The Headingley group were of the Scotch-Indian strain of the Red River Settlement, whose forefathers had come out from the Scottish Highlands and from the Orkneys to serve with the Hudson's Bay Company, who had married Indian women, and who, following years of service, had been given river land by the Company. For them the word "settlers" had a special meaning. As one of the Inkster women said, they were not, like Lord Selkirk's people, "colonials"; they had been fur traders and had then settled. They were people of the land. And they rejected the term "métis," for they were not French-Indian.

Charles Bremner had another and more compelling reason than simply land-seeking to leave the Red River. The year 1881 had been a terrible one for him and his wife, Emily. In the first five months they had lost three of their eight children, a boy and two girls, aged 17 months, 3 years, and 12 years. There had been no epidemic; the deaths were simply part of the high mortality rate among children. The land had become too full of grief for the parents and for the rest of the family. New skies might give new hope. And so, with that mixture of dream and practicality that prompted the great movement of the people, they looked to the west.

In the fall of 1881, after the crops were off, Charles Bremner and Peter Taylor rode north-west on the old trade route to scout out land for their families and their neighbors. They passed the army of heavily laden wagon freighters hauling winter supplies for the merchants of Prince Albert, Battleford, and Edmonton, and they met some of the well-known men of the north. When they reached the South Saskatchewan, Gabriel Dumont ferried them across the river. The famous buffalo hunter, a stocky, deep-chested man of enormous strength, of dark skin and scanty whiskers,[3] was now forty and no longer a hunter, for the buffalo had disappeared. To the Headingley men, he was only a legend, for he was one of the few Métis of the South Branch who had not come up from the Red River after 1870, and who had had no part in the events of that year. But neither was the eastern Saskatchewan his home land. He had been born in Edmonton, where for three generations, the Dumonts had been great hunters for the Hudson's Bay Company. When Gabriel was a young man, however, the family set out as independent traders on the plains. The venture failed, as buffalo hunting had done. With that career ended, the Dumonts, like many other hunters of the plains, turned to farming, and when the Red River Métis moved north, Gabriel, his brothers, and their father joined them in 1870 and took up land there. In 1876, Gabriel put his sturdy, broad-bottomed scow into the water, and there, at Dumont's Crossing, Lieutenant-Governor Alexander Morris had found a hundred carts of traders and freighters waiting their turn as he crossed on his way to negotiate Treaty No. 6 with the Saskatchewan Crees.[4] Since then, from spring break-up to fall freeze-up, Gabriel had added to his income from farming and trapping with the plugs of tobacco, lengths of shaganappi, packets of tea or sugar, and sometimes cash that he received in payment for his ferry-ing. As ferryman to those who travelled to and from the Saskatchewan country—traders, settlers, government officials, police, freighters, land speculators, visitors—Gabriel Dumont had become probably the best known man of the North-West.

Bremner and Taylor rode on to the stopping place at Fort Carlton on the flats of the North Saskatchewan, well below height-of-land. The fort had changed little in the ten years since William Butler had seen and described it in the *The Great Lone Land*: "a large square enclosure, the wooden walls of which were more than twenty feet in height. Within these palisades some dozen or more houses stood crowded together."[5] One observable difference was that all signs were now in French as well as in English, to accommodate the new comers on the South Branch.

Chief Factor Lawrence Clarke, who had attended the Fourth Leg-islative Session (his first) of the North-West Council in Battleford in May of 1881, talked of the effects of the coming of the railroad. It was assumed that it would follow the original survey of the telegraph line, mapped from Winnipeg to Edmonton, but Fort Carlton was not on that route. The fort belonged to an earlier era and way of thinking. The Com-pany had built it on the flats for easy river travel by boat in the summer and by sleigh in the winter, and the choice had been a good one for the fur trade. In addition to scows and sailboats up and down the river (the Chief Factor from Edmonton had travelled to the annual conference at Carlton by skiff) for six years the Company had been using river stea-mers which they had built for heavy freight. Making two or three rounds each summer from Edmonton to Grand Rapids on Lake Winnipeg, fifteen days each way on a good trip, the steamers commonly carried 200 tons of freight and on occasion up to 50 passengers. At Grand Rapids, goods and passengers were transferred to or from lake steamers that covered the rest of the journey, 400 miles, to the Red River. The railroad would change all that. Fort Carlton, as well as the old trade route and Gabriel Dumont's ferrying business, would become obsolete and the Company would have to reconsider its position there.

But Battleford was still the capital of the Territories, and it lay a hundred miles due west. Leaving Chief Factor Clarke and climbing the high, thickly wooded bank opposite the fort, the two travellers rode through a parkland of handsome hills and long, sloping valleys, now golden with turning leaves and studded with lakes and ponds swarming with wild fowl. The air was crisp, and the sky a blue without ending. It was a different country from the flat bottom of ancient Lake Agassiz that they had come from. Reaching Battleford, the men drew in their horses and gazed at the view before them: a steep, wooded incline, the gold touched here and there with white birch clumps, green pines, and scarlet rose bushes, with a river below, and on the opposite side a magnificent plateau high above the confluence of the two rivers, the Battle and the Saskatchewan.

With the horses picking their way down the hill past the government buildings, Bremner and Taylor turned right at the bottom to the log village, earlier known as Telegraph Flats, that straggled along the river bank. This was the centre of communication with the outside world, for here the government telegraph line crossed the river. That had been one reason for Ottawa's having chosen this spot as the seat of government.

Many of the buildings were merely one-room shacks, others were of two stories and more commodious, with fences and garden space around them. In the main street, besides the telegraph office, there was a small Company store near the bridge, three or four other stores, livery stables and harness shops, and the newspaper office. That was the place that the two men made for because they knew of the editor from earlier days. Moreover, he could tell them of the prospects in the surrounding country.

The owner and editor of the *Saskatchewan Herald*, Patrick Gammie Laurie, had come up from Winnipeg only three years before, to start his own newspaper at the source of news for the Territories. After serving his apprenticeship in Ontario, he had worked on newspapers in the Red River Settlement until 1870, when Riel had put a price of 200 pounds sterling on his head.[6] Hunted by Riel's men, he fled overland from the Stone Fort on the Red River to Headingley, a few miles west of the Settlement, where he was given shelter until he got to safety across the border. He had little feeling of friendship for the South Branch settlers, but he welcomed the men from Headingley.

As Laurie and Bremner stood together, they made an impressive sight. Both were tall, six feet or more, black-bearded, broad shouldered, almost of an age, Laurie born in 1833 in the Scotch Highlands, the son of a Presbyterian manse; Bremner also in his forties, of Scottish extraction but of Indian blood too, born into the fur trade on the Red River. They shared the Presbyterian faith and Scots' speech. Both were dominant men, each in his own way, a leader.

When Bremner explained what they were looking for, Laurie told him with some pride that the land was all taken up west of Battleford for five or six miles. They'd have to go further than that to get enough land for the settlement they looked forward to.[7] Then, too, there were many Indian reserves throughout the area. The stretch of country of some two hundred miles from Carlton to Fort Pitt, the land of Treaty No. 6, was old Cree gathering land, and when the bands had come to choose their reserves, they had chosen them in their home territory. The government had surveyed the reserves a couple of years before—Laurie's son had been on the survey team—so that there would be no clash between settlers and Indians here, but anyone coming in would need help in finding suitable places.

Bremner asked how the Indians were getting on, and Laurie replied, "Just now, it's not bad. Crops were good all over this fall, and the Indians who farmed had good returns for their work. But the two years before this were terrible for them—no crops, bitter winter, heavy snow, government supplies held up—there was starvation along the Valley.

"And then, with the buffalo gone, a whole way of living is gone— their meat, their clothing, their tenting, even their harness—all gone. They link the loss, naturally, with the new, restricted life of the reserves. It's all been too sudden, the change from the wide-ranging life of the hunter to the life of the farmer, bound to the earth and the plow. They're bewildered, lost, resentful."

Peter Taylor asked if anyone knew why the buffalo had disappeared. Laurie said, "I don't know, nobody knows. There's no evidence of disease or anything like that. There are no carcasses around. And settlers didn't drive them out, for there are none—none to speak of. Some of the police say that American Indians have been driving them back at the border, but I don't think that's the whole answer. The old men say that the earth opened up and swallowed the buffalo to punish the Indians for selling their land, and perhaps that's as good an answer as any. I don't know. But they're gone.

"The Indians find it hard to believe. Even this spring, Poundmaker and some of his men rode out, scouring the land, sure that there must be buffalo somewhere and determined to find them. But there were none.

When they came back, Poundmaker told his people that the government had given them good advice. They would have to plow the land and sow the seed and get their living from it. But as he told the Indian agent, he's no farmer, no carpenter, no blacksmith, no miller. He needs help with all of these things of the new life, and it's not easy to find help."[8]

As Peter Taylor listened, it came to him that he could help. He was a good carpenter and a general handyman, he wouldn't mind spending the winter on a reserve, and this would be a chance to get a good look at the country and become acquainted with it. The two men rode back up the hill to see Hayter Reed, the new Indian agent for the Battleford district, who had just returned from a tour of the reserves and would know where help was most needed and where the best land for settling was located.

Upper Town, the seat of government, was in great contrast to the log village below. The buildings were handsome in design and built of frame and stone as befitted the dignity of their purpose. There was Government House, the residence of Lieutenant-Governor David Laird, in which the meetings of the five-member Council were held. And there were the judge's house, the land office, the registrar's house, and the headquarters for Indian Affairs, which was also the dispersal point for supplies for the reserves of the North-West.

Hayter Reed, appointed Indian Agent for the Battleford district only at the beginning of May,[9] was a pudgy man with an unoptimistic face, the drooping moustaches following the general downward lines into a thin fringe of beard. Yes, indeed, Poundmaker had need of help and particularly of a carpenter's help to get more houses built before winter. And the farm instructor had gone east for the winter; Taylor could have his place to live in.

As for land, they couldn't do better than the north side of the Battle, across from Poundmaker's reserve, between the two rivers. It was well-watered, with plenty of wood for fuel and building, bush to shelter cattle in winter, farm land not hard to clear, lots of hay. It was on the trade route twenty-five miles west of Battleford, and the government supply trains that rode in to Poundmaker's reserve could serve the settlers too. If space was what they wanted, it was there, unoccupied land stretching west for scores of miles. But they should take a look at it first, meet Poundmaker, see the reserve and decide about a winter there.

Bremner and Taylor rode down the hill, clattered across the wooden bridge, climbed past the log buildings and stockade of the Mounted Police headquarters, emerged onto the plateau and set forth on the Edmonton trail. When they reached the turn-off for Poundmaker's reserve, they turned south, and after a few miles came to the Battle River. It had steep sides, some 250 feet high, some of them grassy, some partly wooded, with a bottom about a half mile wide. Ravines left from old river channels made folds on the south bank. Climbing yet another river bank, they reached the level of Poundmaker's extensive lands.

Poundmaker was—as they had heard of him—tall, strikingly handsome, with great dignity of bearing, his highly intelligent face framed by two immense braids of raven-black hair that hung well below the waist. He was now in his mid-fifties, a vigorous leader of his people. He received the two visitors courteously and the three talked together with ease for Bremner and Taylor were both half-Indian, and both Cree speakers. As Poundmaker showed them around part of the reserve, the cultivated part with the fine harvest of grain and vegetables and hay that had come of their own work and the implements and cattle that the government had provided, he talked in his quiet, measured way of the prospects ahead. Like Chief Factor Clarke, he was concerned about the impending arrival of the railroad.

"Next summer, or at the latest next fall, the railway will be close to us, the whites will fill the country, and they will dictate to us as they please. It is useless to dream that we can frighten them. That time is passed; our only hope is our work, our industry, and our farms."

The other hope lay in the education of the children. He welcomed the government's plan to open industrial schools for Indian children. Two years before, he had sent his eldest son to the mission school at St. Albert.

"Some day he will be able to help himself and his fellow men. He will be able to speak English and French, and he will be able to read and write. Besides, he will know how to work like a white man. The children must be educated if they are to prosper and be happy."

Charles Bremner felt a strong sympathy. His children, too, were being educated, but he could neither read nor write. There was a part of the world around him from which he was excluded.

There were about 250 people on Poundmaker's reserve, most of them still living out in tents, for they reluctantly entered the log shacks even if they did give much better protection against the cold. The shacks were like those in Battleford, except that these had mud fireplaces instead of stoves, and there was no flooring. Cured buffalo hide covered windows and doors, keeping out the cold but also the light. The houses of the chief, the councillors, and the Indian Department employees were a little different. They had cook stoves, floors, and usually two rooms. Poundmaker showed Taylor the house of the absent farm instructor; it had a cook stove, a table, boxes for chairs, other boxes nailed to the wall for cupboards, a bed in the second room with a basin on another box, some nails in the wall for clothing. It would do. Taylor agreed to return for the winter to be Poundmaker's handyman, carpenter, harness maker, blacksmith if need be. Poundmaker shook hands warmly as they parted.

Riding back across the wooden government bridge, the two men looked at the land between the rivers. It was, as Hayter Reed, the Indian Agent, had described it, rich and various. It was also beautiful. The government road could serve them, and the Indian reserves would help to supply trappers and customers for the small trading store that Bremner was planning. For miles around there were no settlers; there was ample room for friends and relatives to join them, to make their own community and to grow. This would be their land.

They rode back to Battleford, wired the families at home to set out at once to winter in Prince Albert for an early start in the spring. They went to the Land Office in Battleford's Upper Town where they described the land they wanted and stated their intention of settling on it. Then they went to Hayter Reed. A train of 32 flat wagon-freighters was assembling to start the next morning on the 270-mile trip to Edmonton, loaded with bacon for the Indian agency there. They could take Taylor's tools, implements, and supplies that Reed had outfitted him with, and drop them off at Poundmaker's turn-off.

While Peter Taylor rode west, Charles Bremner rode east to Prince Albert, where relatives and friends helped him find winter quarters for the families that would be arriving. Prince Albert stretched for about five miles along the North Saskatchewan and boasted twenty stores, six hotels, four churches—one a new Presbyterian church built of brick— and four schools, the one attached to Emmanuel College teaching English, Mathematics, Greek and Latin. It also boasted real and personal property to the value of about two and a half million dollars, and as though to confirm Prince Albert's prosperity, the government had just opened a land office with George Duck, of Duck Lake, as agent.[10]

The winter passed comfortably for the Headingley contingent, three families of Taylors, three of Sayers, and two of Bremners: that of Charles which included his aged mother, and that of his elder brother James. There was plenty of entertainment, sleighing, Christmas concerts for the children, penny readings for the grown-ups—it was explained that a North-West penny equalled twenty-five cents—amateur plays, musical evenings in which Emily and her two eldest daughters sang and Charles accompanied them on his violin, and there was church on Sundays. During these months, the men bargained for cattle, horses, and other livestock that they would need, and they bought farm equipment and household goods to add to what they had brought with them.

About mid-April, 1882, as soon as the snow was gone and the roads were passable, the whole cavalcade of some forty people started west. With the rattling of buckboards, wagons, and carts, and the clanking of machinery, tin tubs, and saucepans, with the whinnying and lowing and grunting and cackling of the livestock, with dogs barking, babies crying, children yelling, men shouting, they could be heard for miles across the hills and valleys greening in the sun. But there were very few to hear.

Their pace was the pace of the cattle, and it was leisurely, yet the day-long jolting of the wagon was exhausting. When they were seven days on the way, Emily began to have labor pains. They had thought to reach Battleford and the police doctor in plenty of time for the birth, but the early onset of labor brought no panic. The whole train halted and made camp. The women in the company were well accustomed to births, they had rarely had a doctor for their own children, and they were experienced mid-wives. They kindled a fire, boiled water, entered the Bremner tent, and looked after Emily. Before long it was over; in the early afternoon of April 25, Emily gave birth to a baby girl. New life in a new land.

In all, they were ten days on the road to Battleford. There, the cavalcade paused for a day to stock up on food for themselves and the animals and on staples for the months ahead. Then they were on their way for the last twenty-five miles of their trek. They had no time to lose. It was now seeding time and they must make haste to get on the land. When they reached the turn-off and the horses moved forward through the breast-high grass and peavine, Peter Taylor was there to greet them and lead the way.[11] The seeking had ended.

Chapter Two

Settling

It was a tent-town at first until they spread out to their individual holdings along the river. The most urgent thing was to clear some land and get the seed in, both grains and vegetables, that would yield the crops that would see them through the winter. They had no one else to depend on.

Then began the building of the log cabins that would be home for some time to come. Some dug out earth for cellars to store the vegetables, others cut down trees for logs, boys cut poplar saplings and peeled them for partitions, girls cut sod for the roofs: no one was idle. Working together, they put up the two-or-three room cabins, filled the chinks between the logs with mud, put up poles for rafters, covered them with tar paper to keep out the wet, and over that the sod roofs. Then each family fashioned the inside of its own cabin. Shortly a delegation was sent to Battleford with wagon frames to bring back lumber for floors and doors, and most precious of all, glass for windows. The windows were only half windows, but they let in the light, and the women hung their curtains and drew down the blinds to suggest full windows. When all was ready, they went from cabin to cabin exclaiming at how fine everything was.

The new land had its dangers. Almost at the time that the ice went out, the prairie fires began. One of them burned through the wooden telegraph poles and cut off communication between Edmonton and Battleford. But whatever might lie ahead of them, it could not be more frightening than what they had just left behind. In Manitoba, a terrible flood came in May. It filled the Red River valley from the border to Lake Winnipeg, and it swept away houses, barns, animals, food supples, haystacks—the life work of many of their old neighbors along the rivers. Water stood three feet deep on Main Street in Winnipeg. The destruction was appalling. Following that, in June the land boom collapsed in Manitoba and many were ruined. The Bremners and their friends had got out at the right time. They put the past behind them and worked for the future.

With clearing, plowing and seeding done, and with the essential shelters up and wells dug, the men and boys cut more logs, hauled them to their homes, and built barns, chicken coops, pig styes, outhouses and feed troughs. They split smaller trunks into fuel for present needs and for the large woodpile that would be needed close at hand for the long winter months. In July, there was hay to be cut and stacked. In August and September, the ducks came and geese honked overhead, and the hunters were busy before dawn. For the rest of the day they cut and stooked their grain crops, harvested the vegetables, and filled the root cellars. Meanwhile, the women and girls cooked and scrubbed and washed and mended, looked after the children, milked the cows, made the butter, tended chickens and weeded gardens. They also made up parties to go berrying to pick the wild fruit for preserves—strawberries, raspberries, pincherries, chokecherries, saskatoons, gooseberries, cranberries both high and low bush—that were there in profusion. It was a rich land.

The season was good, and the crops on the new land were phenomenal. Even the few flower seeds that the women had brought along produced pansies and sweet peas of astonishing size and beauty. Over the river, their neighbor Poundmaker had had similar success, and the excellent crops of wheat, potatoes, and turnips rewarded the work of his people. "He's making a good farmer," Peter Taylor said, "there will be no want this winter." With treaty payments in September, Charles Bremner did a brisk trade in his little log store. The large clearing in front of it was often crowded with the horses and dogs and children and wagons from the reserves and from his own neighbors.

It was almost exactly a year after Bremner had set out from Headingley to seek land that he started back over the trail. The valley papers reported his trip with satisfaction, for the doings of settlements along the river were great news. Laurie said, "The Bremner and Taylor settlement is doing well. The settlers expect many of their friends to join them next summer. Bremner is doing quite a trade, and some of the men returned to Manitoba for more supplies."

But when they reached Battleford, they found that it was no longer the cocky little place that they had known; it had been dethroned. Great changes had come during the summer months, and the whole pattern of the Territories and of settlement within it was shifting. The railroad had abandoned any plan to follow the telegraph survey line that had led along the old fur trade route to Edmonton. Instead, they were laying rails due west, just above the international border, at a rate of three miles a day. With the westward progress of the line, the government was persuading wandering bands of Indians to go north to the Saskatchewan country, where many of them had come from. The government hoped to lessen the friction between Canadian Indians and Indians south of the border, who were engaging most of the attention of the Mounted Police with charges and counter-charges of horse-stealing. They also hoped to lessen friction between the Indians and the railroad people, between Indians and cattlemen who were establishing ranches in the south along the Bow River, and to avoid incidents between the Indians and the people from the east who were hurrying in to take up land left empty by the disappearance of the buffalo.

The spring census had given the total population of the Territories as 56,446, the majority being newcomers in the south. Of the 20,000 Indians included in the total, the majority were in the Saskatchewan country, and their number was growing with the bands sent up from the border. There seemed to be an increasingly sharp division in the nature of the population as between north and south. An Order-in-Council of May 8, 1882, had further divided the region into four provisional Districts: to the east, Assiniboia in the south, Saskatchewan north of it; to the west, Alberta from the 49th to the 55th parallel, with Athabasca north of that.[1] And Regina had been proclaimed capital of all the Territories. Along the Saskatchewan valley, a deepening sense of isolation spread from Edmonton to Prince Albert.

The appointment of the new Lieutenant-Governor in December, 1881, had added to the unease in the North Saskatchewan valley. The highly respected, accessible, though often ineffectual David Laird had been replaced by Edgar Dewdney, an Englishman trained in England as an engineer, who, after coming to Canada had had a successful political career in British Columbia.[2] After the return of the Conservatives in 1878, he had been appointed Indian Commissioner, and he had made an official tour of the Saskatchewan reserves in 1881, but he knew little of the people of the Valley and had even less interest in them. And it was he who had chosen Regina as the site of the capital for the Territories. For Macdonald's main purposes, Dewdney was unquestionably a good choice: he would be valuable to the railroad builders, and he would be an effective liaison man between Ottawa and the new province on the Pacific.

In Battleford, government offices and officials with their files and their staff had gone south during the summer. Upper Town had almost disappeared, and work had already begun to refashion Government House and the official residences for an industrial school for Indian children. The Battleford Indian Department had gone to Regina, and Hayter Reed had gone with it as Assistant Indian Commissioner.

This move aroused misgivings in the surrounding reserves, and before Reed left, a delegation of the chiefs had visited him as Laurie reported: "We have heard that you are going away and we are sorry for it. We know you and you know us and everything that has been done. If a new man comes we will not know him, and he will neither know us nor what has been done. We are afraid that if you go away matters will not go smoothly. If it rested with us you should not go away."

The residents of Battleford were alarmed too. At the same time that the government with the judiciary and police headquarters were on the way south, restless, disgruntled Indians who had been along the border were being moved north. The combination of moves was filled with the promise of trouble. Big Bear arrived at the beginning of July, "hungry but saucy," Laurie said, and his twenty-five lodges were still encamped around the village. They were giving the new Indian Agent a hard time. Big Bear declared that they had been promised that if they came north they would have "grub and no work," but the agent had received no extra supplies, and if he had, he had no authority to give supplies of any kind to Indians who refused to accept the treaty or to take up a reserve. Big Bear refused to do either. But he and his band had no means of livelihood for the coming winter.

Big Bear had another side to the story, which Frank Oliver published in the *Bulletin*.[3] It was told by Peter Erasmus, whom the Indians had chosen from among them for their interpreter in the 1876 Treaty negotiations, and who, this time, had gone south at the request of the government to persuade the Saskatchewan Indians to return to their own land. He was, according to Oliver, "the only man in the country who could have accomplished the mission successfully." Big Bear had two grievances. In the south he and his men were accused of stealing horses, but their horses had been stolen first, and when they complained, they were told to do the same. Then they were accused of making trouble. They no longer trusted white men. "How can we have faith in men that we know do not take an interest in us? If we steal a horse, very serious; if a horse is stolen from us, too bad. Our word is as the wind to the white man." The other grievance was that the promises of food and support if they went north were false promises: "If we don't get the grub we'll go back," he said.

Big Bear and his men were angry and hungry, the Indian Agent was frustrated and helpless, and the people of Battleford were fearful. With the departure of government and police personnel, Battleford had shrunk; the village in the flats was meaner. Another of the frequent spring floods had demolished many of the old shacks, and the debris still littered the river banks. There was little spirit for rebuilding. But the stores were still there, although their trade had dwindled, especially after the loss of government business. The newspaper was there too.

The moving of the capital had been a heavy blow to Laurie, who had thought that he would be in at the beginning of a rapidly growing little city, the hub of the north. Instead, he found himself in the midst of the tattered remnants of a village. But his faith in the country was still strong, and characteristically his first reaction had been to get out a circular to send to southern and eastern papers, extolling the soil, the ample supply of wood and water, the acreage yields for grains, and even the climate of the Saskatchewan Valley. He also saw immediate improvement. Alexander Macdonald, the most prosperous merchant in the whole region, on seeing the spring destruction, had offered to give his claim on the land of the elevated plateau between the two rivers to all villagers who chose to build there.

"His offer was taken up at once," Laurie said. "Streets have been laid out, and they will be fine. The streets will go east and west, 99 feet wide, the avenues north and south, 66 feet wide. There'll be plenty of room for buggies and wagons to pass, and for hitching. It will be a good thing to get out of the flats anyway. There is no room for growth there. And the site—it adjoins the barracks—is magnificent, unsurpassed in the country."[4]

It offered protection too. Headquarters of the North-West Mounted Police had been moved to Regina, but the stockade, the buildings, and a small contingent of men remained in Battleford. Apart from the young men among the police, however, the place seemed middle-aged. Most of the young people had left and there were no more coming in.

When Bremner and his companions arrived at Carlton, they found a disarray in the flats similar to that at Battleford. As the government capital had been shifted, so the trading capital of the area was moving, for the Hudson's Bay Company was vacating the post and sending all goods to Prince Albert, where its trading would be carried on—at least for the time being. The police would move into the empty fort. Further along the trail, Gabriel Dumont was facing the end of his ferrying career as the railroad and the new trade routes branching from it developed. Altogether, it was not a cheerful journey.

But their own spirits were high, with a sense of much accomplished. In Winnipeg they bought their supplies, Bremner made arrangements with fur traders he knew, and they handed out Laurie's circular. In Headingley, old neighbors who had been devastated by the flood made plans to join them, among them two of Bremner's relatives, Louis Caplette, whose mother was a Bremner, and Alex Bremner, another cousin.

By the time they returned through Battleford, even Laurie had something to rejoice about: the railway was now complete to Swift Current, in the spring a scow was to be put into the Saskatchewan at the Elbow directly south of Battleford, and the village would then be only two hundred miles from the railroad and its supply depot. Passage of goods to and fro would be quicker and easier, and that would be a boon to the Indian Agent as well as to the settlers. Charles Bremner realised that he had made his last trip over the old trade route. It was a thing of the past, and Prince Albert and the South Branch settlements were now remote, in another world.

However, there were disquieting moments in his own world. In the months that followed, Big Bear, in his frequent visits to Poundmaker, became a familiar figure to the little settlement. The two chiefs presented an odd contrast: Poundmaker, tall, reserved, aristocratic, handsome; Big Bear, short and powerful of body, with a large head, broad forehead, shrewd black eyes, a long prominent nose with flaring nostrils and deep lines beside them, a firm mouth and square, resolute jaws—in his blanket, the likeness of a Roman caesar.[5] In his youth he had been known as the greatest warrior of the Cree nation in their wars against the Blackfeet, and at sixty he was still proud, independent and defiant.

Among those who accompanied Big Bear was the strange, disturbing figure of his war chief, Wandering Spirit. He was unusual even in his appearance, "whereas the hair of the ordinary Indian is as straight as falling water, the plaits of the war chief, while long and black like any other Indian's, stood out about his head in thick curls, forming a sombre background for his dark, piercing eyes."[6] A member of Big Bear's band said that his greatest pleasure was in fighting, "and he has killed more Blackfeet than any warrior, not excepting Big Bear." Wandering Spirit was in his forties, a generation younger than Big Bear, but he was without purpose. The Indian wars had been ended by the government and the Mounted Police; the last big fight between Indians had taken place in the south three years before, in 1879. The Indians had made a pact of peace, Poundmaker had been adopted as a son by Crowfoot, the Blackfoot chief, and there was now no career for the warriors any more than there was for the Gabriel Dumonts, the buffalo hunters. The changing life was strange and empty for many of the people of the plains.

The Indian leaders were all middle-aged or older. Poundmaker could see the future and was trying to adapt to it. Big Bear refused to acknowledge it. For him, the Crees were still the lords of the north in number and in potential power, in a country more vast than Rome. He would not go gently into the night of obscurity. And his men wandered in and out of Bremner's store, with angry, baffled eyes.

Despite the rich harvest of the fall, the winter of 1882-83 was hard. Bitter cold and deep snow made trapping almost impossible, and horses and cattle wintering out could find little food. Supply freighters, whether for Indian or white settlements, could not get through the heavy drifts, and when they did get through, essentials were unaccountably missing. There was privation all along the valley. On January 6, Oliver reported from Edmonton, "The grocery famine was relieved by the arrival of a large train of sleighs, but they brought neither bacon nor coal oil." On January 20, "Weather cold, grocery famine continues, empty shelves in stores, beef non-existent." From Battleford, Laurie wrote on February 3, "Coal oil and candles out of stock. No relief in sight." Dark came at about 3:30 in the afternoon and all business stopped until light returned at about 9:30 in the morning. All evening meetings were cancelled, so were entertainments. Three weeks later, "No coal oil either at Battleford or Edmonton. No candles for sale." On March 10, coal oil was $3.50 a gallon. As for the reserves, "Destitution is now general among the Indians."

The Indian misery was such that nine chiefs and headmen wrote from Fort Edmonton to the Minister of the Interior:[7]

> Cold and hunger induced us to make this final attempt . . . if no attention is paid to our case now we shall conclude that the treaty made with us six years ago was a meaningless matter of form and that the white man has indirectly doomed us to annihilation little by little.
>
> When the treaty was made how simple we were! We have found to our cost that the binding exists all on one side and the impunity all on the other. We have never yet been supplied with one-half of what was promised in the treaty. . . .
>
> We who send you this letter represent seven different bands. . . . We were once a proud and independent people and now we are mendicants at the door of every white man in the country, and were it not for the charity of the white settlers, who are not bound by treaty to help us, we should all die on government fare.

Both Oliver and Laurie sympathised with the Indians' plight. Both were fearful of the bitter fruit that it might yield for the tiny white settlements along the valley. Charles Bremner wondered. They were friendly with Poundmaker and his people—Peter Taylor had especially cordial relations with them—but they were vulnerable and a long way from any source of protection from desperate men. There was tension in the little community.

But by the end of March, the rabbits were changing color, the geese began to fly north, the hunters were busy, and the people feasted on fresh meat. The world began to stir again: spring break-up came, the ice went out, travel began once more on the trails and on the rivers, plowing was underway by mid-April both in the settlement and on Poundmaker's reserve where, this spring, full supplies of seed had arrived promptly from the Indian Agency.

Another note that came to cheer the spring was a measure of reassurance about the ownership of land, squatters' rights. At a public meeting in Edmonton towards the end of January, a delegation headed by Father Hippolyte Leduc of St. Albert—one of the Oblate missionaries from France who were posted throughout the Saskatchewan country—had been chosen to go to Ottawa and present the problems of the district.[8] Returning in May, Father Leduc stopped over and reported not only a friendly reception in general, but in particular a commitment that the settlers of St. Albert would be allowed to keep their old style of land division along the river; it would not be interfered with.

Meanwhile, the Dominion Land Survey had been completed in Edmonton, and the ownership of land there would be decided shortly. At the other end of the river, the old settlers of Prince Albert were assured that patents would be issued to them immediately, allowing them 160 acres free, and beyond that land at $1.00 per acre. In Battleford the government survey of both the heights and the flats had been completed, and the residents could apply for titles. The *Herald* announced, with some fatherly pride, "R.C.Laurie, D.L.S., has orders to start subdividing in this district" from Battleford to the Elbow on the Saskatchewan to the south-east, where the new ferry was now in operation. Other areas, Bremner was glad to hear, would be surveyed as soon as possible so that land title rights would be made secure.

Early in the June of 1883, the *Herald* reported, "At the Bremner settlement the crops are all in and most are off to Winnipeg for machinery, supplies, and relatives. Land in the vicinity of this settlement is all taken, though it is not surveyed." This time, Charles Bremner did not join the company, but instead sent his son Andrew to conduct the family's business for the store, the farm, and the household—as well as for his own farm and its needs.

This time, the travellers went south by the new ferry, then overland, and at Swift Current they had the thrill and the luxury of riding by train for 550 miles of the journey to Winnipeg. Returning with relatives, they shipped all goods to Swift Current and had only the two hundred miles to cover by wagon. They were not alone on the trail. As the Winnipeg *Times* reported, "The trail between Swift Current and Battleford is alive with traders' carts."[9]

The land was moving. Regina, which they saw from the train, now had a population of 1,100, with two hundred buildings reported. At Swift Current they had heard of plans to build one or more steamships to ply the South Saskatchewan north to Prince Albert. At the beginning of August a weekly stage was started between Calgary and Edmonton, fare each way $25, baggage allowance 100 pounds. It was operating in time to meet the first train that reached Calgary on August 10.

There was movement in Battleford too. On the plateau, the post office, the telegraph office, a new Hudson's Bay Company store, and a boarding house were going up and would shortly be in use, and Laurie was preparing to move his printing press there. On the south side of the Battle, the former Government House was about to have its official opening as the Indian Industrial School, with an Anglican clergyman, the Reverend Thomas Clarke, as superintendant.

Other moves were not as welcome, however. Big Bear's lodges were still camped in the neighborhood of the village, and other chiefs were bringing more lodges up from the south. By the end of the summer of 1883, about one thousand unsettled Indians would be converging on the Battleford agency. Already new arrivals were pilfering in gardens and outlying fields, stealing the fruit of the settlers' labor, which was to have seen them through the winter. Laurie had an angry editorial against the government: "The fact is that men, red, white, or any color, are going to seize food if they are hungry."

The travellers had many things to recount when they arrived home, but Andrew Bremner had the biggest surprise of all. He had returned with a totally unexpected bride. Thinking that his father would rejoice in his new-found happiness, he had spent the money entrusted to him on gifts for his bride and furnishings for their home. He had no supplies for Charles Bremner, neither for the store, the farm, nor the household. There was coolness ever after between father and son. It was Louis Caplette who became, thereafter, Charles Bremner's store clerk and accountant.

But the attention of the settlement was drawn to another development. Big Bear, in an unaccustomed mood of compliance, had agreed to go upriver from Battleford to Fort Pitt, near where he was born, and to take up a reserve beyond Fort Pitt, near Frog Lake. A new Mounted Police post was to be opened at Fort Pitt under Captain Francis Dickens, son of the famous novelist. More police recruits were also being sent to Battleford, and the Indian Department, almost as an afterthought, bought 32 oxen to be distributed among the reserves.

But such minimal measures, even though the pressure eased a little when the lodges moved off from Battleford, were hardly reassuring. Laurie's angry words were echoed by Frank Oliver, who had recently been elected to the Territories Council, now including eight elected members, which was to meet in August. There, aided by the new member for Lorne, a balding, long-faced Scot named David Macdowell, a merchant from Prince Albert, he hoped to focus attention on the potentially dangerous situation along the North Saskatchewan.

Oliver was a slight, fierce little man, clean-shaven, with sharp eyes and a brush moustache that seemed too large for his face. His attitude towards the Macdonald government and all its doings was such that he seemed constantly to have small fists up. Like Laurie, he had come to the North-West via Winnipeg and more specifically the *Manitoba Free Press*, where he had known Laurie though Laurie was twenty years older. But Oliver was a George Brown Liberal from Ontario. He had served his apprenticeship on Brown's Toronto *Globe* and he had never ceased to worship him. In Regina, his antagonism was automatic towards the gifted, erudite Irishman, Nicholas Flood Davin, who had begun the Regina *Leader*, the third newspaper of the Territories, shortly before, in March. Davin was not only a Tory; he had defected from the *Globe*, and worst of all, as a lawyer, he had defended George Brown's murderer—unsuccessfully, it was true, but nonetheless brilliantly, so report went.

In any case, the people of the Saskatchewan got both sides of most questions, for if Oliver could say nothing good about Macdonald's doings, Laurie could see no wrong in them except in the greatest extremities and then it was not Macdonald but his underlings whom he berated.

At the Bremner settlement, however, the summer had passed uneventfully. Helping the newcomers to get established with barn- and house-raising bees, clearing more land, the women and children gathering the lush harvest of berries, they followed the inevitable pattern.

Presently the season turned again, the geese were once more flying south, the high bush cranberries spiced the woods, partridges whirred up from the ground, threshing was brisk. So were the prairie fires.

Charles Bremner's little store flourished in spite of Andrew's profligacy. Tea, sugar, tobacco, raisins, oatmeal, flour, rice, dried and evaporated apples, hardware and household utensils, dry goods, overalls, shirts, under-drawers, socks, hats, boots—all tumbled over each other on and off the shelves. Beyond that, his fur trade was bringing wealth. He not only had good relations with the trappers from Poundmaker's band, he had established his own trap lines—putting up flimsy shacks for winter protection—and they were bringing in a fine haul. His connections with fur dealers in Battleford and in Winnipeg assured him of good markets, and the northern fur was at a premium. In addition, his herds were growing large and fat.

The year seemed to end peacefully. There was a long, open fall in 1883, with Indian summer temperatures of 50°F in mid-November. New Indian arrivals from the south were paid promptly at Battleford and went on to reserves at once. Little Pine chose land adjoining and upstream from Poundmaker's, and Lucky Man went somewhat further west. Reserves now stretched for ten miles along the bank opposite the settlement. Big Bear and his band were living near Frog Lake, and, although he still avoided committing himself, it was expected that he would take up his reserve there. The Hudson's Bay Company had opened a new trading post at Frog Lake in charge of a veteran officer, James Simpson, who had had good relations with Big Bear, and Simpson was giving him some freighting jobs to help him through the winter. Also in the little post was William Cameron, who became well acquainted with Big Bear and his men. The Indian Department had opened a sub-agency at Pitt under Thomas Quinn, of mixed Sioux and Irish-French blood. Things were altogether more peaceful than the settlers had dared to hope.

Christmas was quiet, but there were celebrations for the New Year according to Scottish custom, and on New Year's Day, 1884, the Indians came visiting as they had done at Hudson's Bay posts for generations. They came in gaily decorated sleds gleaming with white rabbit robes, and they went from house to house having tea and cakes and exchanging good wishes for the New Year. There was a great gathering in the square outside Charles Bremner's house, for he had killed a steer and presented it to Poundmaker for a New Year's gift. Presently the Indians moved off bearing their treasure to dress the meat and prepare their New Year's feast. "New-Chi!" they cried.

The Bremner young people looked forward to a greater excitement, for on January 2 a ball was to be held at the police barracks in Battleford. On that morning, the whole countryside around Battleford moved in, and sleighloads of Bremners and Sayers and Taylors set out early, gowns and dancing shoes carefully packed for the evening. It was a brilliant day with the sun glistening on the snow, sleigh bells jingling, gay ribbons flying from the horses' harness as they sped through a fairyland of snow-laden trees and rainbow-tinted hills. Over two hundred arrived at the barracks that night.

The police had prepared three of the barracks rooms, one for the ball room, one for a supper room, and the third partitioned into a dressing room for the ladies and a smoking room for the gentlemen. The ballroom was "tastefully decorated with evergreens, mottoes and Chinese lanterns," Laurie reported. Music was provided by the newly organised police band whose instruments had arrived, by great good fortune and wagon freight, only a couple of weeks before, and it was supplemented by a violin, a banjo, a harmonium, and a piano. The music began and the company danced. They danced the quadrille, the waltz, the polka, the cotillion, the lancers, the Highland Schottische, the Virginia Reel. And they danced all night and until six o'clock in the morning.

The spirit of celebration continued. There was now a considerable group of people in the new settlement, and they thought it time that they had a formal name. The adults met in the long building that they had raised for school-house, church, meeting place and dance hall, and, after a number of suggestions and rejections, they decided that this place would henceforth be known as Bre-Say-Lor, honoring the three originals. On the first page of the next issue of the *Saskatchewan Herald*, February 9, there was a lengthy piece about them:

> BRESAYLOR. The Taylor Settlement Named.
>
> A meeting of the residents of the Taylor Settlement was held Sunday evening, with Alex. Taylor appointed chairman, to take into consideration the present isolated conditions and to devise a remedy. Resolutions were passed and a petition adopted to be sent to the Post Office Inspector at Winnipeg, asking for the establishment of a post office, and to the Minister of Public Works, praying for a telegraph station. Application was also made to the Department of the Interior to have that part of the country subdivided at as early a date as possible.
>
> By a vote of the meeting it was decided to call the

settlement Bresaylor—a name combining part of the names of some of the earlier settlers.

This settlement is about 25 miles west of Battleford, between the rivers, in the midst of one of the finest agricultural districts in the country. As it is on the line of the telegraph, and on the main trail to Edmonton, the only expense to be incurred in giving them the means of communication asked for would be the cost of maintaining the post office.

The present population is about 200. There are some 50 farms, all well provided with stock and implements, and they contain in themselves all the elements of a prosperous community.

The four Taylor brothers, along with their brother-in-law, A.R. Chisholm, made up the largest family block, and hence the reference to "the Taylor settlement." Peter by now was on his own farm and went over to Poundmaker's reserve only when there was need. Over the winter, the Taylors were joined by their brother William of Edmonton. As the *Herald* reported, "he came down to take his brother back with him, changed his mind, married a young lady of the place, and will settle at Bresaylor."

The young lady was Margaret Bremner, and the wedding, the first wedding to take place in the settlement, was cause for more celebration. The bride's gown was ordered from Winnipeg, the couple went to P.G. Laurie for their license—for he was also Issuer of Marriage Licenses for Saskatchewan, according to an ad in the paper—and, there being no Presbyterian minister at Battleford, they asked the Anglican Thomas Clarke to come to perform the ceremony. It was a great day. After the ceremony came dancing and feasting, the fiddlers—including Charles Bremner—spelled each other off until morning, and no one was denied. The *Herald* carried a formal announcement: "Married. At Bresaylor, March 11, by the Rev. Thomas Clarke, Rural Dean, William Taylor of Edmonton to Margaret, eldest daughter of Charles Bremner of Bresaylor." Two of the first families were now linked by marriage. And so were the rivers, for William Taylor took up a farm on the south bank of the Saskatchewan, so that Bresaylor settlement now stretched all across the land between the two rivers.

Other newcomers arrived in the spring. On March 22, Laurie noted, "A family named Slater arrived from Prince Albert last week and will take up land at Bresaylor. They are the first immigrants to arrive this season, and they report that many others will follow soon from Prince

Albert."

Among the spring newcomers were a few families from Batoche and St. Laurent, in-laws of Bresaylor settlers. Their coming was a great joy to the unhappy young French Oblate, Father Louis Cochin, who, two years before, at age 26, knowing no Cree and no English, had been sent to Poundmaker's reserve by Bishop Vital Grandin. At first the children had come to him, as he ingenuously explained, for the good bread he gave them, but by 1884 they no longer came, and he had nothing to do. So when the little group of French-speaking Catholics arrived across the river, he moved over to Bresaylor and they gave each other comfort—he holding mass for them, and they speaking in his own tongue. He was further heartened by the gift of a small portable organ for him to play for his services. Like Peter Taylor, he went over to the reserve at intervals. At the end of May, Laurie had another item: "The Roman Catholics of Bresaylor have built a neat little church in that settlement. Rev. Father Cochin officiates there in addition to his mission work among the Indians."

The large majority of the settlement, the Presbyterians, held weekly Sunday observances in the long log building whether or not an itinerant minister happened to visit. The men who could read took turns reading from the scriptures, Emily Bremner gave the note to begin the hymns, and Charles Bremner pronounced the benediction.

Early in April an answer came from the Minister of the Interior to the Bresaylor petition for a survey of their district, promising that the work "shall be taken up at an early date." At the same time word came from the South Branch that Batoche had already been established as a post-office, and also that Gabriel Dumont was trying to sell his ferry. The reason for that move was clear. As Laurie reported, "The next trip of the mail to Edmonton will be the last by way of Battleford. The Edmonton mail will then come from Calgary every two weeks. Battleford and Pitt mail will come from Swift Current."[10] The last tie with the old overland trade route from Winnipeg to Dumont's Crossing to Carlton, to Battleford and on up the river was ended. The new pattern had taken shape.

Chapter Three

Thirst Dance

At the New Year of 1884, the Bremners had danced the polka and the Schottische on the heights of Battleford, but in mid-June they witnessed another kind of dance on the neighboring flats of the Battle River. Many strains had come together for that dance.

One of them was the changed course of the railroad, which had led to the increased Indian population along the Saskatchewan, to the north-south striation of communications, and which involved other developments. In the same April issue of the *Herald* that announced the new mail routes, there was another item: "A detachment of police have been sent to Poundmaker's reserve. Big Bear and his band are at that reserve. It is said that a large body of police is on route from Regina to increase the strength of the post here." The "it is said" sentence was a sign of the uneasiness of the residents of Battleford and of the neighboring farmers. The increase in the police force (although only 40 men, who arrived in May) indicated at least some uneasiness on the part of the government.

And that uneasiness had already been present at the meeting of Charles Bremner and his neighbors about "the present isolated conditions," when they petitioned for a telegraph station. With the growing number of Indians and the growing number of reserves, the little community began to feel hemmed in and vulnerable. The great expanse of unsettled land that had given promise of freedom was taking on a different face. With Big Bear's young men riding through and around their settlement, Bresaylor people kept a more careful watch on their livestock.

Sporadic incidents added to the disquiet. But if disquiet was growing among the settlers, discontent was growing among the Indians, and the basis of it was food. There had been trouble at Fort Pitt, only a morning's ride away, at the beginning of March. Several of Big Bear's men had gone to Pitt and demanded food and rations from the farm instructor, John Delaney, who refused them. One of the Indians then drew a knife on Delaney, "and others of the band conducted themselves in such a manner that three of them were arrested,"[1] the *Herald* reported.

It was a complicated situation. A Hudson's Bay Company officer would probably have given the food, and the Indians would have accepted a debt charge for it. That was what they were accustomed to. But the Indian Department of the government was not in a creditor-debtor relationship with the Indians.

The government's concern was to see that the Indians had some means of livelihood now that the buffalo had gone, and to see that they got their own choice of land and settled on it before large scale immigration began. To that end, they supplied animals and equipment to help the Indians to become self-sufficient, and undertook to send to the reserves men who could teach them skills that, as Poundmaker had pointed out, were foreign to them. While the Indians were learning to make the earth work for them, the government would provide food. Food was the paramount concern now as it had been when the Treaty was made in 1876.

At first, the Indian Department had given out treaty money and supplies at a few key points. A problem developed. Some Indians went to several payment centers, giving different names, and got payment and supplies several times. The Department stopped that gambit by having the farm instructors on the reserves give out the rations, and by having the district Indian agents pay each band separately at the home reserves. There followed a logical ruling that Indians who did not belong to a particular reserve would not be given food from the allotment for that reserve. Neither, of course, would bands who had not signed the treaty be given treaty money at the annual fall payments. The measure also helped to keep the Indians at home on their reserves.

The system brought extraordinary pressures and responsibilities on the farm instructors, who doled out the weekly rations of bacon and flour, and who had to render account for them to the Indian Department. Inevitably, they became the focus of resentment on various reserves, and even where there was no outright hostility, the farm instructor's lot was not an easy one. Robert Jefferson, on Poundmaker's reserve, gave some idea of the harassments that the instructor suffered:

> At first I had trouble with the rations, which were now given out daily in order to make the issue coincide with the work done; from morning till night they would come straggling along, so that it took nearly all day rationing. I gave out that I would issue nothing after six. They countered this by coming as early as daylight would let them, thinking to sicken me of my attempt at efficiency. I told them they could not come too early for me, and they gradually fell into arriving about six, which left me the

whole day in which to make my rounds. Thus we managed to get about a hundred and fifty acres under crop, which was quite an accomplishment when all things were considered.[2]

The Indian Department could not count on getting instructors as sensible as Jefferson. They recruited them hither and yon, and the turnover was great. Some were lumberjacks from the Ottawa valley, who at least had had experience in dealing with men; some were romantic young men with a dream of living with exotically garbed Indians in a free wilderness. One such had been Jefferson's predecessor on the Poundmaker reserve: disillusioned and wretched, he had left after a few months. The government had no pool that they could call upon of intelligent, suitable men to send to the reserves; the Indians had to suffer the presence in authority of men sometimes ignorant, incompetent, loutish. It was a difficult time for everyone.

But at least John Delaney at Pitt had put in several years of successfully aiding Indians around Frog Lake to produce good crops. He was a farmer, but was never intended to be a quarter-master sergeant. The flare-up in March was the result no doubt of truculence on the part of Big Bear's men, but the friction had a wider base and they had come through a hard winter. By the fall of 1883, Big Bear had accepted the treaty and treaty money, and the understanding had been that, in return, he would take up a reserve near Frog Lake. Thomas Quinn, sub-agent at Pitt though living at the Frog Lake center, had carried out the very touchy negotiations at that time. Half-Sioux, half-French-Irish, a broad shouldered, well built six-footer with a sense of humor and a knowledge of Indians, he was holding Big Bear to the bargain, and Big Bear was not keeping it. As Oliver reported in the *Bulletin*, "When the band came there last fall it was with the understanding that they would take a reserve in that vicinity, and if they did so, they would be rationed during the winter by the government, since they had had no opportunity or time to lay in supplies for themselves. But they refused to take a reserve."[3] As a consequence they got no rations. In January, Quinn had said, "Big Bear's band have not received one ounce of any kind of provisions since November 1883, and will not receive any until they settle on a reserve."[4]

As for Big Bear, he had broken the agreement, and he knew that. But this was the land that he and his forefathers had ruled as chieftains, and now he was expected to accept a minute portion of it from strangers for a paltry bit of money. The thought galled him, and his conviction grew that the treaty had not been a good treaty, that they must get a better one. He declared that, seeing how little faith had been kept with those Indians who had taken reserves, he would not take one until he had further assurances that the promises of the Department to him would be carried out. In the meantime, he got no rations, and in spite of the Hudson's Bay Company's freighting jobs, the band was close to starvation all winter, trading off their horses and other articles of value for food. When spring came, the *Bulletin* reported, "they were flat broke and they scattered in all directions, only two or three tents remaining." They had paid a price for their convictions. It was turning into a battle between Quinn and Big Bear: no work, no grub, versus grub and no work. But Quinn and Delaney were marked men.

Following the Delaney fuss at Fort Pitt, however, there was a general shake-up of farm instructors in the district, in the course of which the Indian Department issued an extraordinary fiat: "In the future only married men will be appointed instructors, and their wives will be required to teach the squaws to bake, to make butter, and to instruct them in household management." As though it were not already difficult enough to find men to take the jobs, the government was now setting up marriage qualifications for the women. However desirable such wifely instructors might be, someone was dreaming.

It was in this shake-up in April that Robert Jefferson was appointed to the Poundmaker reserve. He was indeed married; he was married to Poundmaker's sister, and their son had been born on March 15 at the Eagle Hills Mission south of Battleford, where he had been the school teacher on Red Pheasant's reserve for six years. Though he knew nothing of farming except what he had picked up in those years, he could teach and he was fluent in Cree. He was an Englishman, age 26, two years younger than Father Cochin, and like Father Cochin he became a frequent visitor in Bresaylor. His counterpart on the adjoining reserve where Chief Little Pine had recently settled was John Craig, a phlegmatic young man from Ingersoll, Ontario, who knew about farming, having been brought up on a farm, but he was unable to speak the language of the people he was supposed to instruct. His doling out of rations was a daily ordeal on both sides.

When Big Bear rode south to Poundmaker in April, Little Pine and Lucky Man came over to join them in conference. According to Jefferson, with the 250 in Poundmaker's camp, the two neighboring reserves, and Big Bear's men, there were altogether some eight or nine hundred Indians across the river from the little settlement whose boasted 200 now seemed pathetically few. The Indian Department's census recorded 16 bands in the Battleford district, numbering 1697. The surroundings were scarcely the haven of peace that Charles Bremner thought he was coming to.

Word came out of the meeting of the chiefs that they planned a gathering for the following spring of all the chiefs who had come under Treaty No.6—not the Battleford district alone, but also the Carlton and Pitt districts—all the chiefs of the old Cree gathering ground along the Saskatchewan. They would make a concerted demand for a new treaty. They would demand contiguous reserves throughout the area, larger reserves for each band, and more treaty money. The thought behind the plan was the possibility, which Poundmaker had said three years before was impossible, of reclaiming their country, or at least of presenting a consolidated front of power. The fact that the railroad had *not* come north as they had expected, and so there had *not* been an influx of immigrants was in their favor. Now was their moment.

If the incident at Pitt had sparked this considerable reaction from Big Bear and the other chiefs, it had also caused a flap in eastern newspapers, particularly Liberal ones, whose scare headlines provoked an angry response from Laurie: "There is no truth in the report of a past or probable rising of the Indians in this district, nor any other that we know of. The noble red man may try to intimidate an odd storehouse keeper, and in an emergency capture a bag of flour or a side of bacon; but as to a general uprising, he has strong reasons for letting that job out. He has neither horses, without which he cannot move; nor arms and ammunition, or any means of buying them; nor has he any provisions to carry him over campaigning; above all there is an absence of unanimity among the bands such as is necessary to insure success in case of a conflict with the whites." Laurie's protest revealed very clearly his own anxiety.

Alarm in the east was sufficient to send Lieutenant-Governor Edgar Dewdney, who was also Indian Commissioner, on an urgent visit to the Saskatchewan country, where he arrived on Friday, May 6, 1884. The reception committee of Battleford business men, which included Laurie, gave Dewdney a luncheon and an address, in which they assured him that, "The Indians of this district, on the whole, are peaceably and industriously inclined." To suggest anything else would be a hindrance to immigration. They were somewhat nettled, therefore, when, in the afternoon at a public meeting in the old Government house, Poundmaker and Big Bear, who had ridden over, spoke to the assembly. Poundmaker asked that the cattle and other property with which the government supplied his reserve be turned over to him to dispose of as he saw fit. Big Bear, Laurie grumbled in his report, "spoke for an hour, rambled about and said nothing." The Lieutenant-Governor said that he did not make laws, but that he would report their suggestions to the government at Ottawa. Yet Dewdney did accept the estimate of the situation from the local business men, and reported it to Ottawa, particularly since it reflected well on his administration of Indian affairs.

His reply gave little comfort to the chiefs. As Laurie had said earlier, "Big Bear has come to the conclusion that something is wrong in the management of Indian affairs. He has seen and conversed with many chief officers of the Department, but none of them seems to be 'the head.' There is always someone higher. To settle who this higher power is has now become the one object of his life." But it was now seeding time again, and the crisis passed while everyone was busy getting in the crop—everyone except Big Bear and his men.

Along the river, Bresaylor people breathed easier, but not for long. Seeding done, preparations began south of the Battle for a great gathering, probably mooted in April and crystalised by Dewdney's visit. Messengers were sent to all Indians in the district, calling them to join the bands of Little Pine, Lucky Many, Poundmaker, and Big Bear in a Thirst Dance and conference in mid-June. The site chosen was on the flats of the river about four miles upstream from Poundmaker's camp, on the border between his reserve and Little Pine's. Jefferson said that in a few days, more than two thousand Indians were camped there, and an immense tent was raised in the midst of them. Bresaylor farmers along that stretch had front row seats.

The Dance of Thirst, as Father Cochin said, was "a religious feast of the faithful Cree." It was held usually in June, beginning on one evening and continuing for the next two days. It served many purposes. Sometimes it was a thanksgiving—such a dance had just been concluded in Edmonton, giving thanks for the recovery of a sick child. Sometimes it was to ward off evil spirits with token sacrifices. It was also an initiation rite, a coming of age of young warriors. Again it was Father Cochin who reported: "During the night and the following day, many young people had made incisions in their chests, inserting thongs by means of which they suspended themselves, dancing and pulling until the flesh tore off."[5] Sometimes, as on this occasion, the Thirst Dance was primarily a solemn council to view the future.

There were both men and women dancers and many drums ceaselessly beating. The first evening was taken up with speeches of the chiefs summing up the past year and giving advice, the next day was the initiation of the young men and afterwards a general council about policies to be followed for the common good. On the last day came the war dance of the tired warriors.

It was a ceremonial vaunting of great deeds such as Homer or the *Beowulf* poet would have recognised. Oliver described it in the *Bulletin*:

> Fantastically ornamented with paint and feathers, the warriors marched to the tent to the music of drums, sleighbells, and firearms. They formed a circle around the pole (in the center of the great tent) and began a war dance, which resembled a Red River jig except for the noise . . . the leader going round shooting off his rifle, and the men dropping down one by one at each shot, representing the men he had killed in battle. Each of the warriors told of his valiant deeds and loud cries of approval rose from the onlookers. . . . The leader gave an account of his brave actions, the principal one being the killing of seven Blackfeet in one battle a few years ago. Others among the braves made speeches of similar import. During the recital of these brave deeds, howls and moans might be heard from the old women who had lost their relatives in battle and to whom these old tales brought sad memories.[6]

But this Dance of Thirst, on the Battle River, had not run the usual smooth course. Father Cochin told of the strange and unforgettable day of June 17, 1884, on Poundmaker's reserve: "On that day, the Indians appeared as if wanting to draw nearer to me; I went into the midst of them, and without making reference to what had passed, I visited the sick and taught the catechism to the children. Soon after, I saw the families from the reserve depart one after another, and at the end I found myself alone." No doubt the Indians had sought the goodwill of Father Cochin's god before they started on their own rites. He followed them on horseback to the great tent.

Jefferson also had gone over to the Thirst Dance site, where his wife had joined Poundmaker's two wives. "The police were moved up to Little Pine's, where they would be nearer the heart of things, and in a better strategical position for observation. The Indians seemed absorbed in preparations for the dance; already the tent was nearly ready, and quiet promised quiet, when a metaphorical bomb fell and burst in our midst. Craig, the instructor on Little Pine's Reserve, was assaulted by two of Big Bear's men."[7]

Father Cochin, who had left the crowd and the big tent, arrived at Craig's house at the moment of combustion.

> A group of Indians happened to be there. They were talking

loudly and appeared very excited. In advancing to greet the instructor, I saw his elbow stained with blood.

"Who did that?" I asked. Immediately an Indian shouted to me, "It is I who struck him with the handle of this hatchet."

I severely scolded the aggressor for his violence. Fortunately, the greater part of the Indians present were of my opinion and told him he should not have done that. There were only two or three scoundrels who seemed to have encouraged him.

Several policemen had arrived at the camp about the same time as I. Having no order to seize the criminal, or fearing their ability to do so, they contented themselves with keeping guard over the instructor. Then, fearful for their own safety, they sent to Battleford for reinforcements.

The next morning, Superintendent Leiff Crozier arrived from Battleford with the Indian Agent John Rae and a few troopers as escort. Craig had heard that the two brothers who had attacked him were among the dancers, but Jefferson said, "Paint and dress have so much to do with an Indian's appearance that Craig failed to find his men." As it grew late, Crozier devised a plan of strategy, sent Craig and the agent off to get some ox-teams, loaded all the bacon and flour from Little Pine's storehouse onto the wagons, and started off for Jefferson's place. "In the dusk of a mid-June evening we left the instructor's shack. The procession was led by the police, the ox-teams following, with Craig and myself driving in the rig with the agent, bringing up the rear."

As they got underway, the Indian teamsters deserted them. War whoops and whizzing bullets urged them on. At the creek, the wagons got stuck in the mud and all the bacon and flour had to be unloaded and carried to the far side. "The yelling and shooting at last died down and we reached my instructor's house physically unscathed, to unload the wagons in the early dawn."

When Father Cochin, who had spent the night with some Indians near the dance site, started back to his mission house, he met Poundmaker "whose humor was not as usual. He was tattooed, or rather, his face was partially painted red. His garments consisted in a brocaded vest, in the Indian fashion, and trousers. An animal's head, surmounted with some feathers, served as his helmet. From his right arm hung a huge tomahawk trimmed with nails and armed at the point with knife blades in place of a hatchet. His long braided hair waved in the wind." Poundmaker may have sent his son to a Catholic mission, but he himself was a firm adherent to the Indian faith, and not only in its marriage customs.

Crozier, having sent two men to Battleford for reinforcements, and having built a 'bastion' at each end of Jefferson's little two-room house, returned with the agent and Jefferson to the big tent. When they reached it, Jefferson said, "The dance was at its height; the drum sounded its monotonous boom, and the singing was in full vigor. . . . Fifty or sixty Indians on horseback with all their finery and arms and arrogance" escorted them to the tents of the chiefs, where Crozier and Rae tried to persuade Poundmaker and Big Bear to give up the wanted men. "Both chiefs talked quite reasonably, but neither would undertake the job. As a matter of fact, neither was able to do it." However, neither Poundmaker nor Big Bear wanted trouble. "Big Bear at length made the proposition that if Crozier would defer his attempted arrest until the dance was finished—which would be that same evening—the Indians would go to Poundmaker's in a body, when the police might take the men if they could."

Reinforcements arrived from Battleford, consisting of all the detatchment left there and a number of volunteers, making altogether about one hundred men. When the dance was over, the Indians began to arrive. First the Sweet Grass band came by. Their reserve was down-river about half way to Battleford. They wanted no part of the fracas and they hurried on their way. Then came Big Bear's troop. Jefferson was fascinated with the procession and with the attempt to intimidate the waiting police: "First arrived the horsemen, tricked out in full war costume, yelling and racing up and down near our camp. Those on foot followed, halting a couple of hundred yards from the buildings and making the air reverberate with their cries."

Then came the moment of crisis. Leaving the body of men to guard the bastion, Crozier marched out with three or four police into the midst of the yelling mob to arrest the two offenders. Cochin recalled that Indians around the soldiers were seeking "by every possible means, to tease them by snatching their guns and revolvers." Jefferson said that the police "were immediately lost in the moving crowd of Indians, as they marched to-and-fro in their search. Luck that day was on our side. The police were under orders not to take the offensive or to use their arms; they met with a good deal of hustling that they might not resist." One false step by the police, even one glance aside, could have precipitated a massacre. Jefferson went on, "It would be impossible to describe the excitement that prevailed during all this time—it was not more than half an hour from start to finish, but it seemed ages—the tension, the shouts of incitement of the young bloods to finish us off without delay; the cautioning of older heads, to let the white men begin the fight—the racing to-and-fro—and the piercing war whoops—all combined to make an indelible impression on the memory. Events were on a hair trigger for a while—yet nothing happened."

That was the important thing, the miraculous thing, nothing happened. Crozier made his way steadily towards the man who had struck Craig, arrested him, got his companion, and made his way back through the mob to Jefferson's house. Then he and John Rae, the Indian agent, set about to appease the crowd and to get away without a clash. They threw open the store-house and dealt out provisions. Under cover of this exciting diversion, the police withdrew with their prisoners. Before Crozier left, he asked Jefferson to stay and behave as though nothing had happened out of the ordinary. "He did not want the Indians to regard the affair as anything greater than an incident." With the police gone and the provisions dispersed, "the crowd of Indians dissolved into the gathering dusk," Jefferson said, and there was peace. Not a shot had been fired—except into the air. The Indian who had struck Craig was given one week in jail for assault.

Across the river, there was little sleep in the Bresaylor settlement in those short nights of June. Watchers were posted at the bridge and at fordable points on the river to warn of untoward movement. All along the river bank, the settlers could hear the ceaseless drumming, the wild chants, the firing of guns, the war-whoops, and they feared an explosion of Thirst Dance celebrants at any moment. Men kept their guns handy.

Movement was as ceaseless as the drums: the police messengers galloping out to Battleford, pausing long enough at Bremner's store to tell of the Craig incident; in a few hours Crozier and his escort galloping back, with Rae coming along in the buggy; more messengers galloping out the next morning; the main detachment galloping in that night; the following day the yelling, war-whoops and gunshots converging on Poundmaker's reserve; the Sweet Grass Indians departing in haste; and finally the whole company of police, with their two prisoners, going quickly, but this time not racing, on their way back to barracks. An eruption by the Indians might come at any moment, but the day passed and it did not come. When Father Cochin came over on Sunday and poured out his tale, and when Jefferson dropped in a day or two later, the settlers knew that their fears had been justified. They moved warily for some days.

As the tensions relaxed, Charles Bremner reflected on what a near thing it had been. As Laurie said, "The Indians did not want to fire first, and they knew the police would not, but an accidental shot might have set a war going." Yet the accident did not happen. Even under extraordinary pressure, the Indians had not approached the settlement. Inflamed by religious exaltation, thrilled by tales of war glory, and frenzied by the presence of the police, the Indians had not attacked nor even troubled the fifty farms. Even after the police had gone and the settlers were unprotected and vulnerable, there was no move against them. Bremner concluded that they had been spared not out of friendship nor compassion, but rather because of their dual blood. That was their protection and their insurance, and he felt secure in it.

It was less than two weeks later, however, that other disturbing news came from the half-forgotten and far-off South Branch world. News came by telegraph to Battleford that Louis Riel was on his way to Duck Lake and would arrive on July 2.

The Bresaylor settlers had not been among Riel's supporters in the Red River in 1870, and they did not now welcome his coming into the new land. But he was 150 miles away, and the doings of the South Branch need not affect them. Moreover, Riel and all of them were middle-aged now. As Jefferson said, "The Bresaylor settlers were mostly of a superior class; they were fairly well off, owning quite a number of stock, they had no need of and expected no government assistance; they had seen all they wanted to see of fighting the government in the rebellion in Red River; what interest they took in the agitation of their poorer relatives at Duck Lake was neither a warm nor a personal one."

Laurie didn't welcome Riel either, having had to run for his life at Riel's command. In an editorial entitled, "My Dear Riel," he noted that "For a long time past a quiet agitation has been going on and secret meetings held at Prince Albert, Duck Lake, St. Laurent, and other settlements on the South Branch," and continuing, "That Riel has come in on the invitation of his friends to be their leader is freely admitted, but no open declaration lately has been made as to just what they want. It is a suspicious circumstance, however, that immediately following his arrival in the country, threats of armed rebellion should be indulged in, and that stories of the co-operation of the Indians should be put in circulation, as they now are. . . . We do not believe these rumors will lead to anything."

Big Bear had heard them too, and when he left Poundmaker's camp in July after his lengthy visit, rather than going back north to Pitt, he headed east to consult with the Duck Lake and Prince Albert people. No doubt this visit was an extension of the recent Thirst Dance council, looking forward to a comprehensive gathering the following spring, but

Big Bear also wanted to have a look at the new arrival who was causing so much disquiet. However, when he went back to Pitt after spending most of August in the Duck Lake area, Laurie reported, "The old man does not seem to have been favorably impressed with the prospects held out to him there."

In the broader sphere, at the moment that Riel was arriving on the South Branch, the Territorial Council was assembling in Regina, where Lieutenant-Governor Dewdney opened the session on July 3. The foremost demand of the elected members of the Council was for responsible government. Just as Poundmaker wanted control over the farming equipment allotted to him by the government, so the Territories wanted administrative control over the public works funds allotted to them by the government. Their other insistent demand was for representation in the Parliament of Canada, where at the moment they had no voice. Related to the question of federal representation was a demand for the revision of the terms of representation within the Territories on the Council itself. Along the Saskatchewan, Edmonton and the District of Lorne were represented, but the Battleford district was not, since there were not one thousand non-Indian adults in a one-thousand-square-mile area at that point. Neither the residents of Battleford nor the settlers of Bresaylor had a vote. The government for them was as far off and inscrutable as it was for Big Bear.

The settlements of the South Branch, on the other hand, had voted in the elections of their representatives in 1881 and again in 1883, which made the more curious Riel's declaration at a mass meeting called in Prince Albert on July 19. What he advocated was what their member, David Macdowell, absent at the council session, and the other elected members had been demanding and were continuing to demand at the very moment in Regina: the creation of Assiniboia, Alberta, and Saskatchewan as provinces and their admission into Confederation, responsible government, more favorable terms to settlers, scrip for half-breeds,and redress of grievances. There was nothing novel in Riel's proposals except that he stipulated that all these matters be embodied in one petition to be taken by a delegation to Ottawa, ignoring the fact that, unlike the situation on the Red River fourteen years before, there already existed in the Territories the governmental machinery for such action. He made no attempt to consult with or to support the efforts of the Territorial Council. He seemed to be reliving 1870.

On the Battle River, meanwhile, the settlers of Bresaylor had drawn even with their erstwhile Red River compatriots in at least one area of recognition: on September 1, Bresaylor, like Batoche before it, became a post-office. Another sign of growth and prosperity was the communal threshing-machine that they had bought, which worked busily up and down the river in October. They were serious agriculturalists, particularly in animal husbandry. They had a goodly number of horses, some three hundred or so cattle, and Peter Taylor had been experimenting successfully with sheep. He had a small flock that had come through the previous winter plump and healthy, his main problem being to keep them from getting too fat. The climate, certainly, was no hindrance to them. Once more, with the hay stacked, the oats and wheat garnered, the potatoes and turnips and cabbage and onions stored, and with farmyard chickens, cows, and hogs to provide meat, eggs, and milk, the community was well prepared for the winter. The land would take care of the wintering-out livestock.

But Bresaylor was unusually fortunate. Along the river generally there had been a crop failure. Beginning with a late spring drought, a hot dry summer had shrivelled grains and vegetables. Battleford had to send to Bresaylor for hay to feed their animals. As for the Indians who had farmed, they were bitter. This was another of the white man's promises that had been broken. They had been told that if they worked and put in seed, this new way of life would provide for them. They had worked and they had nothing. But at least the reserves that had farmed got rations. Isolated settlers had also worked, they also faced hunger, but no one took responsibility for them. They would get no rations. Neither would Big Bear and his band.

Charles Bremner, like his community, continued to prosper. Merchant as well as farmer, he had made his trading preparations during the summer. He had had goods shipped from Winnipeg to fill his shelves with necessaries in food staples, in clothing, in piece goods, yarns and sewing needs, in blankets, and in hardware. He had invoices that fall on the railroad from Winnipeg to Swift Current for $150.00 and for overland freighting from Swift Current to Bresaylor for $400.00 at the general rate of 4 cents a pound. His freighting was done and the goods in place in time for treaty payments in mid-October. Under the treaty, chiefs received $25 each, councillors $11, and all others—men, women, and children—$5 each. A family could collect a fair amount towards blankets or clothing or a gun. The Indians were becoming much more conservative and practical in their purchases than they had been.

This was the season also when Charles Bremner, fur-trader, set up debt accounts following the custom of the Hudson's Bay Company, advancing credit to trappers to see their families through the winter, to be charged against the furs they brought in in the spring. He had been reaching out. As he said, "I traded fur from all round, some from Turtle Lake, Cold Lake, the other side of Frog Lake, from Chippewa Indians and from the Big Mountains south of Fort Pitt." He traded with neighboring reserves, and within his community, "I had three men and myself trading."[8]

It was a good winter for trapping. W.J.McLean, recently moved from Qu'Appelle to take charge of the Company post at Pitt, had an excellent first winter there. He reported a collection of furs worth $20,000.00 by spring. Charles Bremner's was on a smaller scale but yet noteworthy. He packed the furs in carts as they were brought in to him, and by March he had nearly twenty packs of furs in his yard. They ranged in value from three silver foxes at $50 each to 1,836 muskrats at $1.00 a dozen, and they included fisher, lynx, wolf, bear, wolverine, martin, beaver, mink, skunk, red fox, cross fox, otter, and badger skins. They were all ready to be moved south in the spring, when he would sell them in Winnipeg.

Other Bresaylor farmers turned wagon freighters for the winter. A large brigade of sleighs belonging to Henry Sayers set out for Swift Current on November 21 to bring up the machinery for John Gowanlock's grist mill to be installed at Frog Lake. He contracted to deliver it there by December 27. Alex Bremner left for Swift Current on December 19 with another large brigade of sleighs to bring up freight for the Battleford merchants, Mahaffy and Clinkskill. He contracted to make the round-trip in twenty days, boasted that he would make it in fifteen, but arrived back on January 19, just one month after he had set out. He had been held up by storms and heavy snow, which had caused a pile-up of freight at Swift Current. At the beginning of January the *Herald* reported, "The first part of a large brigade of sleighs from Bresaylor left for Swift Current yesterday, and others will follow. There is at present more freight lying at the railway than can be moved this winter, to say nothing of the numerous quantities that will be required for the spring trade."

The winter was not all work in Bresaylor, however. The settlers trapped and cut wood, but they also played cards and danced and tobogganed and skated and drove in cutters visiting up and down the Battle River. Charles Bremner's violin was busy. And there was another special celebration in his home too, when his second daughter, Ellen, married Louis Caplette. She was now nineteen and eager to be mistress of her own home. The son-in-law Louis became more of a son to Charles Bremner than Andrew was.

Since they had achieved the dignity of a post-office, the Bresaylor people for a while considered applying for status as a school district, but they decided to postpone that for a time. A school teacher named Joubert, a Métis from Duck Lake, had arrived in the fall, who could work with the children in both French and English, and so the settlement was content for the winter. Shortly, however, they noticed something strange about him. He had uncanny swiftness of communication with Duck Lake. As Robert Jefferson said, "He appeared to be in constant communication with Duck Lake and broadcasted all information that came to his hands during the winter. It was from this source principally that we on the Reserve heard what was going on."[9]

The school teacher, along with a few others from Duck Lake who had come with him, found only a small audience to respond to their appeals for support for Riel. They were confined to "a few of the needier among them," Jefferson said, "more intimately connected with the Duck Lake people, who only waited an opportunity to join up. These thoroughly believed in Riel and the programme of the discontents, but for this their poverty and their ignorance were all to blame." These few, nevertheless, created a division among the small Métis section of Bresaylor, and also, of course, with the large majority of non-Métis; and this division, however small, made cracks in the one-time homogenous nature of the settlement, in its objectives and in its independence. The activities of the South Branch element attracted Laurie's unfavorable attention, and though the *Herald* continued to commend the Taylors and their doings, it became noticeably cooler to Charles Bremner, apparently associating him with the Métis element, though the reason was not clear.

Nevertheless, in the district the winter passed peacefully. Big Bear was at Frog Lake and quiet. In Battleford the only activity was in some small changes. There was some building. The survey had been completed with nearly 7,000 lots marked out, 5000 between the two rivers and 2,000 on the flats, where most of the homes and some businesses yet remained. The police barracks were expanded, several buildings added and the stockade enlarged. And the first number of the *Herald* for 1885 was issued from Laurie's new office on the heights.

But there was an undercurrent of uneasiness. On New Year's day there were no friendly visits by Indians at either Battleford or Edmonton. The police force had been increased to 200, distributed among Pitt, Battleford, Carlton, and Prince Albert. At the end of February, Laurie took occasion to draw attention to Battleford's vulnerable situation among the reserves of the district: Red Pheasant (the chief, a moderate, was dying) 20 miles east; Stony, 20 miles south; Moosomin 14 miles nearly north; Thunderchild adjoining Moosomin; Sweet Grass 18 miles west; Poundmaker 35 miles west, with Little Pine adjoining him and Lucky Man not far beyond them. At the beginning of March the drums began. "We don't want to interfere with what little happiness falls to the share of the Indian," Laurie wrote, " but it would be a blessing to the public if he could be persuaded to desist from beating the tom-tom all through the night."

Officially, there was unanimous word of peace. Indian Agent John Rae went up to Pitt in January and returned in company with Thomas Quinn, both reporting everything quiet in that area. Hayter Reed came up from Regina, visited some of the reserves, and reported everything calm. It was not surprising then that, at the new session of Parliament at the end of January, 1885, the Minister of the Interior reported, "Matters have maintained their normal, satisfactory condition during the year. The Indians induced to go north from the Boundary have, with few exceptions, settled on reserves and are making fair progress in farming." He noted also that the amount credited to the Indian fund this year was $2,281,910 an increase of $121,380 over last year.

There were a few, however, who were alarmed. Oliver, in his paper in Edmonton and from his seat on the Territorial Council, angrily insisted that no such happy state existed, that the Indians were discontented, and awaited only a chance incident to set them off, that the Craig affair the previous June had been a forewarning.

Chapter Four

Captivity

By mid-March of 1885, both Father Cochin and farm-instructor Jefferson reported restlessness among Poundmaker's people, a sense of waiting for something. Before the end of the month, the reason was clear. Word came with great speed of a clash on March 26 at Duck Lake between the police and the Métis led by Gabriel Dumont. The police had been routed. The possibility that, if the police were destroyed, lawlessness would rule was something that did affect Bresaylor. Tensions mounted within the settlement between the handful of Riel supporters and the Scotch majority.

Duck Lake was the explosive incident. Almost immediately, the Indians of the Battle River swept out of the reserves and rode over the trackless land south of the river to council at the Sweet Grass reserve about eighteen miles down river. Since only a handful of women and children were left behind, Jefferson and Craig followed after the riders to hold their own small conference with Joseph Mackay, farm instructor with Sweet Grass,—"a man of the country and of much experience, whose judgement in a crisis like the present, we might safely follow," Jefferson said.

The Indians held a big council that night. Two of Riel's emissaries were present, urging the Indians to join forces with them. They told of the fight at Duck Lake, of the cutting of the telegraph line, of the imprisonment of several white men, of the secession of the Prince Albert people from the movement, and of the determination of the Métis to fight to the end. They were fighting the Indians' war as well as their own, they said, they were all of one blood, and the Indians should rise with them to fight for their rights as true owners of the land.

When the council was over, Mackay called Sweet Grass into his house. The chief was reticent. Jefferson said, "He said that he was not altogether in sympathy with the meeting, but he could not separate himself from what the whole people seemed to have set their hearts on doing, and that on the morrow they intended going down to Battleford to interview the agent, since they deemed that this was a crisis that would give their requests the force of demands. He did not anticipate any trouble. They did not seek it."[1]

After the chief left, the three instructors decided to "bluff it out," Jefferson said. After all, though the Indians had been greatly excited the previous June, nothing had come of it. The next morning, therefore, as the host poured over the prairies to Battleford, Jefferson and Craig returned to Poundmaker's and recounted what they knew to the anxiously awaiting Bresaylor people. The next thing that they heard was from Mackay himself. The bluff had not worked for him. A few of the Sweet Grass men had stayed behind, and after everyone else had gone, they attacked Mackay in his house. His mixed blood was no protection. They plundered the stable, ransacked the storehouse, and led Mackay, his wife, and their children to the chief's cabin, leaving an Indian in charge. Their guard, however, pitied them and allowed them to escape. "With only the clothes they had on, and nothing else, they made their way through the wood and sloughs without any trace of a road, tramping now in water, now in snow and ice. By a miracle they arrived at the house of relatives in Bresaylor,"[2] Cochin said. On hearing this tale, young Craig lit out for Battleford. His reserve days were over.

News was coming in fast now, and always it was worse. On Monday, March 30, the Indians sacked Battleford. The day before, when word came that the Indians were advancing from the Sweet Grass reserve, outlying settlers had fled before them to the protection of the police barracks. So had the people of the flats, including the Indian agent Rae and the Laurie family.

"The river was at its most difficult stage," Laurie said, "virtually impassable, with a deep strong current running on each side of the heavy ice in the centre. The day being far advanced, the refugees had all they could do to cross, without attempting to save any of their property."

On the south bank, the government people—Judge Charles B. Rouleau and his brother Dr. Rouleau, the overseer of Public Works, and Mrs. Rae—had ridden south to Swift Current. When the Indians arrived at the government buildings early on Monday morning, only the cook was left. He fed them until supplies ran out.

The purpose of the safari was to present demands to the Indian agent, but he was not where they had expected him to be. Poundmaker sent a message across the river asking Rae to meet with him. Viewing some hundreds of Indians milling about below, Rae sensibly said he would meet Poundmaker halfway between the barracks and the Indian camp. But before he and his two companions would come within speaking distance, some hot heads[3] fired on them and they returned straightaway to the barracks. The Indians' purpose was defeated, and by their own people.

As the chiefs were pondering what to do next, Stonies and Red Pheasant men poured over the heights from the south. They brought bad news. Two white men had been killed. One Indian bearing a grudge had killed the Red Pheasant farm instructor, James Payne. Worse—three young Stony hoodlums had come upon a white settler, Bernard Tremont, alone and greasing the wheels of his wagon, and they killed him. They had done what the chiefs had tried to avoid: Indians had fired first. Dismayed, the chiefs realised that the murders had changed the whole situation.

A council was held in the afternoon at which Poundmaker was chosen chief over them all. They were now on the defensive, inextricably involved. Their intention of gaining concessions from the Indian Department was frustrated, their journey useless. They would have to return to the reserves to prepare against reprisal attack, their advantage lost.

The inescapability of what they saw ahead of them produced a kind of frenzy. That night the looting and burning began. They burned government buildings, and the log village in the flats. That night and all the next day, the Indians loaded goods of all kinds from the stores and from private homes on to crates, wagons, and pack-horses and took them to a camp a couple of miles away. They drove all loose cattle and horses before them. The Battleford people, watching from the heights, saw all of their possessions, their homes, their work destroyed, and they were helpless. "We *looked very hard* at them," said Laurie. As the mob fanned out over the countryside, they destroyed everything in their path, burning houses, storage bins, hay stacks; the livestock they took with them. The nights of the spring sky were lit with the fires of settlers' homes.

There was panic in Bresaylor. They were the only settlement in the path of the returning marauders. Police were twenty-five miles away at Battleford, thirty-five miles away at Pitt. The settlers gathered in Bremner's large yard, the men grim, the women anxious, the children excited. What to do? Some were for making a break for Battleford. Others, considering the dangers of that journey with roving bands of Indians in their way, were for staying put, taking a chance, and defending themselves as best they could.

Charles Bremner was of their mind. He argued that they were on friendly terms with Poundmaker—even at the height of the excitement last year, not one Indian had troubled them. Unlike the white population of Battleford, they had the protection of their Indian blood—Joseph

Mackay had had trouble, true, but he had been a farm instructor and that was a special case. Furthermore, the Battleford situation was a special one. The Indians had been denied talk with their agent. They had been rebuffed and frustrated, and therefore they had destroyed. It was part of their continuing problem with the Indian Department. There was no such situation at Bresaylor.

Bremner's tall, imposing figure and his strong Scotch voice were impressive, and his arguments were good. Besides, he stood to lose probably more than anyone else if he were wrong. This was one of his own special reasons for not wanting to take off over the dangerous twenty-five miles to Battleford. A great part of his money was tied up in the goods in his store and in the carts of furs in his yard. Then there were his horses and his eighty head of cattle. And seeding time was near. If he were to leave he could count on the store being looted, the furs destroyed, the livestock seized, and he would have no crop for the coming year. By their own work he and his family, like the other settlers, had achieved a comfortable and independent living. He was not willing to give it up. Another very special reason was his aged mother.

But that night, those who had not his confidence decided to move. About ten or twelve families, including all the Taylors, set out for Battleford. Charles Bremner said, "We were notified by Edward Paynton at midnight that they were hitching up, and that if we wanted to get away, to come then. But my horses were eighteen miles away, and my own mother, 95 years of age, was with me, so I asked him to wait until the next night when I could get my horses in; but he said he could not wait, 'There is quite a stir, and the Indians are coming and will kill us all!'"[4] They travelled at night to escape wandering bands; Joseph Mackay and his family left with them. Charles Bremner and those who thought like him remained. On Wednesday, April 1, Laurie noted, "A number of settlers came in from the upper settlement this morning."

The same day, Poundmaker rode over to Bremner's place. He had about twenty men with him. His purpose, according to Father Cochin, who was present, was to reassure them that he did not want to harm them. On their side, the settlers said that "they wanted to have peace and cultivate their lands. Poundmaker made that understood to his Indians, and they went away again." Bremner's judgment seemed to be justified.

Whilst they were debating, a single horseman came galloping from the north. According to Father Cochin, he was a half-breed named John Kisiskatchewan,[5] and he told of the horror of Frog Lake. Big Bear's men had killed the white men, including Delaney, Dill, Gowanlock, even the two priests who were in the mission. Two white women were taken prisoner. The warrior chief, Wandering Spirit, had started the massacre by shooting Thomas Quinn and killing him. The Indians had looted the Hudson's Bay Company's store and burned all the buildings. Gowanlock's grist mill was destroyed. Frog Lake was no more. They would go down river to Fort Pitt next; it was protected by Inspector Francis Dickens and twenty-five police. The horseman galloped on to Battleford.

Once more the settlers gathered in Bremner's yard, this time with their wagons and possessions. Father Cochin had packed his portable organ, some of the women had packed their sewing machines, bedsprings stuck out at crazy angles. Charles Bremner got his horses in. But they were still afraid, afraid to venture into the no-man's-land to Battleford. They sent a messenger to ask for a police escort. Laurie's account was: "At midnight Alex Bremner came riding hastily from Bresaylor saying that that settlement was in danger and asking for an escort to bring in the people and their cattle." He was not believed, and Colonel Morris locked him up.

Bresaylor waited for his return with the police. They did not come. But neither did the Indians. Not that day nor the next, nor the day after that. The Bremners began to relax and so did the camp of about fifteen families on their grounds. After all, Poundmaker had, in effect, given them assurance of his protection if they did nothing antagonistic. Then there were their homes and livestock; to leave now would be to invite looting and the loss of their years of work. Even Father Cochin, shaken as he was by the murder of the Frog Lake priests, advised staying where they were: that atrocity was the work of Big Bear's men, and it was nearly seventy miles away. There had been no outrage nor sign of action from the neighboring Battle River reserves, to which the Indians had now returned. Perhaps the crisis had passed. Rather than exciting attention by trying to move, it might be best to stay quietly where they were and do their usual work as they had told Poundmaker they intended to do. The strategy of everything as usual was the one that Superintendent Crozier had used the year before. And it was now seeding time.

Laurie's note on Monday, April 6, was a sour one. "The Bremners and Sayers refuse to come in, alleging that they are safer there than in barracks, but very anxious to know what is going on here." Whoever is not with us is against us.

The settlers had not yet dispersed to their farms when two men came riding in from Battleford. As Charles Bremner later recounted, "About a week after the sending of our letter to Captain Morris, Angus Miller and Edward Spence obtained a pass and came to the settlement to look after their property. They said the police could not have spared any of their men to help, and that some were suspicious about our designs." They reported the road hazardous, but "we decided to attempt going to Battleford with them."

Before the settlers could get underway, however, two Indians rode into the camp to tell them that Poundmaker had sent them ahead to say that he was sorry but the Indians were excited and he could not stop them. Miller and Spence galloped off. Quickly following the messengers, two hundred or more armed horsemen surrounded the Bremner place. Poundmaker arrived. Cochin said, "He told Mr. Bremner and the half-breeds in my presence, 'They come to take you.'" It was significant that Poundmaker addressed himself to Bremner as the leader of his group.

"We refused to go," Bremner said. "That night they broke into my stable and took all my horses. The next day they went into my store alongside my house and took my goods, and told us to get ready and go with them. So we had to go. They demanded our guns and we said no, we'd shoot it out first, so they let us keep them. They hitched up for me and started to shoot the dogs, pigs and hens. I saw a lot of new hats and clothing on the Indians when they came out of the store." But Bremner managed to get the carts of furs brought along with them. They were his insurance for the future.

He continued, "They took us away, driving with them at the same time about 300 head of cattle at least, mine among the rest. They shot some of our cattle along the way to camp. There were about 15 families taken then; they had all camped about my place, and we were all taken over Battle River to Poundmaker's reserve. We remained there until the fight of Cut Knife Hill."

Father Cochin was herded along with the others. "They dashed on our tents in every direction, overthrowing them, seizing the horses of the half-breeds and all they could carry, stripping my chapel of all I could not save from their furious rapacity. To have our lives safe, since we had neither enough ammunition nor arms, we were forced to deliver ourselves to our aggressors and follow them."[6] No one was left behind as a messenger or a warning voice. "The people lost all of their property; all lost their animals and property. Mr. Bremner had a large band of cattle, about 80 head, and had merchandise in his buildings as well. It was not a very large store, but I think it was all pillaged."[7]

It was not Poundmaker who was in charge of the horsemen; it was Delorme, Riel's agent. Joseph Delorme had been a member of the Scott court-martial in Fort Garry, and he had been one of Dumont's chief men in the rout of the police at Duck Lake. His appearance was an ominous one to the people from Headingley. "Delorme told us that if we did not go," Cochin said, "there would be bloodshed over it. Poundmaker promised Mr. Bremner and the other half-breeds in my presence that he would protect them all the time."[8]

It was in April three years before that the cavalcade had come, full of hope, from Prince Albert. The procession to Poundmaker's reserve was almost a parody of it. Alice Maude Gertrude, born on the trail, had her third birthday in the Cut Knife reserve. From April 14 to May 2, over two weeks, the Bresaylor people, as Father Cochin said, "were kept as prisoners under guard. The camp was all guarded around and we could not escape."[9]

The rounding up of the Bresaylor settlers coincided with Big Bear's attack on Fort Pitt. By April 15, he had taken Pitt, the police were routed, the McLeans taken prisoner, and Pitt burned.

After the foray into Battleford, all of the Battle River reserves, including those south of Battleford, came to join Poundmaker. The site of the great camp was on a flat, bordering Cut Knife Creek. As Robert Jefferson described it, the creek cut through Poundmaker's reserve, coming from the south west, skirting Cut Knife Hill, and going north to join the Battle. "The country is more or less broken by depressions that deepen into ravines as they reach the creek. Poplar and willow scrub screen the coulees up to their very edges. The creek meets the Battle River three or four miles away, running through impenetrable willows the whole way. The banks are steep and there are few fords."[10] It was excellent defensive terrain.

Here the bands waited, for they knew that there would be reprisals. There was no peaceful way out. They were preparing themselves. A warriors' tent was organized, with Fine Day as war chief. "About once a week, camp would be moved," Jefferson said, "but never very far and always in sight of the creek about three miles from the hill which rises above a surrounding plateau."

Emissaries came at intervals from Riel, one delegation shortly after the camp had assembled, bringing a letter from him. A council was held in the afternoon in the warriors' tent, which Poundmaker asked Jefferson to attend, and he sat beside the chief. After the warriors had gathered, one of the delegates read the letter, translated it into Cree, explained it and answered questions about it. Then he handed it to Poundmaker. "Arrived at his own tent, the chief pulled out the epistle, gave it to me, and asked me what was in it. He did not place implicit faith in Riel's emissaries. I translated the letter for him, substantially as the Half-breeds had given it. The letter went, "Rise, face the police. If you possibly can, take Battleford. Destroy it. Save all the goods and provisions and come to us. All that you do, do it for the love of God under the protection of Jesus Christ, of the Blessed Virgin, of St. Joseph and of St. John the Baptist. Be certain that faith works wonders."

Poundmaker, not overly moved by the appeal to Christian saints, asked Jefferson what he thought of it. "I said it read as though the Duck Lake people wanted help. Poundmaker made no remark, but I could see that the idea was not at all to his fancy. The first messengers had conveyed the impression that Riel and his Duck Lake following were going to carry all before them, and that the Indians' part was to sit quietly by, and yet participate in the benefits to result. Also, nothing had been heard from the other parts of the country—and much had been expected— from the west, from the north, and from the Blackfeet. The worst was to be anticipated from this ominous silence."

Riel's men were not content with the formal council meeting. They spread the word among the teepees. Jefferson was invited to the tent of a man from the Red Pheasant reserve, who regarded him as a proven friend after his years as school teacher there. A strange Indian was giving an account of the doings at Duck Lake and Batoche and outlining Riel's plans for the future:

> First the railroad was to be broken up, so that no assistance could come from the East; then all the police in the west— caught like fish in a weir—were to be eliminated. Riel would start at Prince Albert and march up the Saskatchewan River, taking the various posts on his way. The Blackfeet were to attend to the south. After all vestiges of government were wiped out, the United States authorities were to be called to a conference somewhere on the plateau near the South Branch. Arrangements would be made for the disposal of the country, in which the interests of the original inhabitants were to be adequately secured. The Indians asked me what I thought of it. I told them that all this harangue was only a fairy tale; that from Riel's letter the Half-breeds felt themselves to be losing ground and wanted the Indians' help.[11]

Meanwhile in camp there was the matter of daily living. There were provisions for a time. Jefferson, from his erstwhile position as rationer, was interested in the dispersal of them: "The Indians had taken all the flour and bacon from the store houses on all the reserves before leaving, but that amounted to very little among so many, as there was never any great store kept on hand. Nothing in the way of food was looted from Battleford, so that the whole camp depended on beef"— Bresaylor beef. There was great disparity among the Indians, for there was no organized distribution of food. Some had a great deal, some little. "Beef was almost the only food. I do not think I tasted bannock six times during the six weeks' adventure, and no salt."[12] The Bresaylor people looked on with chagrin at their cattle being slaughtered, especially since, Bremner said, the Indians made them pay for their food. They did not fare well.

They had to keep a constant look-out around their tents, for they were frequently harassed, and Poundmaker and his councillors had to intervene a number of times to stop incipient quarrels. But Father Cochin had one consolation: "I had been able to save from their vandalism, by the kindness of a friend, my small portable organ, and this my Christians had the courage to transport with their luggage, from encampment to encampment." Every night, under the clear spring sky, they sang hymns together in Cree, in French, and in English. It was scarcely a Babylonian captivity, but at least it was not regimented. From the other world, from the warriors' tent, came the beating of drums, repeated chants, the cries and shouts of admiration for recounted deeds, of the war dance.

Chapter Five

The Dancing Tent

On April 30, camp was moved again, but this time out of the flats and up on to the high plateau where, in the middle of the reserve, Cut Knife Hill raised its head above the surrounding country. This time the camp, Jefferson said, "was arranged in a semi-circle facing the east, flanked by ravines on each side, and sheltered by massed poplars and willows behind."[1] The Bresaylor camp-within-a-camp was about a quarter of a mile from the Indian tents, towards the creek.

The Indians were edgy. In the morning, as they were preparing to move camp up the bank, Father Cochin sat down while he was waiting and began to write a few notes in his journal:

> This was enough to throw suspicion on me. The report rapidly circulated in the camp and excited them all. Soon I was surrounded by twenty insurgents, saying to me: 'Traitor, go then and publish your information on the poles that edge the road as far as Battleford.' The anger was painted on their daub faces of scarlet red. Although a little excited, I laughed at their mistake, and afterwards tried to explain to them the purport of memoirs, but they did not want to understand, and I saw in a moment that the same fate was to befall me as that of the Reverend Fathers Fafard and Marchand at Frog Lake. But the good chief Pound-maker, who had protected me since the beginning of my captivity, heard what was passing and came in haste, reproved severely the young aggressors, and threatened anyone who would dare to say to me one word. All drew back, shame-faced.[2]

Two days later, there was a shout at dawn, "Friends, to arms!" It was May 2, the day of the battle of Cut Knife Hill.

The look-out, an old man called Jacob, on mounting the hill, heard the rumble of wagons as they crossed the flats below. Apparently, word in Battleford had been that the Indians were still in camp in the flats, and Colonel William Otter, recently arrived to raise the siege of Battleford, thought to surprise them and end the Indian part of the rebellion. He mustered a variety of troops—his own force, the Mounted Police, and volunteers—together with the transport teams, a few mounted scouts, two cannon, and a Gatling gun. They travelled all night and arrived at the camp site just before dawn. They found no one there.

The look-out, Jefferson said, saw the scouts, "along with the rising sun" riding up the hill from the former camp. "He saw mounted men following them, and he saw wagons, wagons, wagons, filled with soldiers, winding towards him from out of the distance behind them. From where he stood he was visible to the whole camp, so that his alarms and demonstrations quickly roused the sleepers, and when the first soldiers came to the summit of the rise, they saw the Indians—like ants disturbed in their hill—streaming in all directions away from the tents.

Jefferson was among the Indian tents. With his ambivalent status as Poundmaker's brother-in-law and the government's farm instructor, he was given a tent beside that of Poundmaker whenever the camp was moved:

> On that memorable morning, I was awakened by the yells, by the rattling of the Gatling, and the shrieks of shells. I dressed hastily and hurried outside. All was confusion as people poured forth from their tents, but it was the confusion of everyone attending to his or her own business, and that was to reach some place of safety from the coming onslaught.
>
> The deep voices of the men, the sharper tones of women, and the crying of children, all mingled as the crowd filed off behind the tents toward the south. They took nothing with them; the tents and their contents were left just as they stood. A wooded ravine that came up from the creek skirted the northern base of Cut Knife Hill and lost itself on the level of the plateau. Down this depression the Indians poured and in a wonderfully short space of time were lost to sight. . . .
>
> I lost no time getting to Poundmaker's tent. He was just performing his toilet and appeared in no way perturbed by the unexpected attack. . . . He donned the fur cap that he always wore and proceeded to invest himself in what looked like a patchwork quilt. In my ignorance, I ventured to ask him what it was. . . . With great dignity he informed me that it was his war-cloak; that it rendered its wearer invisible to an enemy. Then he got up and stalked out of the tent without another word. . . . As soon as I saw his tall form mingle with and lose itself in the streaming crowd of fugitives, I hurried over to the Halfbreed tents, which stood at a short distance, grouped together at the end

of the semicircle of teepees.[3]

In the captives' section, Cochin had been roused by the commotion and ran out of his tent. "I perceived several Indians, guns in hand, running in confusion towards the slope which descended to the brook. Five amongst them had arrived at the summit of a hill and were already disappearing when a shot from a gun was heard, immediately followed by a volley intermingled with cannon shots. I saw two of these Indians fall." Cochin ran in the direction of the soldiers, hoping "to make myself known to them, and to obtain safety for my unfortunate companions."[4]

Charles Bremner, too, saw a hope of deliverance and was trying to make contact with the troops. "Our little camp was about one-quarter of a mile from the Indian camp; the troops were about three-quarters of a mile across a big bridge from us. We sent down Tom Dennison as a messenger to let the police know to come for us, and to say to them not to shoot at the square tents. I put up a big white flag.

"The second cannon ball came near our camp. I then hitched up the horses and sent my family away to hide themselves in a deep ravine."[5] Father Cochin's black robe had no more effect than Bremner's white flag. "Reaching a small hillock at the edge of a grove, I found myself in the midst of firing. I wanted to shout, but I had not the time; a shower of bullets fell around us. I briskly threw myself on the ground in a hollow.

"The soldiers, numbering two or three hundred, were on an elevated level ground, flanked at a good distance by a great number of small excavations. Indians in little groups had squatted in the shelter of these excavations, as in trenches, and from there they could shoot without exposing themselves to any danger.

"Little by little they surrounded the soldiers. The shells and grape-shot which fell among them made them anxious. Nevertheless at each cannon shot they replied by joyful cries, joined with ironical exclamations. Many seemed so little aware of the danger that they loaded their guns with their pipes in their mouths."[6]

Cochin returned to his tent. "I found the Half-breed prisoners preparing to lead their families out of the reach of the shells and in an opposite direction to that of the Indian families. I followed them during the time of the battle."

Jefferson arrived at the same moment. "They were making preparations for flight from the danger zone. I had got quite chummy with the Half-breeds. They were in a different class from the Indians, and there were many points on which we were in sympathy. Very few of them were in sympathy with the rebellion, and I had ample means of finding out.

"Four of us, when the Half-breeds had left, went to a ravine a little distance on our left and lay down just over the edge, among the brush. Here we stayed for hours, one or other occasionally rising to peep over the top of the bank, to mark any change in the fight."[7]

Having seen his family to safety, Charles Bremner with some of the other men "went up on to a high hill on horseback, intending to go to the police, but they fired at us twice with the cannon. I saw some of our Half-breeds get ready to fight the police, and I shouted to them: 'The first Half-breed I see shooting at the police, I'll blow his brains out!'" But the hope of deliverance was gone. Like Father Cochin, Bremner returned to his camp.

Jefferson and his companions watched. "The soldiers were so slow in taking advantage of their surprise attack that their opponents succeeded in establishing themselves in a ravine that flanked the east side of the road up the hill. There, though only a few—not more than fifty—they kept up so continuous a sniping that the advance was stopped and the result practically determined. The Indians, gradually working down the ravine, improved their position until they were potting the soldiers from behind as well from the front and side. . . .

"This state of affairs continued until about noon, when the troops were practically surrounded. Soon their retreat would be cut off. For seven or eight hours the fight had continued and Otter had not advanced a step. His men were wasting ammunition, shooting by guess-work at imaginary Indians. Every minute he stayed increased the perils of his situation. He gave the order to retreat."[8]

Cochin noted, "The battle, one of the most spirited of the rebellion, lasted from five o'clock in the morning to one o'clock in the afternoon. In going over the battlefield, I saw only five Indians killed and a few wounded."

Bremner called his people up from their hiding place in the ravine, and at one o'clock they ate their meal in their camp. When the soldiers began their retreat, Jefferson and his three companions came up from their shelter and climbed up behind the deserted Indian tents. They watched the retreating forces: "The crossing by which they had come was no longer available. The willows were full of Indians. Pushing ahead they luckily reached a ford lower down before the evening, and, crossing there in haste and disorder, took the road back to town. There was no pursuit. A number of Indians had mounted and were about to start after the retreating soldiers, but Poundmaker would not permit it." Charles Bremner took some of the credit for that. "A lot of Indians got ready to follow them, when I told Poundmaker to stop his men and he said he would."

Jefferson and Cochin agreed in their accounts of Poundmaker's explanation to his people. "He said that to defend themselves, their wives and children was good, but that he did not approve of taking the offensive. They had beaten the enemy off; let that content them." Jefferson added, "So there was no pursuit. Poundmaker had now no hope of the rebellion succeeding." Cochin had a different slant. "I believe that at that time the poor chief sincerely deplored the battle which came unawares, and which he would have preferred avoiding."[9]

But there was no doubt about the victory celebration. It was near sundown when Jefferson ventured back to the Indian camp. "The people were all assembled. Some of the tents stood ready for occupation; the rest were in course of erection, and everywhere fires blazed and kettles boiled in preparation for the evening meal. I made my way to Poundmaker's tent, which was already established. He had doffed his war panoply and had regained his unrestrained manner and talked quite good humoredly."[10] When Jefferson told him of his flight up the coulee, Poundmaker laughed and said that many others had run away, and some had got such a fright that they had not yet returned. But gradually they came back, and over the fires and the feasting, the fight was fought over again. Long into the night the deeds of heroism were rehearsed, the shrewd manoeuvres were retold, the victory savored.

The battle of Cut Knife was over. Poundmaker and Big Bear between them controlled the Saskatchewan country from above Fort Pitt to beyond Battleford, even to Carlton. They ruled once more their native land. It was as though the rumored plan coming out of Big Bear's visit to Poundmaker two years ago had taken form, come to a planned moment of action, and had been achieved—contiguous reserves across the land. The only white outpost in the Cree country of Treaty No. 6 was Battleford.

The next day, May 3, was a day of messengers. First, two messengers came from Big Bear who, having routed the police from Fort Pitt, was presently exasperating Major Sam Steele and Major-General T.B. Strange, who had come from the west, in skirmishes around Frenchman's Butte. So far, Big Bear seemed to be having the best of it. No one learned what message they brought, for their talk with Poundmaker was within the chief's tent, and Jefferson could not hear. One thing would be sure—Big Bear was not asking for reinforcements.

But messengers arriving from Riel towards night did come for help. The letter that they brought, Cochin said, "recommended the

Indians to respect the prisoners and not to kill anyone. The leader of these newcomers, Mr. Charles Trottier, addressed the Indians. He reproached them, in energetic terms, for the plunder and the massacre. Then, this Charles Trottier took the command and we had nothing more to dread from the rebellious Indians."

Jefferson, too, noticed a difference from the truculent Joseph Delorme: "These were a different type of man from the arrivals hitherto, and their bearing gave a respectable tone to the whole proceeding." And he saw a different message. Even though Riel had checked General Middleton at Fish Creek on April 24, about ten days before, the messengers "could not disguise the fact that Riel was now getting the worst of it." He urgently needed help. But that had not been the Indians' understanding of Riel's plan and their role in it.

The moment of glory in defiance of enclosing fate did not last long. In the days that followed, as they pondered what came next, Poundmaker's host moved camp every other day south of the creek, awaiting a possible onslaught. With Middleton on the South Branch, Otter and the police at Battleford, and Strange's column on the path of Big Bear to the north, it could only be a matter of time before another force was sent against them. They could not stay where they were. They lacked any source of ammunition, they lacked any source of food supplies; they could be starved out.

A split developed in the discussions as they moved from camp to camp. Poundmaker and a few others were for going west to seek sanctuary with the Blackfeet, to stop fighting. The majority, and the warriors' tent was with them, argued that that would only postpone the end and spread the struggle. They were for going east to join Riel. They wanted decisive action, arguing that, with a strong enough force, they might yet be able to wrest concessions from the government. After several days of argument and a number of dances in the war tent, the warriors' view won and the whole camp moved east along the Battle River, keeping to the rough, broken country that borders the prairie.

The Indians had been used to a semi-nomadic life until only a few years before. This trek was a welcome relief from the restrictions of reserve life, otherwise it was nothing extraordinary for them. That was not so for the Headingley farmers who, perforce, went with them. "We had to follow the dancing tent," Charles Bremner said. Behind them, most of what they had worked for was destroyed. It was not three weeks since they had been forced out of their homes, constantly having to move from one spot to another, constantly on guard against possible malice that Poundmaker could not forestall, and which had become more open since Bremner's attempt to make contact with the troops.

Once more they struck their square tents, piled them and all their goods, including Father Cochin's organ, on the wagons, and distributed people as best they could. Charles Bremner determinedly kept the furs with him, a symbol of hope, and more practically a means of regaining a livelihood for his family when this ordeal was over. They started east over the rough ground. It was a dreary, wretched time for all of them, but particularly for Bremner's aged mother. On the first day out, she died. The Bremners and the Sayers, their old friends, held a simple ceremony as they buried her in the land that was lovely, green, and fragrant with wild fruit blossoms. Once more, Charles Bremner pronounced the benediction.

With the warriors as the vanguard, the whole mass, in a long, straggling line of hundreds on horseback, in wagons, on foot—one old Indian woman shambled beside a fat, spotted dog that pulled a travois holding all her possesions—stretched in an advancing wave towards Duck Lake, struggling, stumbling, forging on over rough land broken with hillocks, ravines, ponds and brush.

South of Battleford, on the second day, they had an unexpected windfall. "A train of freighters, bringing provisions from Swift Current to Battleford, ran right into our long-strung-out line," Jefferson said. "From this time to the end, our fare was varied with corned beef and hard-tack. I had eaten no bread since the trouble began, and hard though the biscuits were, I relished them." [11] One of the teamsters, a young Scot named Neil Brodie, gave another perspective in a brief account that the *Herald* published many years later:

> On Thursday, May 14th, 1885, about 10 a.m., I and twenty others, who were freighting supplies with twenty-one yoke of oxen for Col. Otter's column, were about twelve miles south of Battleford in the Eagle Hills, where there were several small bluffs of poplar, when Poundmaker's warriors surrounded us.
>
> There were about three hundred well-armed Indians and Half-breeds, besides a great many more with shot guns, war clubs, tomahawks, and knives; perhaps eight hundred altogether. . . . We went back to the Indian camp and they held a council to decide what to do with us. The chief, minor chiefs, and principal councillors, sat down in a circle. Each speaker rose and gave his opinion, which was not hard to understand although we could not speak their language. If the speaker wanted to kill us he would dance around with his rifle in the hollow of his arm and

speak loud and fast. If he was willing to spare our lives, he would leave his rifle on the ground and walk around the circle and talk quietly. Finally they agreed to keep us alive if none of us tried to run away. If any did, then the blood thirsty had the privilege of killing the rest.

We of course, accepted the terms. Then Chief Poundmaker, with an interpreter, had a talk with us. He said our lives were safe and advised us to thank God.

Shortly after this the whole camp started moving southeast. A minor chief selected me to drive his oxen. His wife and I occupied the front seat; just behind me was my guard, armed with a three and a half foot cutter bar of a mowing machine, all the sections removed but five. . . . We were travelling in five columns, covering about one quarter section each way. . . . I was driving the lead team of the left hand column. We camped about 5:30 o'clock.

My host killed a calf for supper. His wife, her sisters, and mother, prepared supper of peeled potatoes, boiled meat, bannock, hard tack, tea, milk and sugar. We sat on our heels, tailor fashion, in the teepee around the food. I sat on my hostess' right, and she saw that I got plenty to eat. This ended the first day.[12]

Jefferson picked up the ongoing story. "On the evening of the next day, we found ourselves at what was called 'the end of the hills,' that is, where the broken ground gives place to open, more or less level, prairie. Here, a rider came in hot haste from Duck Lake with news of the fighting there. He said that a desperate battle was in progress, that the Half-breeds had kept their enemies at Fish Creek for three days, but had been forced back to Batoche to make their last stand. They must have help at once or it would be no use.

"The Indians were far from unanimous as to the course to be pursued. We did not move."

They had been wise not to move. More messengers arrived. They told of the fighting at Batoche, of Riel and five hundred followers against General Middleton and fifteen hundred troops. At last, on May 19, two more galloping horsemen came. The conflict was ended. Riel had surrendered. Dumont had fled. The General had granted peace to the Métis. Jefferson said, "They furthermore requested—and advised—the Indians to make terms, and bring peace to the suffering country."[13] Such was Riel's message. Poundmaker called everyone to council. To most of the Battle River Indians, Riel was a name; not even Poundmaker had ever met or seen him.[14] He was a disembodied voice that came and went, a voice sending messages telling the Indians what to do or think. It had been evident for some time that Poundmaker did not place great trust in Riel nor in his movement. Whatever Riel's motives or ambitions, his main interest in the Indians was to use them to set up his governance, which included his strange religion. Métis demands for land were demands on Indian land; they were as eager to occupy it as any other strangers were, even as the more recent newcomers, the Bresaylor people were. However interwoven family relationships may have become, both groups were still outsiders. They were not treaty people. They were part of the closing net.

The Indians must now turn away from outside involvement; they must chart their own course, face the consequences of their own actions. Poundmaker called Jefferson in to a meeting of the chief councillors. "What is to become of us?" he asked. Jefferson gave his opinion: "I told them I thought only the Stoney murderers would be hanged, and that he and some of the others would get off with terms in prison, but that all the others would go free. This would have been harder to tell, but that they appeared to expect that they would all be massacred."[15] The men in the tent resolved to accept their fate for the sake of the rest of the people.

The dismal details of surrender must now be taken in hand. Poundmaker dictated a letter to Jefferson for General Middleton asking "upon what terms he would receive their capitulation." Another such letter was prepared for Colonel Otter at Battleford. Jefferson was sent east to find Middleton and deliver his letter. Several of the Duck Lake people, recent arrivals in Bresaylor, including the school teacher Joubert, went with him to return to their South Branch homes. Charles Bremner, as the leader of his people, together with Father Cochin, who could read, were delegated to take the other letter to Colonel Otter. With them went the twenty-two teamsters, whom Poundmaker had immediately released, three or four Bresaylor men, and two of the Sayer girls. Bremner wanted Poundmaker to come with them, but he would not. "He was scared," Bremner said.

The chief probably *was* scared and wanted to test the reception he would get. No doubt also he was reluctant to give up his command and his country to become subservient to another. He would await word from the other commander-in-chief.

At Battleford, as the company rode down the south bank, clattered across the bridge and climbed the hill to the barracks, Laurie recorded their arrival. "Just as the sun was setting Wednesday, May 29, four wagons filled with people and bearing a white flag, drove down the hill from the direction of Poundmaker's encampment. It was composed of the twenty drivers on the freight train captured by the rebels last week, and Charles and James Bremner, Alex Sayer, Louis Caplette, and Rev. Father Cochin, emissaries from Poundmaker with overtures for peace, and two women of the families of the so-called prisoners."

Laurie had made up his mind that all of the Bresaylor people who had not come into the barracks were Riel supporters and rebels. His hand and voice were against them, and especially against Charles Bremner. As he looked down from the plateau at the results of six weeks of Indian mutiny, he did not restrain his bitterness:

> In the town inself, or that part of it lying south of the Battle River, there is only enough left to remind the sufferers of their once comfortable homes. Their crime was that they were white; the penalty imposed was death. Very few farms are unharmed. There is not a home that has not been raided, scarcely a house that has not been burned. They are afoot and the marauders are mounted; their dairies are bare while their herds are being ruthlessly slaughtered by thieves, with no thought for the morrow. The Indians have shown themselves without gratitude. The Half-breeds who instigated the rising are much worse.

The Half-breeds were betrayers of the worst kind. They knew the pain, the hardships, the long hours of work without reward that were part of the settlers' life. That they would help to destroy their neighbors was contemptible, and Laurie was convinced that Charles Bremner was such a one. What Charles Bremner would be rebelling against, or why a well-to-do farmer, livestock raiser and fur trader would be interested in rebelling were questions that he did not seem to ponder.

For the Indians, it was a fierce, despairing defiance of the inevitable. There had been one wild, unbelievable moment of triumph; there would be poems of the glory of it. But now, the young warriors had torn their flesh out for the last time to prove their manhood. The dancing tent was folded.

Chapter Six

Surrender

Bremner and Cochin were received civilly by Colonel Otter and by Colonel William Herchmer, police commandant, who was by his side. Otter said that he would not do any harm to the Indians, whoever they were, provided that they themselves did not do any harm to the soldiers. He told them that he was not authorized to negotiate and that Poundmaker would have to wait for the arrival of General Middleton at Battleford. The next day about noon the two men rode south to deliver Otter's message. Poundmaker released all of the Bresaylor people, and the next morning sent Cochin back again, carrying a letter containing a statement of unconditional surrender and entire submission to be handed to Middleton when he arrived.

In the meantime, Jefferson had caught up with Middleton at Carlton, where he was about to embark on the river steamer, the *North-West*. "I delivered the letter. He said he would grant no terms to rebels but demanded unconditional surrender. He committed his ultimatum to writing and gave the letter to me to deliver to Poundmaker." When Jefferson returned to camp, he read the letter to the assembled Indians. It was brusque:

"Poundmaker,

I have defeated the Half-breeds and Indians at Batoche, and I have made no terms with them, neither will I make terms with you. I have men enough to destroy you and your people, or at least to drive you away to starve, and will do so unless you bring in the teams you took, and yourself and councillors meet me at Battleford on Tuesday, the 26th, with your arms. I am glad to hear that you treated the prisoners well and have released them.

Fred Middleton"[1]

As Jefferson said, it was what the Indians had looked for, "except that it was rather roughly put." When the letter had been translated and read, Poundmaker addressed his people:

You all, as many as you are, behold me. You all call me today as your leader. Listen well to what I will tell you.

Today there is the question of not fighting, and it matters not either to think of saving your own life. See all these women; see all these children; see all these young people who surround you. They are the ones that we must save.

I know you are brave. In fighting against the whites you can hinder them very much. But we will yield to the number, and something tells me that our children will have their lives safe.

I prefer to surrender myself at the risk of being hanged rather than to shed streams of blood by a resistance which has no more reason to be.[2]

They turned back towards Battleford. Jefferson said:

The last camp was made at the foot of the Eagle Hills, eight or ten miles out. It was a sad camp; gloom of the deepest clouded every face; all conversation was direful speculation as to the form the General's vengeance would take; they were to be disarmed so as to be completely at the soldiers' mercy.

The guns and rifles were loaded into two wagons for transport into town, and a miscellaneous assortment they were. Every kind of firearm ever sold by the Hudson's Bay Company since they came to the North-West, up to Sniders looted from the white men, flint locks, sixteen bore single-barrelled, double barreled, eight- and fourteen-shot Winchesters, were included in the delivery.

Along with these two wagons—some riding on horseback, some walking and some driving—came the whole body of men to make their surrender. A halt was called in the sand hills just south of the town partly to enable the laggards to catch up, and partly that all might be cautioned against talking too much.[3]

As the melancholy host was moving forward to acknowledge their defeat, the Bresaylor caravan was arriving in Battleford. It was early morning, May 26. When they came to the top of the south bank of the river, they looked with joy across to the plateau, to the police barracks, where they had laughed and danced. There were many tents on the plateau that had not been there before. They would be the tents of nearby settlers and neighbors and friends and relatives whom they had last seen nearly two months ago. The plateau looked like a shining and beckoning promised land. At last their ordeal was over; they could rest.

When they climed the hill to the barracks, Charles Bremner went into the commandant's office, and Herchmer told him to make camp on a large, flat space just to the west of the barracks. The rest of the morning was spent in once more setting up their square tents in what they hoped would be their last camp before they returned to their homes.

But there was little welcoming. Their own people stayed aloof; from others there was outright hostility. They were guilty, even that day, of having eaten the teamsters' provisions that had been intended for the strictly rationed refugees. In front page headlines of the next issue of the *Herald*, Laurie laid open the anger, malice, suspicions and exaggerated rumors arrayed against them.

> THE REBEL HALF-BREEDS. The army of half-breeds from the upper settlement who latterly lived in Poundmaker's camp posing as prisoners came into town on Tuesday, with their flocks, herds, household effects, and families. The appearance of the procession as it crossed the bridge gave the lie to their story of captivity, because on every wagon there were articles of furniture such as bedsteads, tables, chairs, and sewing machines— proof positive that they had been allowed plenty of time to prepare for their entry into bondage. . . . They were put into camp a little west of the barracks and a search of their outfits was instituted by the police.[4]

The sewing machines caught Laurie's eye, for his wife's had been destroyed in the sacking of Battleford. It was a precious instrument among settlers. But he didn't mention Father Cochin's organ, nor the fact that the livestock were being herded in for the Indians.

The foundation for that bitter welcome had been laid by the *Herald*'s report of the Cut Knife fight, a report undoubtedly contributed by Laurie's son William, who worked on the paper and who was one of Otter's volunteers on the scene. Its implications had festered in the minds of the besieged refugees.

> We found the camp deserted, climbed the hill and met with fire from the Indians who appeared on the edge of the thickly wooded coulee 200 yards away. . . . The Indians were able from their shelter in the wooded ravines on both sides of the troops and from the summits of surrounding hills to pour in a harassing fire. . . . Hour after hour the battle waged, always with success on

the side of the troops, until about 10 o'clock, we decided to dislodge the enemy on the right. . . . An hour later it was deemed necessary to dislodge a party of Half-breeds who had posted themselves in a deep ravine on the left. . . . A large number of Half-breeds, including many whose faces were familiar on the streets of Battleford, were recognised under the paint with which they had bedaubed themselves, and not a few of them paid the penalty of their perfidy. . . . During the action both the cannon became useless through the breaking of the carriages, and it being useless to follow them without artillery, it was decided to return to Battleford.[5]

The account noted in continuation that "The enemy was completely hidden in the numerous thickets, the puff of smoke, followed by the sharp whistle of their Winchester bullets, being the only indication of their presence."

William Laurie was possibly disconcerted by the encircling harassment so that he could not estimate numbers accurately, and too busy to see clearly the assailants hidden in the rifle pits or in the willow bushes. The only half-breeds clearly visible were Charles Bremner and his companions on horseback on a promontory, waving a white flag and being shot at. The casualty list reported five dead Indians. No half-breeds. Some of the confusion apparently came from lumping together the Bresaylor settlers with the handful of Riel's men who were mixed with the Indians. In any case, this damning report, that passed sentence by innuendo on Bremner's people, not only caused the hostility on their arrival at Battleford, it was copied by other newspapers and was often taken as a reliable, almost official account of the affair: Colonel Otter had scored a famous victory in spite of the perfidy of Bresaylor men in fighting against their own people.

In Battleford, the excitement of the arrival of the Bremner company was quickly superseded by that aroused by Poundmaker and his hapless host. They appeared at the top of the south bank at noon. Jefferson was with them. The village had changed considerably, and not only in the charred remains of the official buildings on their right as they started down the hill.

> The flat between the Battle River and the barracks was covered with the tents of soldiers—a most imposing array—and into the midst of these the Indians were now to wend their way.

Quite a large concourse of people were on hand to take in the
spectacle, but there was nothing in the appearance of the
Indians—except their unusual numbers—to indicate that they
were conquered supplicants for peace.

Their bearing did not lack dignity; they appeared quite
unconcerned—some even had a truculent look. Nothing, in
short, was provided on the part of the Indians to give the event
the character of a show. Poundmaker and the principal men led
the way.

The steamer *North-West* was docked by the bridge where it had
arrived on Sunday morning at 8:15 with General Middleton and his
staff. They were now in formal array at the edge of the hill. There was
silence over the whole scene as the conquerors watched the slow ascent
of the defeated. Cochin was there. "The General waited for Poundmaker
surrounded by his officers and by a strong party of the garrison." So was
Brodie: "General Middleton sat on a chair facing west; at about fifteen
feet sat Peter Hourie, the interpreter, on a chair facing east. The Indians
sat on the ground to the south. I stood about fifteen feet north of the
General, inside the soldiers' lines."[6]

Poundmaker and the other chiefs had sat in another such semi-
circle less than nine years before, at Carlton or at Pitt, negotiating a
treaty. There had been another tent, with the flaps open so that all could
see and hear everything that passed. The red coats of the police had
added a splash of color then too. But then it was the whites and the
governor with friendly eyes and kindly smile who were the suppliants,
and it was a parley between equals.

Poundmaker was now, not just a spokesman, but the commander of
the host, even if a commander in defeat. He rose from his place and
came forward to greet the general, holding out his hand. Middleton
waved it aside with contempt, "I do not shake hands with rebels."
Poundmaker gathered his blanket about him and resumed his seat.

Middleton, a man of average stature well-filled out, with ruddy
cheeks, walrus moustaches, a swagger in his mien, sat with his sword by
his side and legs spread apart, stiffly, to receive submission. Cochin was
dismayed,

> The manner in which Poundmaker was received by the
> General somewhat surprised me. The Indians had remained mas-
> ters of the field at Cut Knife, having lost only five men. They
> could have resisted a long while yet, and caused considerable

damage, or scattered themselves and taken refuge in the United States as others had done. Poundmaker delivered himself up voluntarily. He was the only chief who thus exposed his life to stop the bloodshed and re-establish peace in the country. This was the main motive which made him act. It was on the part of an Indian a generous act and heroic, more worthy of pardon and even of reward, than of prison and fetters.

But Middleton was not a generous man. A man of minor achievements and close to retirement, he was experienced in assisting at the subduing of indigenous people, in putting down rebellious Maori chiefs in New Zealand, or in overcoming mutinous Sepoys in India. Lately the ruler over cadets at the Royal Military Academy at Sandhurst and now the victor over some 500 Métis farmers at Batoche, he was intent on imposing the authority born of superior force and dominant race. He reprimanded Poundmaker for taking up arms and murdering innocent settlers.

Poundmaker rose again. "I have murdered no one. We defended ourselves when we were attacked at Cut Knife, which I believe we are entitled to do. We now come to give ourselves up. You have us in your hands to work your will upon us. We have submitted to you our unconditional surrender. All that we ask is that the women and children may go unharmed."

Two Stoney Indians came forward, one who had killed the farm instructor on Red Pheasant's reserve, the other who had killed the farmer Tremont south of Battleford. Each confessed his guilt. Middleton ordered the murderers into custody along with Poundmaker, his brother Yellow-Mud-Blanket, Break-the-Ice, Lean Man, and a few of the head councillors. He told the great mass of Indians to go back to their reserves. He was following the policy of the government as he had done with the Métis of the South Branch. The leaders were taken for trial, the followers sent back to their farms. It was a sensible policy. The police escorted their prisoners into the barracks. As the afternoon wore on, the Indians began to disperse morosely, starting back to their reserves. The affair at Duck Lake was on March 26, the surrender of Poundmaker was on May 26. Two months of struggle.

Middleton's scornful rebuff rankled in Poundmaker's mind, and when Cochin visited him in prison that evening, he said, "If I had been in the place of the General, I could never have allowed myself thus to treat a white, who would have acted as I did. I'd rather be hanged than be so treated."

The crowd of spectators drifted off—Battleford residents, refugee settlers, police, soldiers, Bresaylor newcomers. Charles Bremner went back to his tent. At its entrance, a soldier who had been searching the tent came out, holding a rifle in his hands. He demanded to know where Bremner had got it. Bremner replied that he had bought it a few days before from a neighbor. And where did the neighbor get it? Probably bought it from an Indian. The rifle was army issue and must have been taken from a soldier—or from a soldier's body. Bremner was taken into custody.

He was not the only one. As Laurie reported, "Most of the men of the party have been arrested on various charges, principally appropriating property belonging to others." Jefferson was shocked: "Several of the Half-breeds from Bresaylor were also made prisoners as rebels, but there was not one scrap of evidence against them." Father Cochin tried to intervene but without success, "In spite of my protestations in favor of some Half-breeds, my companions in captivity, many of them were also taken and thrown in prison." And so Charles Bremner and his neighbors rejoined Poundmaker, but this time they were all prisoners.

Middleton was preoccupied. "After making a prisoner of Poundmaker, I was informed that some half-breeds had come in from his camp and that there was some reason to believe them to be rebels."[7] He told the police to hold them.

And then there were Bremner's furs. As soon as Charles Bremner was seen being taken into the barracks by the police, soldiers and others began drifting by his tent to help themselves to skins from the heavily laden carts. Louis Caplette tried to stop them, but they laughed at him. Bremner was a rebel, wasn't he? Then the furs were fair game. Emily and the girls, bewildered and frightened, watched from inside the tent. Caplette appealed to Middleton. Again the general was off-hand. "That same day, I think, it was reported to me that the people were carrying off furs belonging to these half-breeds, and it was suggested that the furs should be sent to the police barracks, which I believe I ordered to be done."

There was another witness, one with a better memory. Ronald Macdonald, of the Home Guard, a contractor in Battleford, had been acting as assistant to Quartermaster Warden of the police in rationing food to the civilians. From the windows of his office in the large storeroom for supplies and provisions, he looked out to the Bremner tents about two hundred yards away. He had known Charles Bremner for some time, and when he saw what had happened, he strolled over to see the collection of furs that had become a magnet for so many sudden passersby. He estimated its value at between $5,000 and $7,000, and noted that it included beaver, bear, fisher, mink. That evening from his office, Macdonald saw General Middleton and Colonel Otter talking with Louis Caplette beside the fur carts and shortly after there was action:

> In the evening of May 26, several loads of fur were brought into the quartermaster's store from Mr. Bremner's camp. They were brought in by teams in the employ of the Government, by the police, who had charge of them. After they were brought into the barracks they were brought to me and I placed them in rows. I should judge over fifty, perhaps even a hundred beaver skins were packed together, worth $7 to $8 a skin. The furs were placed by themselves and covered from view to ensure protection from theft.

Charles Bremner and his furs were now both locked up, but at least they were safe. And Bremner was confident that when the confusion subsided and he got out of this unbelievable mess, he would have his furs as capital to start over with. At the moment, the prospect was grim for all of the settlers on the plateau. The army would not let anyone out into the countryside yet with Big Bear's men still at large, and with no crops in, their buildings, implements, supplies destroyed and their stock driven off, the winter would be hard. Their resentment grew against those who had caused the hardship, or who were thought to have caused it.

Towards the end of the week, General Middleton left by steamer for Fort Pitt, to join Major-General Strange in the pursuit of the elusive and baffling Big Bear, who was playing tricks with the troops in the northern swamps and heavy woods. The rebellion was not over yet.

Neither was the confusion. Charles Bremner found that the situation, which had seemed to be a joke, if an unpleasant one, had become deadly serious. Inspector Francis Dickens, having lost his post at Pitt, was sitting for the police as a Justice of the Peace and conducting daily preliminary examinations of the Indians and the Half-breeds who had been arrested and, as Laurie reported, "committing for trial such of the prisoners as the evidence warrants. There are now thirty in the guard room awaiting trial at the coming session of the Saskatchewan court." That court was to be opened by Judge Charles Rouleau on June 26, but it would be "only for the trial of those accused of robbery, theft, and minor charges."

Meantime, most of the Bresaylor men who had been arrested were dismissed, but five were held. The five who had stood on a promontory at Cut Knife waving their white flag. On June 1, Laurie reported progress: "The following cases have been disposed of by Inspector Dickens: Baptiste Sayer, Henry Sayer, Charles Bremner, James Bremner, William Frank have been charged with treason felony and remanded for four days."

Treason felony. Charles Bremner. This was a world gone mad. He looked down on the man sitting at the desk, the man whom Big Bear had allowed to escape in the night on a river scow from Fort Pitt, and protested that he was not a rebel, but loyal to the Queen. Dickens brushed him aside. Father Cochin tried. "These people are not rebels. I have lived with them for over a year. They were my fellow prisoners in Poundmaker's camp. They had no part in the battle."[8] Dickens' reply was that Cochin had not known all that had gone on, either in the community or in the battle itself. Cochin was dismissed.

The five returned to the guard room to await word from General Middleton about what would be done with them, for they were, after all, prisoners of war, not prisoners of the police. The general was with Strange, chasing Big Bear through the marshes, and could not be reached.

Emily came to Charles in the guard house in great distress; the families of the prisoners were being harassed. "Little Emily," as she had been known, had grown in girth with childbearing, and she was expecting another in the fall. She told Charles of refugee children and Battleford children running through the camp yelling "Thieves! Traitors!" sometimes even darting inside the tents. Louis couldn't stop them. The girls were heart-broken. What to do? Nothing but wait it out.

On Saturday, June 6, a public indignation meeting was held in the barracks. In the bright, clear summer evening the prisoners could hear the hubbub of the gathering as both villagers and famers crowded in. Primarily they were angry with the government for its miserly offer of help. "The Indian Department lends out grain to the farmers on condition of a bushel and a half being returned in the fall for each bushel lent," and it was now seeding time. The Edmonton *Bulletin* took up their cause. "All but two or three of the Indians were sent to their reserves, rationed and allowed to keep their plunder, while the people they had robbed were allowed seed grain on Shylock conditions, or to fish for themselves as best they might. They have lost everything."[9]

The meeting passed resolutions. *Resolution:* To express much dissatisfaction with the manner and leniency of the acceptance of the surrender of the Half-breeds and the Indians. *Resolution:* To declare that the offer of the Indian Department to settlers of seed grain to be repaid in double quantity in the fall was most ungenerous. *Resolution:* To prohibit Indians from roaming at large. *Resolution:* That the government be requested to appoint a commission to investigate rebellion losses.

Day was still bright in the sky when the meeting ended and Louis Caplette went to Charles Bremner to report on it. The part that hurt most keenly was the reference to "the surrender" of the Bresaylor Half-breeds. Loss, arrest, and more—bitterness from one-time friends. The long growing days of June, now wasted, passed slowly.

On June 19, Middleton returned to Pitt after a vain chase for Big Bear, and received messages left for him. "It was sometime between then and the beginning of July, that I received some information confirming the opinion that those Half-breeds who had come into Battleford from Poundmaker's camp were rebels. . . . I remember that a rifle, belonging to one of the men killed at Cut Knife or Eagle Hills, had been found in the possession of this very Bremner, and it was probably then that I ordered the whole of these Half-breeds to be sent to Regina." The venue of Riel's trial had been set in Regina, to Laurie's chagrin, who thought it should have been in Battleford.

On Friday, July 3, over a month after Bremner had been arrested, the *Herald* reported, "Colonel Herchmer left for the south with the police and scouts belonging to that section. They took with them the following prisoners, arrested by order of General Middleton, all of whom are to be tried at Regina or sent to the Manitoba Penitentiary." The list included the Bresaylor five. The day before, Big Bear had given himself up to the police at Carlton, far from General Middleton. The general's work was over in the North West, and he prepared to leave Pitt by steamer for Battleford. The rebellion was finished. The surrenders were complete.

Chapter Seven

Trial

The long, hot, dust-filled summer in Regina began for the Bresaylor men in the square of the police barracks. Their coming was recorded by the Regina *Leader*: "Col. Herchmer arrived on Friday, July 10, with Poundmaker and twenty-two prisoners."[1] They had been a silent, gloomy lot as they were trundled the 200 miles to Swift Current across the empty land, stopping every four hours while the drivers watered and fed the horses, sleeping at night on the floor of stopping houses where their mounted police escort could guard them easily. It was a trip that Bremner and his companions had often taken as freighters, but they were not then in leg irons. At the police station in Swift Current, they were transferred to the train for the final 150 miles across the flat, tree-less, buffalo plains. Word had gone ahead that Poundmaker was arriving and, though it was after 11 p.m. in Regina, a crowd was milling about on the lighted platform, hoping to catch a glimpse of him.

The town that had had a population of fifteen hundred a few months before had swelled with the oncoming of Riel's trial to two or three times that size. The four hotels were full—there wasn't a room for a good-sized flea in any of them, the *Leader* said—the boarding houses were full, the private homes were full. The government was hard-pressed to find accommodation for the legal counsel and their staffs, four of them being put in "the large house on Albert Street." Many of the large body of witnesses had complained, not only of the poor lodging assigned to them, but also of the high prices, for they were paid only $1.50 a day and five cents a mile travel fare. As a result of their com-plaints, the *Leader* reported, "Mr. W. N. Newton, N.W.M.P., has a boarding tent, 3 sleeping tents, and one wash tent erected opposite the Court House for the accommodation of witnesses unable or unwilling to pay more than $1 a day for board. At present nine Crown witnesses are in the tents." The crowd of newspaper men from Montreal, Toronto, Winnipeg, and the United States squeezed in wherever cot space could be found.

The curiosity seekers, drawn by the double novelty of the trial and the prospect of an excursion to see the wonders of the Rocky Mountains on the almost-completed trans-Canada railway, pitched tents in open lots. Tents housed the 350 men of the Montreal Garrison Artillery south of the tracks, tents housed the 100 men of the 91st Battalion north of the tracks near the station, and six square tents had been put up at the barracks to help lodge the 250 police.

Everything was being built as quickly as materials could be rushed in. Wooden sidewalks had already been laid in four of the principal streets, and were being laid in a fifth, several large houses and a Presbyterian church were being built in the residential area, stones for the foundations of government buildings were now on the sites, and bricks to be used in building them were being made in the neighborhood.

Riel, the magnet of the activities, had been quietly brought into Regina over six weeks before, on Saturday, May 23, by sixteen soldiers under Captain George H. Young, of the Winnipeg Artillery, whom Middleton had appointed brigade major in the field. Young was the son of the Methodist minister who had been with Thomas Scott when he was killed and to whom Riel had refused to release the body, which subsequently was never found. Capt. Young was nevertheless on good terms with his prisoner.

By the time Riel was charged on July 6, the crowds had increased to such a degree that, to protect him when he was taken from the barracks to the Court House, he was disguised as a policeman with a long cloak and white helmet. "He was driven down in an open carriage with a corporal and three policemen," the *Leader* reported. "His bushy beard flowed warriorlike down from beneath the white crown." The day before the Battleford contingent arrived, the *Leader*'s owner-publisher, Nicholas Flood Davin, one-time parliamentary reporter in the British House of Commons and member of the British bar, rose to the heights of history:

> Regina is about to be the theatre of one of the most interesting events which have ever taken place in Canada—a state trial; the trial of a leader in a rebellion—a trial in which his life is at stake. For a trial of such importance you have to go back to England to 1789, and Riel stands in the same category as other state prisoners—Charles I, Strafford, Monmouth. . . . Most of these paid for their treason with their lives.

Even Regina society elevated the occasion, and Lieutenant-Governor Dewdney and Mrs. Dewdney held a Government House Ball, 'a brilliant affair,' in the Council Chambers, with music by the Montreal Garrison Artillery band.

Such was the excitement in the air when the train pulled in from Swift Current on Friday night. The ten bound for Winnipeg and the penitentiary stayed on board; the others disembarked. There was no attempt to disguise the tall, proud figure of Poundmaker with the two heavy braids hanging to his waist, but there was an unusually large detail of troops to ward off eager newsmen and to make a way through the noisy mob. For Poundmaker, Bremner, and the others, the sight before them was a shock. It was one thing to be freighted across the plains in wagons, but another—an offensive and humiliating thing—to be paraded as a spectacle for sight-seers.

On their arrival at the barracks, they were taken through a room or large hall in front of the cells, where a shift of police were having a late snack. Here, Poundmaker, his brother, and one or two other chiefs were separated from the rest and put in the cells, which were kept for important prisoners, and where Big Bear would be put as soon as he arrived. The others, including the Bresaylor men, were taken through to the yard.

The scene was a familiar one—several large square white tents, visible even in the dark. They held many of the nearly 70 prisoners who had so far arrived, most of them Métis from the South Branch. Here, as elsewhere, government buildings were being erected, this time a new prison to accommodate the unbudgeted-for lodgers. The Battleford group, now shrunk to only seven or eight, were led to one of the tents.

With the morning came another sense of familiarity. As the Bremners and the Sayers looked about them, they felt as though they had been transported back to 1870 on the Red River. Many whom they saw now they had seen then as members of the provisional government and controllers of Fort Garry which had been seized from the Company. At a short distance they saw Louis Riel when he was brought out to exercise. They had last seen him as master of their lives fifteen years ago. In some incongruous way he was still controlling their lives. They looked without warmth at the slight, dark-bearded, lonely figure with its strange explosive power and messianic convictions. The rebellion suddenly became intimate. It was also, as they saw on the faces about them, a rebellion of the middle-aged, of the unsuccessful middle-aged.

With the Indians there was a difference. Even the *Leader* had already made a distinction between the Métis rebellion and the Indian uprising. The Indians too were rebelling against the inevitable, but specifically against the mystery of the loss of the buffalo, which had made the old life impossible, and against the incomers. And those included the Métis, the Bresaylor Half-breeds, and all the other settlers taking up land, who made the earth grow less. Strange people said you must stay there, in that place—like a tethered horse. For either group it was a rebellion against the intangible and the inescapable.

The long days passed. The notables assembled. Big Bear, his ten-year-old son, and twelve Indians arrived on Friday, July 17, in the custody of Inspector Denymer and twenty-five police, to add to the prison population. General Middleton, a witness for the Riel trial, arrived with his wife, the daughter of a prosperous Montreal merchant, in a private railway car and stayed with the Dewdneys. S.J. Bedson, warden of the Manitoba penitentiary, who had come west with the Wolseley expedition in 1870, and latterly had been put in charge of the transport services for Middleton's forces, came from Stony Mountain. J.A. Ouimet, a lawyer from Montreal, chairman of the recently created Rebellion Claims Commission, in Regina to consult with Dewdney, was staying at the Palmer Hotel before leaving for Battleford. Counsel for the Crown and for the defense had already been present for the arraignment, but now some of their ladies began to arrive.

At last, the trial of "The Queen vs Louis Riel" began, on July 23. Davin set the stage:

> Where three years ago the only signs of life were Indian trails and buffalo tracks, now the highest expression of civilization—an organised court of law presided over by a judge learned in the law, with the most eminent lawyers in the Dominion pleading before him, in gowns and white ties as in Osgoode Hall. Within the bar young lawyers are taking notes. There are generals and famous captains, and in that part made sacred for the fairer sex, fashionable women known in courtly drawing rooms bring youth and beauty. Mr. Sheriff Chapleau, full of dignity, sits in the Sheriff's chair on the left side of the bench, with his under-strappers to do his bidding as in an English court. The scene is sprinkled with red coats where Captain Deane and four or five of his policemen are stationed here and there. A dozen reporters peg away at their notes. The place allotted to the general public is crowded and just as in an English court, there are complaints that the door-keepers are sometimes insolent, ignorant, or both.

On August 1, the trial ended. Riel made a two-hour speech from the dock, the jury retired for an hour, and brought back the verdict of guilty. At 3:30 Riel was sentenced to be hanged in the police barracks on September 18. It was a sombre escort that brought him back to the cells. Word spread swiftly, and deep melancholy hung over the prisoners in the square. The Métis were full of grief for their leader, the Indians fearful for their own fate, the Bremner group tense with the constant uncertainty.

Four days later, on Tuesday, August 4, there was further movement in the square. As the *Leader* reported,

> At 3 o'clock, a small army of mounted red coats arrived in full canter at the Court House in charge of 26 prisoners of war—vanquished heroes of Duck Lake, Fish Creek, and Batoche. Once in the courtyard, the Métis were ushered through the hall and into that memorable little building where, but a few days before, a highly interested and attractive audience gazed on the central figure of the North-West rebellion. . . . The attendance was fairly small, with only one lady in the gallery.

On the advice of their lawyers and of Father André, their parish priest, all pleaded guilty to treason-felony, with the understanding that their punishment would not be severe. They were remanded, and the impressive convoy trotted back again.

There was other activity. General Middleton and his wife left for the east in their private car; counsel for the prosecution and their wives took the train west for the excursion to the Rockies; counsel for the defence began to arrange for Riel's appeal. There was activity even in the jail, where a carload of window-sill slabs from a quarry five miles west of Calgary arrived for the new prison.

There was activity on behalf of the Bresaylor men too. T. C. Johnstone, a Regina lawyer, had agreed to defend them, and he was busy searching out witnesses who would testify for them.[2] Two likely possibilities were Robert Jefferson and Father Cochin, the young Englishman and the young Frenchman, both still in their twenties, who had been called as Crown witnesses for Poundmaker's trial, set for August 15.

Both of them in turn visited the Bresaylor men to give them news of home, for it was now six weeks since the group had left Battleford. Their families were still in the tents near the barracks. Of the other Bresaylor folk, Peter and Herbert Taylor and Philip Macdonald had been the first to return to their farms. But their homes and their farm machinery had been destroyed; they would have to start all over again. The Battleford people were beginning to get things together, and all of the houses still standing in the flats were occupied. At the barracks, now that Big Bear's men had been rounded up, the jail was jammed with over 40 prisoners. The trials of the murderers were to begin in mid-

September, after Judge Rouleau returned. The Indian Department had closed out the farm instructorships, which seemed to have been a source of constant friction, and anyway, it was now almost impossible to get men to go on the reserves. Jefferson, while he was in Regina, was going to see Hayter Reed about a job as interpreter for the Battleford agency.

Father Cochin told of the brief—he thought cursory—hearing into rebellion losses claims, which the commission had opened in Battleford on July 30. In addition to Chairman Ouimet of Montreal, there were Thomas Mackay of Prince Albert, Henry Muma from Ontario, and Captain George Young of Winnipeg as secretary, the last on the recommendation of General Middleton. Father Cochin had written a long letter to them on behalf of his fellow captives of Cut Knife, but the Commission said that they had contributed to their own losses by joining the Indians, and so were not eligible for compensation; and Mr. Laurie had put a piece in his paper saying that Father Cochin did not know all that had gone on. "I think I know as much as Mr. Laurie does about what went on in Poundmaker's camp," the young priest said.

Bishop Grandin had made a tour of his whole parish and had found the Métis of the South Branch destitute, and so he was on his way to Ottawa to try to get aid for them. Father André, who was still in the barracks with Riel, was very angry with General Middleton, whom he had accused of allowing his troops to loot the homes of people of Batoche, stealing their furs and other valuables. The general denied it, and very haughtily said that he would have been justified if he had wiped out the whole village.[3] Father André also said that Riel's rebellion was as much against the authority of the church as against the authority of the government, but that he had given up his new religion and had received communion. He would die in the faith.

After the visits of Jefferson and the young priest, Charles Bremner pondered the nature of the prisoners who had been jailed as a result of the two months' action in the spring, and of the charges against them. What was treason? Treason-felony?

The Indians who had killed—the two from south of Battleford and the ones from Frog Lake—were being held at Battleford to be tried for murder in the district court, for their killings were civilian crimes and not part of a military action. They were not generally accused of treason or treason-felony—not even Big Bear's men.

Riel, yes. He had come in from outside, stirred people up, raised a military force, and led it against the police and the army. Granted amnesty for his acts of 1870, he had returned to organise another insurrection against the government of Canada. Voices of the West, both

Tory and Grit, were agreed on the nature of his action. Davin took for granted the fact of Riel's treason in the view of history. Frank Oliver, a fierce Liberal, took a more immediate view: "Riel should be hanged because from motives of personal aggrandisement he had betrayed his friends to death and ruin, and caused the slaughter and torture of those with whom he had no quarrel, knowing well what he was doing the while."[4] He had had his trial, he had been sentenced, his lawyers were now preparing an appeal based on the jury's recommendation of mercy—all a reasonable process growing out of the fact.

But what about the Indians? True, they had broken a treaty—a treaty that Big Bear had reluctantly accepted only a few months ago— but the treaty was between equals, between two nations. They did not regard themselves as subjects of the Queen—they had no feudal relationship with the Crown—and they did not recognize the legalistic charge of felony. As for treason, as Jefferson had said,[5] that was a concept entirely foreign to them. On the heights of Battleford, when Middleton first charged Poundmaker with high treason, the interpreter had said, "There is no such word in the Cree language," and after some discussion with Poundmaker, he gave as his translation, "You are accused of throwing sticks at the Queen and trying to knock her bonnet off."[6] It was no more absurd than the present trial. The assembled bands who had chosen Poundmaker as leader had sacked Battleford, and he as leader must answer for it. They had burned and looted settlers' homes, they had seized their cattle and horses. In short, they had behaved as they had behaved for generations against the Blackfeet until Chief Sweetgrass had brought them to a conciliation ten years before. In the new life, they were guilty of theft and of destroying property. Poundmaker had been attacked in his own domain and had routed the attackers and their Gatling gun. That was fair. Then against his wish—but again as chief he was responsible—the whole host had moved off the reserve intending to join Riel. That was arguable, for they had not joined him. True, they had captured the freighter train and had seized army provisions. For that theft they must pay. But even that was hardly treason.

And what about them, the five from Bresaylor—himself, his brother James, their two old friends, Henry and Baptiste Sayer, and their neighbor William Frank? Treason-felony? They had harmed no one, they had not taken up arms, they had not stolen. They had been in the company of Poundmaker's host, but not of their own will. They had helped to herd into Battleford the cattle and horses—some of them their own—that the Indians had taken, and they were accused of having stolen them. But even if they had—was theft treason? There was the rifle, of course. He had bought it from John Wells. Where had it come from? The Indians had Winchesters and ammunition for them. But this one was said to be army issue, then it was said to belong to a dead soldier, finally to the one body that the soldiers had left behind in their retreat and that Father Cochin had buried. Treason?

Why were they here, as prisoners of war? Fortunately, their lawyer, T.G. Johnstone, was beginning to find others who felt the same way. Doubts as to the accuracy of battlefield reports by volunteers were surfacing; merchants with whom Bremner had dealt were willing to give character references. The case looked hopeful. But when would they be called? That was uncertain.

The middle part of August was a time of many events. On the 14th, the Métis band were ushered out again to be sentenced in the Court House, for treason-felony. According to the *Leader*, 7 were dismissed, 10 got seven years in the penitentiary, 3 got three years in the penitentiary, 3 got one year in the Regina jail. Those destined for the penitentiary were started on their way by the night train. On the 15th, Poundmaker was escorted to the Court House. He pleaded not guilty and was remanded for two days. In the dock, he aroused Davin's admiration as he had done with many others, and the *Leader* hailed him as "a noble figure, a handsome and truly noble—nay, kingly-looking man . . . brave but misguided. . . . He wore a defiant, intelligent look." On the 17th, he was brought in again, tried and sentenced to three years in the penitentiary. He rose to say, "I would rather prefer to be hanged at once than to be in that place." On the 18th word came from Ottawa that Middleton and Adolphe Caron, Minister of the Militia, had both been knighted for bringing the rebellion to such an expeditious end. On the 20th, Jefferson, Cochin and the other Battleford witnesses left for home. Two or three days later, Johnstone came with discouraging news for his clients. He had assembled some 30 people who would be willing to testify in their defense in the trial, but the Court had ruled against him. He could not call on that body of testimony.

There was a hiatus, then on September 3 another cortege rode out, a smaller one this time, with Big Bear and nine other Indians. They were charged with treason-felony, they pleaded not guilty, their trial was postponed for three weeks to allow lawyers to gather evidence.

At last, on September 7, the Bresaylor five were called in the case of "The Queen vs. Charles Bremner et al." Bremner was officially designated as the leader of his group, and besides, he had had the incriminating rifle in his possession. They too had an escort, though a modest one, as they went the now well-worn route across the bridge over the

Wascana, past Government House, past the Council Chambers, down Albert Street, past the post-office, past the Bank of Montreal, at last to the Court House, there to be led into the now famous little building.

There was no audience. They stood before the judge. Hugh Richardson was sixty, born in England, raised in Upper Canada, called to the bar in 1847, Lieut. Colonel commanding at Sarnia in the Fenian raids of 1866, Colonel-in-command of the 22nd Oxford rifles until 1875. He was a tubby little man with round face and shrewd eyes, brown side-whiskers and moustache tinged with grey. But the formal robes obliterated human traits. He was The Law.

It was a solemn moment, full of apprehension for the five Half-breeds. The Clerk of the Court rose and read the charge, issued on the formal complaint of Captain George Young of Winnipeg, that:

> Charles Bremner, James Bremner, William Frank, Henry Sayer and Baptiste Sayer at Cut Knife on May 2 . . . and on divers other days and times before and after did conspire, consult, confederate, assemble and meet together with divers other evil-disposed persons to raise, make and levy insurrection and rebellion against our said Lady the Queen . . . and later on May 14 to seize and take possession by force of certain goods and merchandises belonging to Her Majesty the Queen, being carried from Swift Current to Battleford.

The prisoners pleaded "Not guilty". The Crown Prosecutor rose, tall, impressive, with dark eyes, black hair and moustache, Britton B. Osler, Q.C. from Ontario, in his mid-forties. He addressed the judge:

> Your Honor, in these cases, the prisoners are charged with having been concerned in the late rebellion. They were in the Indian camp of Poundmaker, and the Crown has evidence against them showing that, to some extent, at all events, they joined in resisting the forces of the Government. In one case, military clothing, and in another case, a police rifle was found in the possession of the prisoners, but we have considered that perhaps the prisoners were in a difficult position. They were brought into camp (Poundmaker's) probably without their consent, by a large body of armed Indians; and having got into that camp, they may have been led into the acts complained of without knowing the serious position they were placing themselves in in so doing.

We have considered that originally the desire probably of all the prisoners was to stay in their settlement. We have considered also that they had their families and their property to protect against uncontrollable violence of the Indians surrounding them. They were in a very difficult position. The Crown considering these things, and not being able to bring home acts of personal violence against any of them, and learning that they were all men of good character before this trouble came, we have considered that perhaps the ends of justice would be obtained by allowing them to be discharged on their own recognizance to appear when called upon for trial; and I may say on behalf of the Crown, that unless the evidence implicating the prisoners with acts of personal violence appears, that as far as that offence of theirs against their allegiance is concerned, the Crown does not propose to call upon them to answer. It will only be in the event of evidence turning up to show that they were personally implicated in acts of violence during the rebellion that the Crown will call upon them to respond.[7]

And that was it. That was all. The Crown, having searched for the two months that these men had been in the Regina jail, had found no evidence against them. The Clerk of the Court recorded: "The prisoners' own recognizance taken and the prisoners were released." After the long weeks of imprisonment, anxiety, torment, with no crops in, no food stored for their families, no chance to get any, with the worry of their families left without care in the midst of antagonism—that was all. And unlike the South Branch rebels, they had no powerful lobby to go to Ottawa to plead their case. These arid, useless months, the solemn charge of conspiracy, of treason—nothing—empty.

As Charles Bremner said, "We were released on bail on our security of $400," and still not told of any grounds for the accusations made against them. They were released, they were no longer prisoners, but they were not cleared. In Scottish law, they would have been under the grey, ambiguous cloud of "Not proven," but they had not even that assurance. They could be called up again and again if anyone thought that he could safely charge them with "an act of violence," even as they had been called up in the first instance. Why? The unanswered question. Middleton had arrested the South Branch leaders and had sent the rest back to their farms. He had arrested the Indian leaders and had sent the rest back to their reserves. Why pick on this handful of settlers to treat quite differently?

Chapter Eight

Homecoming

They reached Battleford on September 18, the day when Riel was to have been executed had he not been given a month's reprieve. But Riel, Regina, and the whole ugly nightmare of the summer were all behind them now. They were free and their lives were ahead of them. When once more they topped the bank of the Battle River and looked down at the golden glory sloping steeply below them and then across at the grand plateau, once more the magnificence of the scene thrilled them. As they rode up the hill to the tent town and got out of the police wagon, their wives and children came running down to greet them.

Emily came more slowly. She was eight months pregnant, expecting the baby within three or four weeks. Charles thought back to the last time, to the child born on the trail three years ago. This time Emily had spent most of her pregnancy without a home, harried from one place to another, never free of anxiety. Her time was near and the nights were frosty—too frosty for her to be living in a tent. He must get to Bresaylor and make ready a place for her.

But the ugly dream had not gone. It had a voice, the voice of P. G. Laurie, who greeted their homecoming in the *Herald* with the notice, "Along with the police outfit that came in from Regina on Friday were the Sayers and Bremners arrested by General Middleton. They are out on bail on their own recognizance to appear and take their trial in Battleford when called on." Then he added on no basis other than his own antipathy, "More probably they are being sent here for trial."

Laurie was much less generous than the Crown Prosecutor had been, but then he wasn't restrained by evidence—or lack of it. He was convinced that his son's eyes had not deceived him at the battle of Cut Knife Hill. He was convinced that the Bremner group were hypocrites. Even Jefferson had remarked on the peculiar swiftness with which the school-teacher Joubert had received news from Riel's headquarters, and Cochin had said that Delorme was in charge of operations. Of the dozen or so families that had gone to Poundmaker's camp, most were Métis families, Father Cochin's flock, that had recently come from the South Branch, some of them openly advocating Riel's cause. These were not innocent victims, and it was improbable that Charles Bremner, an acknowledged leader in the community, was ignorant of their sympathies even if he did not share them. More personally, twice now in fifteen years the Half-breeds of the Red River had destroyed Laurie's work and marred his life. Once more he must build a new life for himself and his family, everything gone except his printing press.

The lawyer Johnstone had been able to find a score and more in the Battleford district willing to testify for Charles Bremner and his companions, but even his very soliciting had sharpened a division among the people. Many of those who had lived out the siege agreed with Laurie that anyone who had not fled to the citadel could be counted among the despoilers who had sacked and burned the village and the farms.

Then the ugly nightmare took on substance. Before Charles Bremner went to Bresaylor to rebuild for Emily and the family, he must first get his furs. They were his credit by which he could buy building materials, household supplies, clothing, everything that they would need for the coming winter. He went over to the police barracks to see Inspector William Morris, who had been in charge when he left, and asked for his furs. The policeman looked up from his desk, disconcerted; the furs were gone.

Bremner looked at him in stunned disbelief. Where were they? Morris didn't know. They had been confiscated. General Middleton had confiscated them a couple of months before, early in July, when the general was on his way to Winnipeg. In fact, Morris had had telegrams from him since then, asking for more. Ronald Macdonald would know more; he had had the job of packing some of them.

Ronald Macdonald had gone back to his contracting work. There was plenty of it. He gave Bremner the same account that he gave later to a parliamentary committee:[1]

> As far as we were concerned, it was a command, a command from the general of the Canadian army. We just did what we were told. It was the day after you left for Regina. A courier came from Pitt. He had a letter from Hayter Reed to Warden, the quartermaster sergeant. It said that the general had decided to confiscate the furs, and wanted some put up for himself, for Reed, and for Bedson, the warden of the Manitoba penitentiary, temporarily on Middleton's staff, just as Reed was. The letter said they were coming down by steamer the next day, and they wanted the furs ready.
>
> So Warden told me to put up two bales for the general and one each for the other two. And they were to be choice furs. I

had laid them out when they were brought in, so I knew what was there. I picked out enough for the two bales for the general, mostly beaver, some fisher, I think, and some otter. Dorion, the store clerk, did most of the packing. When I left the storeroom that night, there were the two bales for the general—I addressed them myself—and one for Reed and one for Bedson of lynx and mink.

Well, the next day was pretty confused. I was never sure what happened. It was Sunday, so I wasn't at the barracks for very long. The boat came in early in the morning, there was a funeral at the barracks—Colonel Williams, who led the last day's attack at Batoche, had died of a fever and was brought to the barracks here—and Middleton and his staff came up the hill to attend it. It was sometime after that, in the afternoon, that I went over. I wanted to talk to the general about some rationing for the Home Guard.

When I went in to the storeroom, there were two big boxes put up, addressed to the boat and with his name on them—boxes that the troops' saddles came in, four foot square and four high. They were also packed with furs, in addition to the bales, with some bearskins on top. Dorion said that the general hadn't been satisfied with just the two bales, he wanted more. And Warden and Dorion had packed the boxes.

[As to how many] . . . I'd say about half of the total. But more than half in value, for the packed furs were the very best ones—it was all pretty jumbled. Up until that day, no one had been allowed in to the storeroom except Warden, Dorion, and myself. But that day, Hayter Reed and Bedson were both in there, mainly giving orders about the packages, I think. The general's furs and Bedson's were to be put on the boat, but Reed had his bundle addressed to him in Regina. It was to be taken down by the police. He was going west to some of the Edmonton reserves on Indian Department business, and he'd be gone for some time.

I didn't see the boxes put on the boat, but Dorion did, and of course, so did the teamsters who hauled them down the hill. Then the boat left for Prince Albert. I heard that Middleton and the rest stayed over in P.A. for a day or so—one of the officers wounded at Batoche was recuperating there, staying at the Macdowells. . . .

[As to the other half] as I say, it was all pretty confused. For the next several days we were handing out furs to officers. They always had signed orders. . . . Some of them came in and made their own choice—out of your pile. The orders seemed genuine enough, written orders—"General Middleton authorises Captain or Colonel So-and-so to select four or five skins," that sort of thing. They were issued—or seemed to be—only by General Middleton or Colonel Otter. We received them day after day. Warden had them. But the furs just went.

Macdonald went with Bremner to see some of the Battleford merchants—Alex Macdonald and James Clinkskill—whom he had dealt with for years and who had offered to testify for him when the lawyer Johnstone came around. They had influential connections and might be able to help find a way out of this morass. Besides, he would have to get credit from them for groceries and other supplies for the winter.

As they walked, Ronald Macdonald said,

There's another thing you should know about, perhaps, an odd thing. It may have something to do with the whole business. The day after Middleton and the boat left—on the Monday morning—Hayter Reed came round to Warden at the barracks and tried to get his letter back. Warden wouldn't give it to him, said he didn't know where it was. He wanted to keep it for his own protection, to have something to show that he actually had an order to deliver the furs, because nobody gave him any receipt for them. He needed something for the police files. But Reed came back later with another letter as a replacement. He said the first one had personal things in it. Well—Warden had showed it to me and others. The personal part, or the part that was changed, was a couple of sentences saying that Middleton had decided to confiscate the furs of "the rebel," and asking Warden to keep quiet about the whole business. Those sentences weren't in the second version. They didn't affect Warden's files, so he gave Reed the original letter. Reed must have had second thoughts.

"That's funny—but Middleton took the furs."

"Oh yes. He took them."

With assurances from Clinkskill that he would get in touch with people in the south who might be able to help, and leaving the women in town for the time being, Bremner and his four companions went to

Bresaylor the next morning to see their homes that they had not seen since mid-April. Bremner looked about him. His place was a shambles. The farmyard was littered with debris, bits of fur and feathers, skeletons and skin of animals that the Indians had shot. The carcass of a favorite dog lay near the door. Weeds choked the garden.

> I found my house and store barely standing. Windows, stoves, furniture were smashed, the flooring gone, the ceilings were torn down. In the store, shelves were torn down and broken, bins overturned, casks smashed. My books were gone; I found some invoices among the rubble, some even out in the yard.[2]

The stables had been demolished, and in the pasture area the cattle were gone, taken by the Indians, the horses were gone, taken by the police. All five men were in the same plight, and they would have to work together once again to build, to cut logs for houses, wood for winter fuel, send to Battleford for doors and windows, but at least they wouldn't have to dig cellars—they were there with their steps intact, although the provisions that they had held were gone.

For Charles Bremner time was short. Repairs to the kitchen above the cellar, and to another room large enough to be partitioned off—that would have to do. He salvaged enough planks to make a rough floor for the kitchen, but the ceiling would have to wait. The tent was struck at Battleford, Emily and the girls, with beds, stoves, and groceries were brought home. The baby, christened Mabel, was born in Bresaylor on October 4. At least this time Emily was in a bed and she had the care of a doctor. There were now four girls in the house: the baby, three-year-old Gertrude, Mary aged ten and Clara, fourteen. He would have to find a way of supporting them over the winter.

The other Bresaylor people, both the refugees in Battleford and those who had been in Poundmaker's camp, had been back since the beginning of August, but there was a lack of friendliness between the two groups, which was the more marked toward the five who had been arrested. Charles Bremner was no longer a leader in the community. He was still under doubt; his integrity had been taken away by the Court, his wealth by the army, his stock by the Indians and police protectors. Even that was not enough. The *Herald* kept up a note of malicious innuendo.

There was no time to brood. Winter would be coming on, and Charles Bremner must take steps about his furs. Leaving the family as well provided for as he could, he set off for Winnipeg, taking Louis Caplette with him.

Part Two

REBELLION LOSSES

Chapter Nine

The Wronged Man

The city editor of the *Manitoba Free Press* looked up from his desk one day early in November of 1885 when a large figure filled the doorway of his office.

"I want to put an advertisement in the paper."

The speaker was a heavily built man of about forty-five years of age, wearing a bearskin coat, which he removed as he took a seat in the room. His whiskers were long and slightly tinged with grey, which, together with his long, curly locks, gave him a semi-half-breed appearance.

"My name is Charles Bremner," he said in somewhat broken tones, "and I have been cruelly wronged by the Dominion Government." His Indian blood was quite apparent, his accent decidedly Scotch.

"Yes, I am a Scotch Half-breed," continued Mr. Bremner, "and I live in a mixed settlement between the two rivers, twenty-five miles from Battleford."

The visitor then told his story. First taken prisoner by the Indians on April 14, released by Poundmaker on May 25 after having led the captured teamsters to Battleford and having returned for his family, arrested by Colonel Herchmer on his second arrival in Battleford, and after six weeks in the guard room, taken to Regina and kept in prison for another two months. He was released without the privilege of a trial and still without knowing the grounds of his arrest. He ended by saying,

"I am a loyal subject and will always remain so, but I have been cruelly wronged by the government."

He put on his fur coat, touched his hat to the reporter, and walked quietly from the room.

The next day, November 6, the *Free Press* published the story, the "advertisement," under the heading "FOUR MONTHS IN JAIL. Cruel Treatment of a Scotch Half-breed. How a Loyal Man Was Kept in

Prison and Refused the Privilege of a Trial."

Charles Bremner had begun his long struggle to gain redress of injury, to cast off the taunt of perfidy which, like leg irons, hampered not only himself and his trial companions, but the whole group of Poundmaker's captives. His first aim was to force acknowledgement of their truth. After that came the money payment for the furs, his personal, singular loss. His life changed. It was no longer a vigorous one of action, building, even violence. It became one of waiting, the power gone out of his own hands, waiting on the talk, the schemes, the decisions, of men far away.

Winnipeg was the place to be in the fall of 1885, particularly in the month from October 20 to November 20. Recovering from the double disaster of a real estate crash and a ruinous flood, the city of thirty thousand was bubbling with activity, much of it the aftermath of the rebellion. As Nicholas Davin had said in Regina, the rebellion had turned out to be not a bad thing at all, for it had advertised the North-West as nothing else could have done, and "three to six thousand young Eastern men have seen it," among them M.P.'s and sons of M.P.'s. Winnipeg had been the base for troop assembling and dis-assembling, as it had been the source of supplies. Army uniforms were still common on the streets, and the faces of Winnipeg business men were plump with pleasure.

There was also a great congregation of journalists, who had chosen the comfort and delights of Winnipeg over the sparse tent-and-log-cabin accommodations of Regina, which they could reach by train in nineteen hours. The trials of rebellion prisoners had ended on October 22, but Riel's appeals continued, and the reporters awaited the outcome. The appeal to the Privy Council had been turned down on October 22, but there was another stay for a sanity examination by physicians. As late as November 10 another respite was announced, and on that day betting was even among the newsmen that Riel would never hang.

Moreover, several officials of the Dominion Government were using Winnipeg as their western base. One was the newly appointed Minister of the Interior, the Hon. Thomas White, who had published and edited the Montreal *Gazette*, and who, it was hoped, would be able to unsnarl the difficulties that had led to the rebellion. He had just returned from Prince Albert on his first fact-finding tour of the affected territory. There, he had been presented with a petition from the residents of "the largest and most important town in the Territories," which had used the fact of the rebellion to reinforce the repeated demands of the elected members of the Territories Council for representation in the Dominion Parliament, for a railway to Hudson Bay—"an absolute necessity"—and for provincial status for the Territorial districts. There were one or two additions. The Province of Saskatchewan should have Hudson Bay as its eastern boundary, with Prince Albert declared a port and its capital. Then too, "the Government should furnish farmers with seed grain for next season on favourable terms." There was nothing in the petition about the rebellion.

There was a War Claims Commission in Winnipeg, appointed to inquire into and recommend upon expenses of the Department of Militia concerning claims by soldiers, by suppliers, and occasionally by civilian freighting firms. Another cabinet minister had come to Winnipeg for that purpose as well as about further plans for the militia in British Columbia. The *Free Press* reported, on November 5, "Sirs Middleton and Caron are en route to the North-West on 'rebellion business'." The Minister, Sir Adolphe Caron, and his lady stayed at the Queen's Hotel.

But the rebellion, or as it was now referred to in *Hansard*, "the disturbance" was over, remote in time and far away, except for the last minute details in Battleford and Regina. What most affected Winnipeg and the future during these crowded weeks was the railway. The gap north of Lake Superior had been closed. In celebration of that fact, the Governor General, Lord Lansdowne, had arrived in Winnipeg on his special train on Wednesday, October 21, at 7:30 in the evening. It was a magnificent occasion. Nearly everyone turned out, lining the streets; a citizens' committee met the Governor General at the C.P.R. station, and the procession began.

"Main Street as far as the eye could reach was one blaze of flickering lights," the *Free Press* reported. "The picture was grand in the extreme. Everybody cheered and brandished torches. The procession was led by police and army bands and the skirl of the pipes." Near Logan Street, a horse ran into the Governor General's carriage, breaking a whiffle-tree, but in moments the horse was taken out of the shafts and eager young men seized them and pulled the vice-regal company the rest of the way. "When the procession turned on to Broadway, the view was enhanced by illuminations along the street. Chinese lanterns were in the houses and grounds. On Kennedy Street the order was given for fireworks and there was a grand display; Government House and the grounds were handsomely illuminated." When the procession passed, the brilliant dark of the starry night took over again.

The exhilaration was prolonged by the arrival, on Monday the 26th, of the first regular through train from Montreal to Winnipeg. Only the gap in the Rockies remained to be closed. Railway men began to gather in Winnipeg, awaiting the climax of their long planning. The reporters awaited it too. Railway executives, soldiers, journalists, bankers, traders, farmers, and immigrants passed briskly along the broad streets of the city.

For Charles Bremner's purposes, everyone was there: the Hon. Thomas White, concerned with settlers' losses; the Minister of Militia, concerned with claims on the army; and General Middleton, his special quarry, who was arriving in Winnipeg on Thursday, November 5. On the day before, he and Louis Caplette had reached Headingley and were staying with relatives. James Clinkskill had started them on their way. He had been in touch with a Winnipeg lawyer who might be able to help them, and he had given them transportation to Swift Current in one of Clinkskill and Mahaffey's empty wagon freighters—empty because there was no produce in the district to export. On the Thursday morning they drove in to Winnipeg with a borrowed horse and buggy.

They were impressed with the thickening settlements as they passed White Horse Plains and Cuthbert Grant's old mill, and crossed Sturgeon Creek, at which point the old Portage Road that they were travelling on became the city's Portage Avenue. Everyone seemed to be building. Everyone was travelling. Along the street there were also smart carriages and fine horses, delivery rigs, and clanging street railway cars on their tracks with a maze of overhead wires at Portage and Main. There the buildings were high and handsome, some brick, some stone.

The first street north of Portage was Post Office Road, and the small, end-stopped street beyond in was Owen Street, newspaper row. At Number 9 was the *Manitoba Free Press*, in a fine new two-story brick building that the paper had just moved into. It was a busy place. The paper had benefited from the influx of newsmen, and from a staff of a dozen or so, it had swelled until now it had nearly sixty—editors, reporters, printers, typsetters—all the workers that went with a modern paper.

Charles Bremner felt awkward at first as he asked his way to the office of the well-known city editor, Arch McNee, to whom he told his story. He told only his story as a settler; the other story, the one about the furs, was separate. He had chosen the paper carefully. The *Free Press* and its men were dedicated Grits, and they welcomed Bremner and his grievance against the Tory government.

When he left McNee, he and Caplett started on the other story. A little further along Main Street, "the second door north of the old Post

Office," the advertisement said, they entered the offices of Archibald, Howell, Hough and Campbell, one of the eleven law firms in the city— another was the firm of Hugh John Macdonald and J. Stewart Tupper— and asked for H.M. Howell, Q.C., a prominent Tory, whom Clinkskill had referred them to.

To him they told the story of the furs, Caplette giving details of Middleton visiting the camp and sending the furs to the barracks. Caplette, being Bremner's clerk and book-keeper, for he could write, had a clear recollection of what furs were in the carts. The lawyer thought the first thing to do would be to get in touch with the Minister of Militia, who was so very conveniently in town. He would try to make an appointment for the following day, November 6.

On that day, Howell and Charles Bremner waited on Sir Adolphe Caron. But that gentleman disclaimed any responsibility for the matter, or indeed concern with it. "When I asked him for information about the furs," Bremner said, "he stated that I should apply to General Middleton for information."[1] The matter involved only General Middleton, not the forces nor any armed action. General Middleton was in town; he was the man to see. That was the end of the interview. Howell said that he would get an interview with Middleton for Monday, and in the meantime, Bremner and Caplette should draw up as complete a list as possible of the furs lost.

The next day, Saturday, November 7, was a day of celebration all over Canada. While Bremner and Caplette were working out their lists, a great event took place a thousand miles to the west. Three trains came to Craigellachie in the midst of the towering Rockies. Two were filled with excursionists; the third, special train, with dignitaries: William Van Horne, manager of the C.P.R.; Sanford Fleming, an old railway builder and chief engineer when the C.P.R. began; Major Rogers, discoverer of the pass; Major Sam Steele, who had commanded the N.W.M.P., protecting workers and railway property throughout the time of building in the mountains; and foremost, the Hon. Donald Smith, Minister of Railways, M.P. for Selkirk, Manitoba, who had risked his personal fortune five years before to save the railroad from collapse. He had been given the honor of driving the last spike.

Nicholas Davin, present among the newsmen, recorded the moment of ceremony in the Regina *Leader*. After all the trains had emptied and the special group had taken their places around the magic spot, "At 9.22 a.m. everything was ready; the Hon. Donald Smith took the maul in hand to drive the last spike. After missing it a few times he drove it home amid cheers from all present." And so the great dream of the "Canadian-from-coast-to-coast-railway" was here and now, a reality. As word rippled along the telegraph wires, the rejoicing began: trains hooted, whistles blew, bells rang, people cheered; it was a great New Year for Canada. The celebrations continued all week-end.

Charles Bremner and Louis Caplette took their list to the lawyer on Monday. They had drawn it up from their memory of what they had caught on their own lines, of what they had paid other trappers, of what Bremner had acquired from Wook Crees and from Battle River reserves, and of how the carts had filled up week by week. To the list they added a horse taken away by the army:

371	beavers, at $4.00	$1,484.00
9	wolverines, at $4.00	36.00
376	lynx, at $3.00	1,128.00
1,736	muskrats, at $1 per dozen	144.66
160	red fox, at $1.25	200.00
494	mink, at $1.00	494.00
5	wolves, at $1.25	6.25
10	fishers, at $10.00	100.00
4	com. fox, at $2.00	8.00
31	bears, at $10.00	310.00
233	skunks, at .75	174.75
19	martin, at $2.50	47.50
23	badgers, at .50	11.50
8	otters, at $10.00	80.00
3	silver fox, at $50.00	150.00
60 days' use of horse by scout		60.00
Value of horse not returned		200.00
		$4,634.00

Howell, Bremner and Caplette called on General Middleton. He denied all knowledge of any part of the matter, of Bremner or the furs: he had no such furs, had never received them, had never given orders for their confiscation, had never authorised them to be given to others, and he had never before known of Bremner. As for asking for furs to be put on the steamer, that was absurd.[2]

Caplette interjected, "But don't you remember, sir, that I told you the soldiers were taking furs from the carts, and I asked you for some protection for them?"

"I remember no such thing, nor do I remember having seen you before. At that time, you know, I was fighting a war. I had just taken

Poundmaker's surrender, and I had other things on my mind than packets of furs."

Bremner tried, "But Captain Morris says he has had telegrams from you fairly recently about furs."

"Captain Morris may say what he likes. I sent no telegrams to him nor any one else there since the operation was concluded. I know nothing at all about this tale. If that is all, gentlemen—"

As Charles Bremner had seen Poundmaker at the moment of his triumph, so he now saw Middleton at the height of his. The knighthood was beyond anything Middleton had hoped for while instructing cadets at Sandhurst or pursuing Sepoys in India. He had a charming and wealthy wife; he had a private railroad car; he was receiving the gratitude of a nation.

The meeting was over. General Middleton left that day for the West, intending to visit the Indian reserves in the south and to set up a flying column as a permanent patrol. Charles Bremner reported that night that he had seen Middleton, who denied any knowledge of the furs or of having any connection with them. "He also stated that he had never ordered my arrest nor that of any of our party."

That left Thomas White, Minister of the Interior. White was staying over for a banquet given by the Conservative Association in honor of himself and Caron. H.W. Howell was on the reception committee. He took his clients to see the minister. They were civilly received and civilly heard, and White said that he would be willing to pass on their problem to the Commission on Settlers' Rebellion Losses, but that he could do no more than that. He expected to be in Battleford in the spring, and perhaps they could talk further then. In the meantime, he would advise that they take an affidavit as to their list.

The last call of the day was on James Fisher, whose office was only a few doors from Howells', who was authorised to take affidavits, and who had been one of the citizens' committee to welcome the Governor General. Bremner was beginning to feel that Winnipeg had a very closely interwoven society.

To Charles Bremner's affidavit, Louis Caplette added his sworn statement:

> At the time of the arrest of Charles Bremner, referred to in his affidavit, I was his clerk, and in possession of the furs as set forth in Schedule A of his affidavit this day sworn, and I know the contents of the four cart loads of furs referred to in his affidavit. The said Schedule A referred to in his affidavit is a true

and correct statement of the furs then owned by the said
Bremner. About that time, the soldiers commenced pillaging the
furs, and I went to the military authorities to ask for protection.
These authorities took possession of the furs and placed them in
the police barracks at Battleford. . . . I have seen the furs several
times at the barracks since then, but I have noticed the pile of
furs upon each visit growing less, and the authorities refused to
deliver them up. I believe the furs are worth the amounts set
forth in the said Schedule A.

The oath taken and Charles Bremner, being unable to write his
name, having signed with his mark, as a "mark-man," Howell said that
he would see that the document got to White and to the Rebellion Losses
Commission. That was all that could be done now. To go any further,
they would need documentation from the police and from anyone else
involved as to what happened—letters, telegrams, receipts—anything to
back up their story officially. He bade them good-bye and good luck.

As they drove back to Headingley for the last time, the horses'
hooves clipclopping on the hard road surface, Charles Bremner began to
feel like Big Bear. Who was the higher power? Who was the top man?
Who could speak with authority? Who made the decisions? The activity
of the last few days had buoyed him up, but now as they drove over the
flat, wintry land, he realised that he was where he was when they began.
He had been able to leave a record. That was all. "I made a statutory
declaration in Winnipeg before James Fisher on November 9. Having
got no satisfaction, I returned to Battleford."[3]

Chapter Ten

Losses

The day of their return to Battleford was the day Riel was hanged, November 16. That event seemed far away and yet it had the presence of the unexpected. As even Oliver commented in the *Bulletin*, "The news that Riel had been hanged came as a surprise to everyone in this part of the Territories." There had been so many reprieves that "it has been taken for granted that his final reprieve was a mere matter of time." In Quebec, riots had begun. Ten days of that November had seen two events in the West that were to affect profoundly the growth and definition of the fledgling nation: the one physical and unifying, the completion of the railroad; the other political and dividing, the execution of Riel.

At Battleford in the barracks square the lumber was already stacked for the single scaffold to be built for the Indians who were to hang for murder on November 27. Among the eight was Wandering Spirit, Big Bear's war chief. W.B. Cameron, said to be the lone white male survivor of Frog Lake, whom Laurie had chosen as a member of the coroner's jury, visited Wandering Spirit in jail. There was a question he had long wanted to ask: " 'Suppose I had been with the other whites at Frog Lake when they were shot, what then?' He considered before replying. 'We were singing,' he said at length. This may seem a mystifying answer, but I understood its significance. He might as plainly have said: 'We were on the warpath. We were not looking to save life.' "[1]

A hangman had been found in Robert Hodson, the McLeans' little English cook, who had been a prisoner with them. He had volunteered for the job. Major Sam Steele, sent in to become the new police commandant at Battleford, said, "He was a very respectable citizen, but more than willing to hang any of the rebels in revenge for the severe and cruel treatment he had received at Fort Garry when he was a captive of Riel in 1869-70."[2] Hodson had something in common with Coroner Laurie, a deep bitterness left from the Red River insurrection, which had been revivified and sharpened by the second uprising.

Crossing the square, Charles Bremner went to Inspector Morris once more and told him of Middleton's absolute denials. Morris "repeated his assertion that Middleton had given instructions as to the disposal of the furs." For the moment, that was a dead end. What next? The Rebellion Losses Commission was a possibility, since Bremner had been in Regina when the Commission had visited in the summer, and so with the help of Morris and Ronald Macdonald, Bremner made a copy of his sworn statement in Winnipeg and added a list of losses of store and household goods. "I sent my first claim to Ottawa about the end of November. I wished to be paid for the furs and goods first. I hoped to find some horses and cattle later."[3]

The intangible loss was ever-present. In the first issue of the *Herald* after Bremner's return, Laurie reprinted the *Free Press* story and declared editorially, "Charles Bremner's version of affairs in and around Battleford during the troubles of last spring . . . is devoid of truth. The story is false from beginning to end. . . . He does not explain why he did not come into the barracks with the others." The power of the published voice of Laurie's antipathy meant the loss to Charles Bremner of his social freedom, of his credibility, of his stature as a person in this small, isolated world.

In Bresaylor the narrowed world was even narrower. The division between those who had sought refuge in the barracks and those who had not was hardened by the action of the Rebellion Losses Commission, who had passed sentence on evidence that the Crown Prosecutor had declared inadequate. None of the claims of those who had been in Poundmaker's camp were allowed; the claims of all who had gone to the barracks were allowed. True, these claims together with all other claims from the whole area of the rebellion had been reduced, even if only by one or two dollars. There was one exception: the claim of the Presbyterian minister at Battleford had been allowed in full—it was for $70.00.

Among the Bremner neighbors, for household goods, farm equipment, and livestock, Peter Taylor was allowed $1,964, Philip Macdonald $2,004, Herbert Taylor $1409, including compensation for three pigs, fifty hens, and a stove, and C.H. Cinnamon was allowed a total of $3,447 including $1,255 for 19 head of cattle. Out of 300 claims submitted in the entire area, 168 were allowed, and the total sum (for the reduced claims) was $131,797.35. Of that sum, $102,791.35 went to the Battleford district. The rest went to Duck Lake, Fort Pitt, and Prince Albert.

Throughout the area there was great dissatisfaction with the Commission's hasty survey and hastier decisions. There was dissatisfaction with the reductions—Laurie had claimed $1,089.60 and was allowed $864.00, though he had lost everything, including blankets, mattresses, bedding, outer and under clothing, winter coats, buffalo robes, china, cutlery, furniture, curtains, pictures, carpets, kitchen utensils, table linen, and the precious sewing machine. There was dissatisfaction at arbitrary disallowances of claims. But most of all, there was dissatisfaction because, by mid-December, no payments of any kind had been made. Laurie sent a telegram to Thomas White, and on December 26 he got a reply: "An Order-in-Council has been passed to pay immediately rebellion losses claims to the amount of half the sum awarded by the Commissioners." For many of the claimants, the minimal sums resulting, when they came, could not provide sustenance through the winter, nor did they impress the settlers with the government's regard.

From Prince Albert came another angry complaint, this time from the farmers against the Dominion Government's demand for mortgages on their farms as security for a proposed advance of seed grain. "Considering that seed grain, food and clothing have been promised free of cost to rebellious Indians and Half-breeds, to demand a mortgage at one year return for less favors granted to loyal white settlers seems like making too much of a distinction with too great a difference." Everyone seemed to be doing well except those who had been on the Government's side, and Laurie's sense of an unfair bias was intensified by a report from the South Branch in mid-January: "All the Half-breeds in distress in this district are being served with provisions, and there is no starvation."

Poundmaker and eleven of his fellow prisoners were released in early March, 1886, and the warden of the penitentiary, S.L. Bedson, entertained the chief at dinner. Also to mark the occasion, a correspondent from the Toronto *Mail* was sent to interview him at the prison. Laurie, still indignant at Poundmaker's short sentence and early release was outraged at these gestures of special favor. Still, he reprinted the interview:

> He has not been well lately. . . . He told me that he was well treated by everybody and especially by Warden Bedson, but that he felt lonesome and wanted to get back to the prairie. His hair has not been cut, and he has lots of tobacco. All that he lacked was his liberty. Just then Big Bear came in—a small-sized, weason-faced chap with a cunning, restless look—and I interviewed him, but without success. He wanted to get home, and had declined to be christened by Archbishop Taché.

I asked Poundmaker, "Didn't Riel want you to join him six years ago?"

"I never saw Riel until I met him in Regina last summer."[4]

Then he went on to say how he wanted to get back to his families—he has two wives.

When the prisoners who were released with Poundmaker got back to Batoche, a public meeting was held there on February 24, instigated by Father André, and both Laurie and Oliver carried accounts of it: "A large public meeting was held at Batoche at which resolutions were passed thanking the Government in warmest terms for the very generous and humane manner in which they had been treated since the unfortunate occurrences of last spring, and for the promptitude with which the Government had sent relief to the destitute and needy, not only in the shape of food and clothing, but by furnishing employment in the way of freighting . . . and also for the universal kindness displayed by the officers and men of the Mounted Police in dissipating the bad feeling aroused by last year's troubles. The presence in the meeting of some Half-breeds lately released from prison, and the kind treatment that they had received while there left a most desirable impression."

Poundmaker's reception when he returned to Battleford was mixed. The settlers were out on the land, trying to repair buildings and to get their farms started again, and for them Laurie recalled another visit. "It was just a year ago when Poundmaker and his men came to Battleford. Now he is back again." But his grudging admiration for the man came through: "By nature a giant in intelligence among his fellows, by his untiring ambition he carries recognition in a larger circle, and now, when he should hang his head in shame for his crimes, he is forced to feel himself a hero and a mighty man." And there was indeed a fanfare for a returning hero on the reserve.

There was little communication now between Bresaylor and Poundmaker's people. Apart from the settlers' resentment at the destruction of their homes, Jefferson was gone, Father Cochin had been assigned to another district, and Poundmaker himself seemed more remote than ever. Occasionally he would say that he was sorry for their trouble and loss, but his very restraint emphasized his unspoken thoughts about his own loss and that of his people. The settlers would recover in a year or so; the Indians would not. What they had lost was gone forever.

But if Poundmaker's reputation was growing in popular favor, that of his captor, Middleton, was declining. The first sign was the fiasco of his plan to patrol the southern reserves. The shrill cries of the ranchers of the Bow Valley echoed across the plains, protesting that Middleton's flying column might so incense the otherwise peaceful Indians that they would fire the prairies. The plan was abandoned. "Like everything else that General Middleton has had to do with in connection with the Indians," Laurie wrote, "this flying column business has been mixed and muddled."

There followed murmurings from Middleton's former comrades in arms when they discovered that he had not cited them for commendation. The Saskatchewan Valley particularly resented his lack of commendation of the police. Indeed, his outright criticisms of them had led to a general shake-up of officers, a number of resignations, and a commission being set up to inquire into the doings of the police during the rebellion. When the commission's report was laid before Parliament in April, Laurie wrote an editorial on it: "The report gives a history of the doings of that body during the late campaign. It contains a number of General Middleton's telegrams and orders to the Police Commission, which prove that all the movements for which the police were condemned were made under his special orders. The General issued so many orders contradictory of each other, directing the police to meet him at times and places at which he so often failed to put in an appearance, that it is a cause of wonder that disaster did not follow. The blame so freely heaped on the Police should really be laid to the charge of General Middleton and his everchanging plans."

Individual accounts began to emerge. One of them was from Coloner Herchmer, saying that after Poundmaker's surrender, "On the 20th I was ordered to proceed to Pitt, taking with me fifty mounted men. . . . On the 28th I was ordered to proceed to Battleford and take all the prisoners from that place to Regina." Oliver in Edmonton was indignant about the "humbugging" of the police, and in particular at the "repudiation" of the claims of Steele's Scouts for losses suffered on active duty. The matter of the police and Middleton broke into the open in the summer, when Major General Strange, also an Englishman, also a former officer in the Imperial Army, also with gazetted honors in India, resigned. Oliver reported, "Smarting under the slights that have been put upon him by General Middleton, [he] has given the public a letter in which he lays bare some acts of rank dishonesty and petty meanness on the part of someone in authority."

Charles Bremner was glad to have confirmation of his experience from such a worthy source, but it didn't help him with the claims commission, which, after the widespread outburst of complaints about their hasty assessments during their brief visit the previous year, had been re-established by Order-in-Council on February 25, 1886, as a Royal Commission to investigate claims in greater depth. Unfortunately, the Government had kept the same commissioners: J. Alphonse Ouimet, now Judge Ouimet, of Montreal; Henry Muma of Drumbo, Ontario; Thomas Mackay of Prince Albert; and as secretary the ubiquitous Captain George Young, Middleton's nomination, who had lodged the official information and complaint for the Crown against Charles Bremner in the court case in Regina. There was little likelihood that this group of men would consider that the original hot-off-the-anvil information that they had received would be faulty, or that they themselves could be wrong. This time, however, there was at least the appearance of an examination in depth. They arrived in Battleford on Saturday evening, May 29, and they stayed until June 10, sitting every day from 10 a.m. to 1 p.m., and from 2 to 5 p.m., to review the claims of the district.

Bremner was called to make his deposition on June 7, towards the end of the Commission's stay: "Personally came and appeared Mr. Charles Bremner, of Battleford, farmer and merchant, forty-seven years of age; married—Claimant." This time, Bremner submitted four documents. Exhibit 'A' contained invoices for the goods that were in his store, receipts for goods bought and paid for at Macdonald's in Battleford, and receipts for freight on goods from Winnipeg, "almost half of this stock remained unsold in my store on the 14th April." Exhibit 'B' was the list of furs, a revision of the estimate made from memory in Winnipeg, adding to the number of furs but omitting the claim for the horse, the prices for the furs being those he paid for them. The total was now $5,364.50. Exhibit 'C' was "my losses in house and on farm separate from the store;" and Exhibit 'D', "the general statement of my claim as at present put before the Commission."

The general statement was, in effect, an account and justification of his action; for before this body, Charles Bremner was in the position of having to prove himself innocent of the charge which Captain Young, busily writing across the table, had brought against him in Regina, that of being a rebel. To the query of why he had not come in to barracks with the others, he cited the unsuccessful attempt to get help or advice from Battleford, Poundmaker's assurance that no harm would come to them, Father Cochin's advice to stay, the horses being out at pasture that could not be found for two or three days, and the fact that "my own mother, 95 years of age, was with me."

Repeatedly, upon questions from Ouimet or Mackay, Bremner insisted that he knew nothing of the rebellion beforehand, that he had had no part in it while it was in progress: "I swear that I never took part in any of their movements, never acted as scout or went away with any party whatever of Half-breeds or Indians."

The official report ended,

> And further deponent sayeth not.
>
> The present deposition having been read to the witness he declares it contains the truth, nothing but the truth, persists therein—and has declared he cannot sign.
>
> Taken, sworn and acknowledge before us, Commissioners duly appointed as a Royal Commission as aforesaid at Battleford, District of Saskatchewan, North-West Territories, on the seventh day of June in the year of Our Lord one thousand eight hundred and eighty-six.

His
(Signed) Charles + Bremner
Mark

On the same day, the Commission took the depostion of Father Cochin, testifying for Bremner:

> At the time of outbreak I was at Bresaylor Settlement. I know all the circumstances attending the capture of Charles Bremner and party by the Indians; I was in the camp at Charles Bremner's place with 10 or 12 Half-breed families, and I say they were not rebels. They did not come here because they did not believe that the Indians would rob or injure them at all. . . . Charles Bremner, I would say, was not a rebel at all. And those people acted on my advice. I told them that probably the best thing to do was to remain and work on their farms. . . . Before this I had written a letter to the Police captain signed by C. Bremner and H. Sayer, asking what we had to do, and we received no reply to this. The Indians forced us to go along with them. I was kept as a prisoner under guard, but not in a tent, but the camp was all guarded around and we could not escape; we were not close prisoners, but our camp was visited frequently to see if we were there. The brother sent with the letter was kept at the barracks and not allowed to return. The people have all lost

property. . . . Chas. Bremner had a large band of cattle and lost many, and he had a large quantity of fine furs. I should say I saw from $2,000 to $3,000 worth. He had about 80 head of cattle, he also had a good stock of boots in his store, and had merchandise in his buildings as well. It was not a very large store, and can't say as to the amount, but I think it was all pillaged, and he has found some animals, but no goods, I think. Many of the animals I saw killed by the Indians.

I was with Poundmaker during the entire time of the captivity of these people, and I did not see any disloyal act on their part.

And further deponent sayeth not.

(Signed) L. COCHIN, O.M.I.

A number of witnesses were prepared to testify for Bremner, but here, as with the court in Regina, they were not allowed to speak for him. The Commission would allow only one—Louis Caplette— to give evidence as the the quantity and value of the furs. They listened to him repeat his earlier sworn statement, and that was all. Two days later, they left for the south by the weekly stage.

Charles Bremner's plight was separating itself into three distinct, though linked themes, as he recognised. First was the damage to his home, the loss of stock and goods—a plight that he shared with many others. Second was the peculiar affair of the purloined furs, not shared by others and not the result of Indian action. Third, and most important, both because it affected the possibility of redress for the other two, and especially because it affected his life and the lives of his family, was the cloud of suspicion hanging over him because of the arrest and the ambiguous release. It was shared in part by his companions, but it focused on him as their leader.

For now, they could only wait for the Commission's decision. The momentous event of the early summer, however, was the death of Poundmaker. After his return to the reserve, Poundmaker had taken a new wife, following the Indian custom, younger than his other wives, and the two of them had left on May 7 to visit Poundmaker's adoptive father, Chief Crowfoot, near Calgary. Laurie was scandalised at this latest evidence of Poundmaker's flouting of the white man's law. They had been gone two months when word came, on July 5, that he was dead. Reports varied as to the cause; one said that he had broken a blood vessel while taking part in a Sun Dance, another that he had been thrown from a horse. The Indian agent for Crowfoot's reserve buried him at nearby Gleichen. Nicholas Davin paid him tribute in the Regina *Leader*: "News we have heard with deep regret. . . . He was one of the heroes of the insurgent side in the North-West Rebellion. A man of large, generous heart, the nobleness of his nature was written on the lofty traits of his mobile and handsome face. He looked a chief, every inch of him—a born leader. . . . A great man of his people had fallen, and we pay him with genuine regret and respect his last tribute—Poor Poundmaker!"[5] Laurie was briefer, but he was evidently deeply moved: "His death practically settles the Indian question in the north on the side of peace, there being no one left clever enough or influential enough to take up the banner he has just laid down."

When the Battleford agent rode out to the reserve with the news, Poundmaker's people refused to believe him. Not until the young wife returned and told them it was so would they accept the fact as true. Then the weird and melancholy death chant began, a people lamenting the loss of their chief and their own loneliness. Their quality of life was changed forever. They would not starve—the Government would see to that; Herbert and Peter Taylor and some dozens of other teamsters were freighting in flour from Swift Current for Macdonald's Indian Department contracts—but both the pride and the fierceness were gone. The next Thirst Dance was a muted affair; warriors were obsolete and the songs of brave deeds were now a lament for the past.

Bresaylor too mourned the passing of their great neighbor.

News came of other figures in the drama. Gabriel Dumont, the feared, the loved, the mighty hunter, had taken up yet another career. He was in show business, with Buffalo Bill's Wild West Show, and Major Crozier, released from the police because Dumont had bested him, now saw his adversary on a stage in New York, exhibiting his rifle skills. Francis Dickens, who had been given "a gratuity of a year's pay" when he was released, died in Illinois on June 11, and the body of the unhappy son was shipped back to England for burial.

By the fall of 1886, Charles Bremner was beginning to get back on his feet. He had trapped the previous winter and sold his furs, he had sown and reaped a crop, he had recovered a few of his animals and had a supply of hay for them, and the chickens and pigs of the farmyard had been replaced. The family would not starve, but the struggle back was hard. All of the considerable wealth that he had earned, that could provide comforts and pleasures for his family, all that was gone.

But that defeat was not enough. Now it was not the nonchalance, the arrogance, nor the malice of men that assaulted him. This time, mindless, uncaring fate got in its crack. On Monday, the 8th of November, an explosion destroyed his house.

Laurie reported it: "A serious accident which came near being attended by fatal results occurred at Bresaylor on Monday by the blowing up of Charles Bremner's house. The building was a double one, part being used as a kitchen, and part as a general living room. The cellar was under the kitchen, and stored in this was a keg containing gunpowder. At the time of the explosion the only inmates of the building were Mrs. Bremner and her infant daughter, who were in the main building. . . . From the appearance of things the explosion must have lifted the roof off bodily, the escape of the gas allowing it to settle almost into its place again. Some of the roof-poles broke, and in their fall bruised Mrs. Bremner and inflicted several deep cuts. By this time she discovered that her child's clothes were ablaze, and in her efforts to save the child, her own dress caught fire, and before she succeeded in putting it out, they were both badly burned about the body and face. The probable origin was that a spark from the stove fell through a crack in the floor. . . . The kitchen is blown to pieces, and the interior of the building and its contents all wrecked and broken. . . . Dr. Baldwin went up and attended to the injuries of the wounded ones."

Racing back from the woods where a frantic searcher had found him cutting logs for winter fuel, Charles Bremner looked with horror at Emily and the screaming baby. They were in the Caplettes' house, and neighbor women were trying to stanch the cuts and soothe the burns, but death had been close. Louis was already well on his was to Battleford to fetch the doctor, but there and back was fifty miles; it would be hours before the doctor could arrive. At least, thank God, they were alive.

He went to look at the house. It was only a little more than a year ago that he had returned to find it vandalised. Now it was even worse; superhuman force had ripped through it, and the fire had followed. Then panic seized him. Where was the money he had managed to scrape together? Where was the tin cash box? In his hand he held out what he found. "Last time I opened it, I just stuffed some bills in; the ends were sticking out. Here are the ends. Just as if they'd been cut off by a pair of scissors. But that's not all; there's no trace of the cash box or the rest of the money. I had about $200 saved up there."

Misfortune was one thing; humiliation was another. Now he would accept help that was offered, not as his due, but out of pity. Yet this latest disaster had another effect. It wiped out lingering hostility, and the Bresaylor people gathered to help, not out of pity, but out of concern for their common humanity, and perhaps a little out of fear. In the fires that swept the prairies every spring, shattered hopes were not uncommon; they might one day be victims too. Moreover, the utter injustice of the blow in a strange way called into question the justice of the other misfortune that Charles Bremner had suffered, and throughout the district people began to reconsider his story. Even Laurie re-established him in the *Herald* as "Mr. Bremner," and once more recorded his doings. Battleford merchants helped.

On Friday, November 26, only eighteen days after the fire, "Mr. Bremner left for Swift Current with a brigade of jumpers to bring in Xmas goods for Mr. A. Macdonald. This is the first winter brigade to take the road." But the weather turned fierce. The sweep of the winds, the bitter cold, the frightening hours of blinding snow without refuge— the earth became the enemy. For a time a new fear arose. On December 13, "Mr. Bremner and his train of sleighs with holiday supplies for Macdonald's ought to be in this week." Macdonald's ad read only, "Xmas Goods in a Few Days. Wait for Them." On December 20, "Bremner, Sayer, and Sandon with their respective freighting outfits were inward bound Sunday." There was a happy ending. The freighters pulled through, children had their toys, housewives had their goodies, and the Bremners had a safe, if meagre, New Year's celebration for 1887. It was among friends.

Chapter Eleven

Politics

The holiday celebrations had been meagre for all the settlers of the Battleford district. Their hopes and expectations from claims for rebellion losses had become a sour joke. Laurie kept the running record. Word had come from Ottawa on July 9, 1886, that "Messers McKay and Ouimet, Rebellion Claims Commissioners, arrived this morning. They investigated over 700 claims in the North-West." In mid-August, "The Rebellion Claims Commission is in session in Montreal, preparing their final report." At the end of September, "The Government has received a warrant for $65,000 to meet the claims of settlers for losses suffered during the rebellion. The Auditor General is busy making out the cheques." At the end of October, the *Herald* reported, "The payment of the balance of claims was made last week by Mr. Nash, Dominion Lands Agent. The sum paid last Christmas was half of the amount allowed by the Commission, but the most inexplicable thing about these payments is that many of the heaviest losers have not received anything, nor can they find out why they are thus treated, nor when their claims will be adjusted."

The settlers were not alone. The Minister of the Interior was baffled too. When he was questioned in the House by Sir Richard Cartwright about the paltry sum allotted, the Hon. Thomas White replied, "This amount is simply to pay the settlers in the neighborhood of Battleford, on the first report of those who went out to investigate the losses. I have telegraphed Mr. Ouimet in the hope of getting an approximate estimate of what will be required, but I have not been able to get an answer."[1]

The Bremner explosion, with the concerted effort to help that followed it, had the unexpected effect of hastening the coming together of the settlers in the interests of all, and turning their strength to their common problem—recompense for losses. The forming of an Agricultural Society helped to organise their efforts, but they were given greater impetus and focus by an important political development which the elected representatives in the Territorial Council had been fighting for: the achievement of representation in the Dominion Government.

The first step came in a Bill introduced by Sir John A. Macdonald and passed in May, shortly before Parliament prorogued. It provided for four representatives from the Territories to be elected to the House of Commons, two from Assiniboia, which was divided into East and West Assiniboia, and one each from Alberta and Saskatchewan. The Battleford district, with a population of 3,603, was one of the divisions in the Saskatchewan constituency, and Bresaylor was a polling centre. At long last, Bresaylor settlers would have a vote.

The basis for allotting representation was in the census figures published in March 1886, which gave evidence of a number of population changes. The total population of the Territories was now 48,362, made up of 23,344 white, 4,848 half-breeds, and 20,170 Indians. For the first time, whites outnumbered Indians, but there was still a severe geographical division, with the majority of the whites in the south along the railway line, and the majority of the Indians and Half-breeds along the Saskatchewan Valley. However, the number of whites in the north had increased considerably. At any rate, the settlers would have a vote whenever a Dominion election was called, and it looked as though it might be soon.

Closer at hand was a development within the Territories. With the increased population came an enlarged Council and a redistribution of seats, whereby Saskatchewan was given four seats, two of them going to Prince Albert with its population of 5,313, and one each to St. Laurent and Battleford. At last the one-time capital of the Territories had a voice in its government, and the Half-breeds of Bresaylor had a vote as the Half-breeds of the South Branch had had for some years. Bresaylor experienced the novel entertainment of electioneering. James Clinkskill, merchant of Battleford, born in Glasgow, educated at the University of St. Andrews, emigrating to the Territories in 1882, was elected to represent the district. He was friendly to Charles Bremner.

With the dissolution of Parliament on January 17, and the calling of an election for February 22, the new year of 1887 brought together in public gatherings the various elements of organisation in Battleford: agricultural, which was local, Territorial, which was non-partisan, and the clubs of the two national parties. The timely coalescence of these elements gave unusual strength to a public meeting held on Wednesday, January 27, about seed grain and rebellion losses. The *Herald* reported, "Mr. Skelton introduced the question of claims at some length, dwelling on the inconvenience, the trouble and loss to settlers, occasioned by the dilatoriness of the government and the injustice of the amount of awards. . . . Mr. Clinkskill spoke at some length, censuring the actions of the first commission for the indignities heaped upon the settlers by refusing to accept sworn or any evidence tendered to substantiate their claims, but in an undignified way to extract, solicit and apparently act upon information from gossips in no way qualified to have any correct knowledge. They had abused the prerogatives and dignity of any royal Commission, and he urged that steps be taken to secure full compensation for our losses."

The meeting only too eagerly took what steps it could: it passed resolutions. One resolution asked for seed grain on reasonable terms. Another said, "We who are loyal citizens . . . request that a Commission be appointed who will properly investigate claims, giving us an opportunity of proving by sworn evidence the real losses we have sustained . . . and that this petition be immediately wired to the Honorable, the Minister of the Interior and that his immediate answer be requested."

On the following Wednesday morning, a telegram from "Thos. White" came in reply, to the effect that the Department of the Interior had to wait for funds until Parliament voted them, but "will cause inquiry at once to be made on this point"—that the settlers had not been permitted to submit evidence. Indeed, the government appeared to have anticipated the petition. At any rate, whatever the authority, an investigator was already having interviews and taking evidence from individual settlers. Unfortunately, the investigator was the unchanged and unchanging George Young, who had been secretary of the former commission.

The meeting, the resolutions, the petition, however, helped Charles Bremner to realise that, although he was as yet no better off, he was not especially marked out as a victim of malice or misfortune. In fact, he and his companions of Cut Knife were in a fair way to becoming a small political "cause," for the first election in which the Territories voted was also the first election since the rebellion, since the execution of Riel, and the subsequent political agitation in Quebec, which had been gathering force for over a year.

As early as December 1885, the *Bulletin* had recorded, "The Montreal *Star* thinks the hanging of Riel will produce a political earthquake in Canada; that the majority of the French Canadian supporters of the government will go into opposition, which will leave the government with a minority in the House and bring on a general election. Of course an almost solid French vote against the government on this subject means an almost solid English vote in favor of it, and consequently its being sustained in power, but on very different lines than at present."

The protest movement in Quebec undoubtedly had something to do with the government's prompt and solicitous care for the South Branch Métis, but that gesture was too slight and too remote to have a deterrent effect on the strong swing to the Liberal party in Quebec. The earthquake was indeed happening, and though Edward Blake, the Liberal leader, declared, "I do not propose to construct a party platform out of the Regina scaffold," and though Wilfrid Laurier was deeply dismayed at the prospect of the French-English fissure, the majority of Quebec Liberals had no such compunctions. Riel's ghost was a political power, and the Quebec vote, which had been habitually Conservative, was to become habitually Liberal. The 1887 election was the watershed. The Quebec figures for the 1882 election were Conservatives 48, Liberals 17; in 1887 they were Conservatives 33, Liberals 32.

Sir John A. Macdonald, now 72, still won the election (Conservatives 123, Liberals 92) but ten of his twenty-one seat majority came from the solidly Conservative West—six from B.C., and four from the Territories. The *Herald* rejoiced in the "Clean Sweep" in the Territories, and in Saskatchewan David H. Macdowell, member of the North-West Council, Prince Albert merchant, age 37, born of gentry in the Scottish Highlands, a minor assistant to Middleton in the rebellion, won handily over David Laird, Liberal candidate and former lieutenant-governor. Yet there were interesting pockets of dissent. In the Prince Albert constituency, in spite of the government's clemency, the subdivision of Batoche voted 27 for Conservatives, 74 for Liberals; and in the Battleford subdivision of Bresaylor, the vote was 12 for Conservatives, 19 for Liberals. Parliament was summoned for April 13.

From either side, or both, Bremner's case now took on political overtones that led to his being championed by the Liberals, while P.G. Laurie's antagonism was cemented in Tory fervor. At the western end of the Valley, Oliver, staunch Liberal, summing up the reasons for the rebellion, castigated the government but refused to sanctify Riel: "The prime cause of the rebellion and its deplorable consequences . . . was governmental mismanagement; Riel's influence was secondary." The passions of Quebec were not those of the Territories.

As for the Indians of the rebellion, Big Bear, having been released from prison a month earlier, arrived across the river from Bresaylor in March, a small, shrivelled, defeated old man. His band was dispersed, his chief men either dead or gone to the United States. The Frog Lake settlement was abandoned, shunned by all Indians. He had no home and he scorned pity. But though his old friend Poundmaker was dead, Poundmaker's people welcomed and honored him. So did the Bresaylor people, as they would a stricken pine. On May 2, the second anniversary of Cut Knife, Poundmaker's men recited the acts of that time and praised famous men.

Meantime, the petition to Thomas White had brought a telegram from him on March 5, "Seed grain as requested will be furnished to Battleford," and the supplies came. The highly respected Thomas White had proved once more to be a man of his word.

From March 26, when Alex Bremner pulled out for Swift Current for seed grain, through April, the trail south was alive with men and outfits. On April 30, Laurie reported, "The whole week there has been a procession of trading outfits into town—from the primitive cart that carries seven or eight hundred pounds up to the string team that handles a carload at a time. Some of the loads were goods for the stores, but most of them were seed grain." The crops were going to get in this year. Hope and energy were alive again.

Before the end of May, hopes were further raised by word that the Rebellion Claims Commission had "closed its labors and reported to the Government. Estimates have been brought down. As soon as they are passed, cheques will go out—welcome news to those who have not yet received any portion of their claims."

And then on May 31, 1887, Charles Bremner's affairs entered Ottawa. A proposal was brought before this first session of the new Parliament to increase the salaries of various officials in the North-West, including that of S.L. Bedson, warden of the Manitoba penitentiary. The Hon. David Mills, former Minister of the Interior in the short-lived Liberal Mackenzie government, rose to ask "whether any complaint has been made to the Government in regard to Mr. Bedson by Charles Bremner, or by anyone on his behalf, in connection with the North-West trouble." He recounted the events of Charles Bremner's captivity, arrest, trial, and the loss of his furs which were said to have been divided "between Mr. Bedson, Mr. Hayter Reed and the General who was in command." Sir Adolphe Caron, Minister of Militia, replied that he had heard no such complaint against General Middleton, that the matter had never been brought before his department, that he had never heard anything about it.

Hansard recorded:

> AN HON. MEMBER: There is not a word of truth in it.
> SIR ADOLPHE CARON: Quite so.

It was possible that Sir Adolphe had not heard the murmurings of the police, nor the complaints of Father André against Middleton, but it is remarkable that he did not recall the visit to him in Winnipeg of

Charles Bremner with his lawyer, who was a prominent Conservative, and Louis Caplette, and their further discussion, at his suggestion, with General Middleton. But the exchange went no further at the moment.

However, three weeks later, on June 22, the question of a small increase for Bedson came up again, and again Mills took the opportunity to bring up the history of Charles Bremner and his furs. This time, he addressed Thomas White, Minister of the Interior, and this time Sir John A. was present. White said that the matter had not been brought to his attention: "There may be something in the report of the commission, but that has not been received." Mills began a denunciation of men in high official positions robbing a citizen of his property. "I believe the Government have in their possession the proof of the accuracy of the statement which I make. . . . I was given a copy of a receipt that was taken by the police at the time this property was taken possession of."

The mention of the police brought John Thompson, Minister of Justice, into the discussion. He too denied knowledge. "If Bremner has been aggrieved in the way the hon. gentleman describes, it is very extraordinary that he has not made a complaint either to the Minister of Militia or to myself. . . . It strikes me as novel and somewhat unwise that an officer of the public service, and, so far as I know, of honorable service, should be stigmatised as a thief when the person he is alleged to have robbed has not laid a single charge against him, and when the officer has not had an opportunity of answering any complaint."

A lack of communication, no doubt. Mills would have to discover which department held Bremner's depositions or claims or if the Claims Commission had retained them. And he would have to change his approach, for it was probable that Bedson had not been named, since he was only a peripheral figure. What Mills had accomplished was to brush the dust off the files, and bring Charles Bremner's story into the open.

May's bright promise of early payment of claims faded as spring passed and summer wore on. The sour joke persisted. On August 20, the *Herald* reported, "The last mail brought about 85 cheques to claimants. There is much dissatisfaction with the reductions which the Claims Commission made. Some refused to accept their cheques. The complaints of unfair treatment are so general that a strong effort will be made to secure a re-hearing. This will be strongly urged on Mr. White."

The "unfair treatment" did not have a political bias, for Mahaffey & Clinkskill, strong Conservatives, whose store in the flats had been sacked, had their claim reduced from $31,602.96 to $24,395.85, and Laurie, whose Tory devotion was unquestioned, got only a small modification—$55.00 of the $225.00 cut from his original claim. Both of these claimants, furthermore, were in the most favored category, Category A "unavoidable direct losses." In this category only Wyld and Bourke, farmers and stockmen south of Battleford, were allowed their own evaluation of $11,234.00. In Category B, "imprisonment by rebels," W.B. Cameron, who had lost everything he owned and had claimed $2,500, got nothing.

But the Cut Knife group were not allowed either Category A or Category B. The Bremners, the Sayers, Louis Caplette, and all who were with them were put in Category C, "Rejected. Claimants party to their own losses." They got nothing; the sentence was irrevocable; they were rebels.

However, to show that they were open-minded and flexible, the Commission did reverse a decision in the case of Malcolm Macdonald of Fort Pitt. They had rejected his original claim for $285.00 "Believing he joined the Indians voluntarily, and therefore he was categorized C. New evidence shows him to be loyal, and in Category A." Nevertheless, his claim was reduced by $15.00. The details were given:

	Claimed	Allowed
House burnt	$100.00	$100.00
Cooking stove and utensils	30.00	30.00
Dishes	20.00	20.00
2 axes	5.00	5.00
Clothing	25.00	25.00
Feather bed and bedding	25.00	25.00
2 prs. boots	12.00	8.00
Wife's clothes	60.00	50.00
2 trunks	8.00	8.00

The uproar at Battleford on receipt of the cheques brought the long-promised and frequently postponed visit of the Hon. Thomas White. On Sept. 8, the *Herald* published an account of it. This was the first time that Battleford had been able to talk to a Dominion minister directly, and they were sensible of the fact that he was one of the finest. The citizens' committee greeted him with the usual address of welcome, followed by memorials, petitions, and Bills of Complaint. After the reception and the banquet, White invited the citizens of Battleford to present their cases to him the next morning, Saturday.

With D.H. Macdowell, their new M.P. in the chair, John Macdonald, merchant, read a memorial concerning the payment of rebellion losses, and respectfully submitted the great dissatisfaction with the reductions made from legitimate claims by the Commissioners appointed to investigate them: "The people are desirous of having the whole question re-opened for a more thorough and impartial investigation." Then followed a dozen or more requests concerning scrip for the Battleford Home Guards, the building of a new bridge, a court house, new police barracks, and a particular request that the government's stipulation that two bushels of grain be returned for every bushel of seed grain received be reduced to bushel for bushel.

White replied that rebellion losses were not always paid, and he made an important point that was to recur, "It is a matter of grace and not of legal right for the Government to pay these claims. And as a minister, I am bound by oath to reserve my opinions." But he promised to look into the matter carefully. He added that "No award was made in the cases of the Bresaylor settlement for the reasons stated in the report, which I shall examine on my return to Ottawa."

To aid him in that examination, the Bresaylor people presented him with a petition with sixteen signatures, headed by Charles Bremner's mark.[2] Their urgent request was for a court of inquiry before which they could prove their loyalty and clear their names, for until that happened they would remain where the Commission had sentenced them—in Category C, rebels and denied restitution: "Although the *onus probandi* [burden of proof] does not or should not rest on us, we have always been ready and are still ready to appear before the Government Commissioners or a jury of our fellow citizens and prove to their satisfaction that we were forced to follow the rebel Indians as their prisoners, and never ceased to be loyal to Her Majesty's Government."

Recounting the circumstances and events of their captivity, however, they made an admission which, though it should have attested to their honesty, worked against them: "Firing was kept up at out tents during the battle. Incensed at what we considered a breach of faith or an unpardonable distrust, a few among us—two or three—decided to take part in the fight against the troops, saying, 'Since the police do not take any notice of our letters and messages, we are not to remain exposed to be killed by both the Indians and the police.' The whole group should not be penalised for the momentary and understandable action of two or three."

Their petition was supported by an endorsement signed by 39 citizens of Battleford, including four clergymen—two Roman Catholics, one Anglican, and one Presbyterian—saying, "the erroneous impressions we had formed of their loyalty have been dispelled on better

understanding" and declaring "That the facts as stated in the within petition are in substance true, and that the granting of the conclusion of their
petition would be an act of justice to which they are entitled, and your
petitioners will never cease to pray."[3]

P.G. Laurie was not among the signators. Rather, in an editorial on
the issue and on the endorsement, he wrote, "We have no desire to preju-
dice or prejudge the case of the Bresaylor settlers in their address to the
Hon. Mr. White, nor to enter now upon a discussion of the truth or otherwise of their statements; but we think some of those who signed it
should have left it to those who were in the country to give evidence as
to the loyalty of the memorialists."

The hidden, unofficial informers were still strong, still in defiance
of the Regina court that could find no evidence of wrong doing. Charles
Bremner and his neighbors were still under the cloud of "Not proven."

The re-creation of the Bresaylor community was well under way.
The post-office had been re-established and Herbert Taylor had qualified
as postmaster. The settlers started a school; they built "a neat and comfortable schoolhouse at their own expense," the *Herald* reported, "and
took the necessary steps to have their district recognised as a Protestant
School District." Trustees were elected and a school teacher found
whom they had all known in the Red River, whose husband was secretary to the Presbyterian church board in Battleford. Early in the New
Year, 1888, the school opened with 30 pupils on the register, among
them Alice Maude Gertrude Bremner, born on the trail from Prince
Albert. The school was "the first rural public school to be established in
the Battleford district," and shortly it was gazetted as School District
No. 111 for the whole of the Territories. And there were marvels, a
marvel of the skies in an eclipse of the moon, and a marvel of human
invention when "a conversation by telephone was successfully carried
on between Battleford and Edmonton, a distance of 300 miles."

There was also terror. On January 11 a blizzard came. "All the way
along the line there was a sudden overcast and snow began to fall.
Towards evening the temperature fell and the wind blew until it blew a
hurricane, the sharp, icy snow drifting in clouds and the thermometer
ranging from 25 to 30 below. . . . Snow was piled in fantastic drifts in
some places and to a depth of six feet or more. The odd forms they
assumed . . . suggest that many of the sand hills and peculiar land marks
to be found on the plains owe their origins more to winds in the days that
preceded vegetation than to water, as is commonly accepted. . . . The
storm rose without warning; fortunately few were out in it." But the

mailman inward bound from Swift Current was found frozen to death about ten or fifteen yards off the trail and not far from his cabin.

The blizzard struck the note of the winter. Beginning Volume Ten of the *Herald* with this new year of 1888, Laurie ruefully observed, "The good things for which we have been waiting have not come along yet; but they will be here shortly." In that bitter January, Bresaylor again heard the death chant from across the Battle river. It was for Big Bear, who died "from a gradual decay of nature," after a long illness.

From all along the Valley came grim stories. The year was a hunting failure, game was scarce, the snow was deep and trapping poor. At Edmonton a group of chiefs went to the Indian agent, "This winter we have no furs, no crop, no game, no fish;" the bands were starving. At St. Albert the police began issuing food to more than 300 destitute people. In Bresaylor, Charles Bremner and his family shared the privation.

In early March, he went in to Battleford to consult with some of his well-wishers. They were Liberals, eager to seize on issues to be presented at the new session of Parliament, which had opened on February 22. It was the first session with Wilfrid Laurier as the Liberal leader, Edward Blake having resigned that position in June. Laurier's right-hand man was James Edgar, member for Ontario West, astute in political affairs, a champion of minorities, and known to Battleford Liberals, some of whom had met him in Ottawa. Moreover, one of his sons had been with Colonel Otter's troop at Cut Knife. He would be the one to approach.

Bremner was ready for action of any kind. Nothing had come in the six months since White's visit, and he was in much the same state as the chiefs at Edmonton. As he told the Battleford men, "I would a thousand times rather die than go through what I have this winter—family half clothed and not half fed."

The proposal of his advisers was two-fold. One, that Bremner, this time, should make out a claim for his total losses—livestock and store goods as well as household goods and the furs. They estimated the sum at about $20,000, using values that the Commission had apportioned to such property in claims already paid. That claim could go as a petition to White, since the Commission had officially concluded its work, and it might help White in urging his colleagues to action. Second, Bremner should have a separate letter prepared about the furs, recounting the reception that he and his lawyer got in Winnipeg from Middleton, Middleton's denials, and Inspector Morris's insistence that Middleton had sent him orders about the furs. That account would be sent to Edgar with a covering letter about the general plight of the settlement at present. With the statement and the letter prepared for him, Charles Bremner signed with his mark and returned to Bresaylor. He hoped, but did not expect, that results would come from the enthusiasm of his sponsors.

The flurry of activity about Bremner's furs stirred the Battleford police, who were emerging as an unexpected and fortuitous ally. Not only were they still smarting at the scorn that Middleton had poured on them, at the slighting of their scouts, at the accusations against some of their officers, but now it appeared possible, if an investigation should begin and Middleton persisted in his denials, that they could even be accused of carelessness at best in the storage of the furs, and possibly of outright collusion in the theft. Having already discussed the matter in the fall with Bremner, Caplette, and others in Bresaylor who knew about the furs, Morris now set out to get testimony that would put the police in the clear. He spoke with the former Quarter-Master Sergeant, Warden, who had pointed out the lack of documentary evidence—even of customary receipts—in the handling of the furs, but at least Warden was able to give him a copy of the letter from Hayter Reed ordering the packing of the furs, which he had kept for his own protection in an action that he had considered extraordinary from the beginning. Morris also asked the civilian who had been assistant quarter-master and who had received the furs to write an account outlining the events connected with the general and the furs. Ronald Macdonald's letter was dated Battleford, N.W.T., March 16, 1888, the same day as the documents were being assembled for Bremner.

The letter detailed the arrival of the furs in the police store-room on May 26; the messenger from Pitt with a letter from Hayter Reed on July 4, ordering packages of furs to be put up for Middleton, Reed and Bedson; the arrival of the boat the next morning when "the General and Reed went to the barracks." It went on, "The General was not satisfied with the quantity of the furs prepared for him and had the packages supplemented by a large saddle box filled with choice furs, which with the packages were sent to the boat. There were a few remnants of fur left, but I am under the impression that they were given out on the order of the General.

"Next day, Monday, Mr. Reed called at the store and asked Warden for the order authorizing the packing of the furs. Warden professed not knowing where it was, keeping it I suppose for his own protection, as there was no other order either for receiving, storing, or disposing of them, and it was generally understood that General Middleton had confiscated the furs."

The winter held on. March 18, "Sunday afternoon, a blinding snow storm from the north-west. Impossible for horses to travel against it. The mail courier coming in had to lie over." March 31, "Both rivers are still solid." April 4, "Heavy snowfall. Roads badly drifted. Gophers running about on top of the snow."

But the worst of the spring was not the weather. On April 28, the *Saskatchewan Herald* had a black-bordered column: "Death of Hon. Thomas White, last Sunday evening, April 22. The news filled every heart with grief. . . . In the territories he will be sorely missed." Liberal Frank Oliver wrote in the *Bulletin*, "His death is a national calamity. The prime minister was prostrated at the news," and he quoted a dispatch from Ottawa, April 23: "In the afternoon, Sir John rose to move adjournment as a tribute to the Hon. Thos. White. He opened his lips to say 'Mr. Speaker,' but the words did not come. Tears stood in his eyes and were already in streams running down his cheeks. He placed one hand on his mouth to choke the emotion, but his grief was too great, and he burst into a flood of sobs and tears. He was not alone in this outburst of grief. There was scarcely a dry eye in the House. Sir John, realising his inability to speak, touched Sir Hector Langevin's arm and, sitting down, buried his face in his handkerchief. Sir Hector moved the adjournment."

For those in the North-West who had looked to Thomas White for sympathy and justice, another hope was gone. The promised enquiry, the review of evidence, would be further delayed, and restitution, if it came, yet more distant. And then—who would take his place? It was now three years since those two months of turmoil, and little healing was evident.

Chapter Twelve

Loyalty and Furs

Things were not as barren as they seemed. Less than a month after the death of Thomas White, when the House moved into Committee of Supply on May 17, James Edgar rose in his place beside the new Liberal leader to present the case of Charles Bremner.[1]

Like Laurier, Edgar was tall, elegant, distinguished in bearing; like Laurier he was born in 1841 and in Quebec—Laurier in a village north of Montreal of one of the oldest families in Quebec, Edgar in the Eastern Townships, descendant of the Edgars of Keithoch, Forfarshire, in Scotland; both were called to the bar in 1864, Laurier in Quebec, Edgar in Ontario; Edgar had first been elected to the House for West Ontario in 1872, Laurier had first been elected in the Eastern Townships in 1874. They made a remarkable pair as they faced across the floor the gaunt figure and craggy features of Sir John A. Macdonald, over twenty-five years their senior.

Edgar began by describing the general plight of the erstwhile prosperous Bresaylor settlers and "the serious grievances and the deep wrongs which I think have been inflicted on these people . . . mostly Scotch Half-breeds of a very high order of intelligence"; and he outlined the circumstances and events of their captivity on Poundmaker's reserve and the subsequent refusal of the Rebellion Losses Commission to indemnify them, "claiming they had been party to their own losses." With an air of candor and fairness, Edgar went on to note the captives' admission that "a few amongst us—two or three—decided to take part in the fight," and even conceded that "there were suspicious circumstances," but that "while the commission had some ground to go upon in their general conclusions, still, on the whole, they came to a wrong decision." Edgar was not, perhaps the strongest champion that the Bresaylor people might have wished for, but he then read from a letter "by a leading citizen of Battleford on the 12th of March," saying that "These people are starving. . . . They have killed all the animals they had and are now so discouraged and disheartened that many would prefer death in almost any other shape than starving."

This situation and the commission's decisions stemmed from the accusation that they were rebels, and Edgar next read from the petition from the Bresaylor captives asking for a court of inquiry to clear their names,[2] and from the endorsement of the petition by thirty-nine worthy citizens of Battleford. He noted that the government had turned the petitions over to "Mr. Young, secretary of the commission, who had examined into the losses, and I have here an enormous mass, amounting to 162 pages, of a report which has been made to the government by Mr. Young on the subject of the petition. The whole effect of this report is to justify the finding of the commissioner . . . against the claims of the settlers." But Edgar contended that one could find, even from within the report itself, "perfect answers to almost every one of the charges made against the settlers or against the Half-breeds."

However, defense of the group of settlers and their claims of loyalty was not Edgar's purpose. It was to press the case of the furs, which had also been thrown out by the commissioners. For Edgar and Laurier—not to disparage their keen sense of justice—Bremner's furs was the little cloud, like a man's hand, that would lead them to Middleton, to the embarrassment of the government, and to political advantage in Quebec. Edgar said, "I contend that this claim for furs of the Half-breeds rests upon a very different footing and a higher footing than other claims, and it is to that that I particularly call the attention of the House."

He continued, "I do not care whether these men were rebels ten times over, this was their private property, and it was taken possession of by the mounted police under General Middleton's directions, and they have not got any portion of these furs yet, nor have they been paid a single dollar on account of these claims. . . . These men may be rebels, but do not steal their furs. . . . More than that, Mr. Speaker, I do not care who the guilty parties are, it is the duty of the Government to bring them to justice, even if it would send somebody to the penitentiary."

To forestall any plea of ignorance on the part of the government, Edgar reviewed the items of information in government files, beginning with the affidavit that Charles Bremner made in Winnipeg in November of 1885 which was subsequently sent to Ottawa, the sworn deposition before the commissioners in Battleford in June, 1886, the re-iteration before Thomas White in August 1887, and the recent submission of March 1888.

"There is no dispute that these furs were brought in by Bremner, and were placed, by General Middleton's order, in the custody of the police at Battleford." Then he read Bremner's account of his frustrating meetings with Caron and Middleton in Winnipeg, of Middleton's denials, not only of knowledge of the furs, but even of ordering the arrest of Bremner and his neighbors. Edgar then played his trump card, a copy of the letter from Hayter Reed ordering the furs to be packed, which was received by Quarter-Master Warden, and dated Fort Pitt, July 4, 1885:

> Gen. Middleton has instructed and authorised me to send you the present letter, desiring that you put up bales of furs for the undermentioned: Two bales for General Middleton, one for S. L. Bedson, and one for myself. Please select the best, and pack them down, as we will be down there by boat tomorrow.
>
> (signed) Hayter Reed
> Assistant Commissioner of Indians

Edgar continued, "As Government officers took charge of those furs, the honor of the Government of Canada is pledged to finding out who stole them and where they are." It was also, he contended, a matter of the honor of the army—one of his sons had been among Otter's troops at Cut Knife—and members of the House had been in action; this was not something far off and learned by report, it was a personal experience.

"There are gallant members of this House, generals and colonels, and you also, Mr. Speaker [Joseph A. Ouimet],[3] who were also in the North-West, and you should see for your honor that a charge of this kind against the force should be cleared up. . . . It is the duty of the Government . . . to investigate this matter further, and to pay these men the value of their furs, to follow up the offenders who took the furs and punish the guilty parties no matter where the punishment may fall."

He sat. The reply came, not from Sir John A., but from the Hon. John Thompson, Minister of Justice and member for Antigonish. He was a formidable opponent, for he was one of the most highly regarded men in Canada. Appointed to the Supreme Court of Nova Scotia at age 38, he had been persuaded by Sir John A. in 1885, in Sir John's effort to bring new, energetic and untainted men into the cabinet, to resign his post and become Minister of Justice and Attorney-General of Canada. He had since won the respect of the House for his integrity. A Catholic, a convert from Methodism, he had shown an even-handed justice between Catholic Quebec and Protestant Ontario in the highly emotional debate over the execution of Riel, and had won a strong vote for the government. He was three years younger than the pair he faced, and he was a brilliant debater.

He began mildly by agreeing that this matter could not be a party question, and he praised the genuineness of Edgar's concern for people whom he believed to be poverty stricken, but he pointed out that it was necessary for the government to protect the nation's treasury against unjustified demands. The government had already paid many claims to the deserving (figures for the cost of the rebellion had been officially presented a couple of weeks before as $5,895,256) and the Rebellion Losses Commission had been entirely in the right to refuse claims of those who had been active in the rebellion against the government of Canada.

Having established a general basis, and with Young's voluminous report before him, Thompson bore in on the weak spot—the admission of the petitioners that "a few amongst us—two or three—decided to take part in the fight against the troops;" and Edgar's concession that there were suspicious circumstances," and that "the commission had some ground to go upon in their general conclusion." With these two admissions supported by details from Young's report, he built up a strong case against the petitioners, reiterating the charges that they had stolen property belonging to their loyal neighbors, and of course, there was the incriminating rifle belonging to a man killed on duty. Thompson declared, "They were themselves responsible for the loss they have sustained. They went into the rebel forces for the purpose of minimizing those losses." They were culpable, and the commissioners "perfectly justified in applying to them the rule that rebellion should not be made profitable."

Edgar tried to protest that, "I carefully said that I was not going into discussion of that. . . . I do not rest the case upon that, but upon the matter of the furs."

Thompson thrust home. "I did understand the hon. gentleman to discuss it."

Once more, Edgar insisted that whether they were rebels or not was irrelevant to the furs case. But Thompson claimed the victory. "I am speaking to the general question of those claims. Then the hon. gentleman and I understand each other to this extent, that there was evidence before the commissioners from which they fairly came to the conclusion which they did. I was about to state what that evidence consisted of, but it is not worth while to press that point, as the hon. member concedes it."

At that moment, the case of the Bresaylor petitioners for rebellion losses was closed. They would get no compensation. The matter had become an abstract debate between two men, neither of whom knew the land or the people, over two bodies of evidence, over which interpretation of facts was valid, the petitioners' account or Young's report. Thompson was convinced that Young's report was irreproachable, and he had 162 pages to back him up.

As for the supportive petition by Battleford residents, he dismissed it. Like the commission itself and like the court in Regina, he refused to admit witnesses for the defence. The Crown's device had been to dismiss the case on insufficient evidence, and so the defence lawyer could not get his witnesses on record. The Commissioners had allowed only one outside witness, Father Cochin, and he was brushed aside as not knowing all that had gone on. Strangely, at no point was testimony for the petitioners allowed to go on record.

But Thompson was not yet content. He went further, much further, in presenting the case against the Bresaylor people, and read into *Hansard* the highly colored, highly emotional account that Laurie had published of the arrival of the captives, in advance of Poundmaker, declaring it to be "corroborative evidence with regard to the position of these men in relation to the rebellion." He took items from Young's report in which, despite Father Cochin's explicit statement, it was declared that the Bremner group "refused to remain at Bresaylor or to go to Battleford." The visitation of Poundmaker assuring them of no harm, and the later appearance of Delorme with two hundred Indians were stated to be "consultations with the hostile Indians and with rebel emissaries from Batoche, and as a result of those consultations they moved, with all their animals and movable property, to the Indians' camp."

The distortions were patently clear when the Minister of Justice moved on to deal with the matter of the furs, and made the astonishing declaration that "Mr. Bremner was a very prominent and active rebel in the field." He pursued his attack. "In the first place, the commissioners had evidence before them that the prices were excessive; in the second place, they had evidence that the number of skins claimed exceeded even those which were in the stores of Hudson's Bay posts of considerable size; and, in the third place they ascertained by the evidence that there was no fur trade on the settlement where Mr. Bremner was, which could have possible furnished such a store of furs as he claimed to have."

Thompson was obviously intent on destroying any vestige of credibility in Charles Bremner's statements. Ignoring completely the startling and irrefutable fact of Hayter Reed's letter that Edgar had read to the House, he attacked "the assailing of men in high positions . . . on the statement of a person who was not only disloyal, who was not only found with stolen Government goods in his possession, but who was found armed with the rifle of a recently slain public servant; and I think to have assailed men in high position, on the statement of a person who made, as this person undoubtedly did make, claims grossly exaggerated against the Government, only reflected discredit upon those who rashly did so."

Thompson's sledge-hammer attack on Bremner was a shock, especially as it came from a former judge of a superior court, and the present Minister of Justice. As though thinking that perhaps he had gone too far, and to suggest that the government was a compassionate one, Thompson ended more quietly. Summing up his attitude to the Bresaylor petitioners—who included Charles Bremner—he said that the government had investigated the truth of the statements made by the petitioners, had found the commissioners' "fair and proper" decisions upheld, and had not found any new evidence "which could lead us to arrive at a different conclusion now." On the matter of the furs, however, "I think the claim for them stands on a different footing." White had been investigating the claim, but no one knew how far the enquiry had gone. "I ask the House, therefore, to understand that, as regards that claim, the enquiry has not been concluded and will be pursued."

It was as though a tacit trade had been agreed upon between Thompson and Edgar—the petitioners' claim for Bremner's furs. Laurier, who now rose to speak, crystallised the division, one which Bremner himself had made at the beginning. As for the petitioners' claims, "It must be evident that it is not beyond possibility of doubt that these men were not rebels. . . . I have always protested, not only after the event, but before the event, that these men were not rebels." So one man believed that they were telling the truth; the door was not irrevocably closed on Poundmaker's captives. And in that regard, "One statement is that they were there of their own accord, and the other is that they were taken prisoners by the Indians. Even if the first statement is correct, that cannot be made an act of rebellion, because those Indians were on their own reserve, and as long as they remained on their own reserve, none of their acts could be construed as an act of rebellion." In case of doubt, Laurier urged, a claimant should get the benefit: "There must necessarily be a good deal of bitter sentiment among these people, and the best way to cure that and bring them to their dutiful allegiance is to extend the best consideration to them which is possible."

As to the other question, "As far as Charles Bremner is concerned, it seems to me that his claim has been rejected for reasons altogether of a frivolous nature . . . it is not satisfactory to hear, as we have heard from the Minister of Justice, that the Government are not at present prepared to consider the question. . . . This is the great court of enquiry, because this is the place where public opinion can be called to the fact, and this is the very place of all others where the charge should be made. . . . It does not do to say: You have no right to accuse this or that man. I do not accuse anybody, but I say the Government should see that ample justice should be done to this man, and that the property which was confided to the Government should be restored to him."

Hansard recorded: "It being six o'clock, the Speaker left the Chair."

So ended the first formal attempt to bring Bresaylor matters before Parliament, and to get some response to the petition that had been presented to Thomas White, asking for a court of enquiry to hear evidence in public; in effect, to put the petitioners on open trial. John Thompson, the righteous man, had declared them to be rebels; he had declared the Commission's findings to be entirely justified; he had delivered the verdict and passed the sentence. As long as he was Minister of Justice, the petition would not be granted and the petitioners would have no hearing.

As for Charles Bremner and the theft of his furs, which was outside the rebellion altogether, the fact that Thompson had declared in the House that Bremner was "a very prominent and active rebel" gave little hope that Thomas White's investigation would be followed up with any enthusiasm or promptness.

Laurier had brought Thompson's fierce denunciations back to a level of reasonable consideration, but that was all he could do. The Liberals could not force the government to act, and the matter was now indisputably a party affair. Hopes were dashed once more. Charles Bremner would get no money this year.

During the summer of 1888, there were changes in high places in Ottawa. A new Governor General arrived, "His Excellency, the Right Honorable Sir Frederick Arthur Stanley, Earl of Fife, recently married to Princess Louise, eldest daughter of the prospective King of Great Britain," who became a noted hockey fan. John Thompson, who had succeeded in negotiating a treaty favorable to Canada in the fisheries dispute with the United States, was knighted, though almost immediately Grover Cleveland, President of the United States, repudiated the treaty and imposed an embargo on Canadian trade.

Within the government, Sir John A. Macdonald appointed Edgar Dewdney as the new Minister of the Interior in White's place, to the bitter disappointment of Nicholas Davin, M.P. for West Assiniboia, who had hoped for the Interior Ministry for himself, and to the outrage of Frank Oliver, who despised the man: "There has seldom been so high an office attained by a man of so little merit."[4] But at least he would no longer be sitting on the Territories Council in Regina. To take the place of Dewdney as Lieutenant-Governor of the Territories, Macdonald appointed the Hon. Joseph Royal, who had founded the newspaper *Le Métis* in Winnipeg in 1870, had become Attorney-General of Manitoba, and later M.P. Hayter Reed was given Dewdney's office as Indian Commissioner.

In the smaller world, P.G. Laurie received a cable from England with the news that he had come into "something over $5,000 as his share of an intestate estate just distributed." The fairy-tale gift helped to mellow his attitude to Charles Bremner as he came to appreciate what $5,000 meant to the well-being of his own family. In Bresaylor, a new school was built with a shingled roof—in fact, sod roofs were becoming rare—Henry Sayer imported a 12-horse-power thresher, and he and A.R. Chisholm were elected directors of the Battle River Agricultural Society at its annual meeting, December 17.

At the meeting, the Society, as usual, passed resolutions. The first was "to send the Government a memorial pressing for the abrogation of the fee of a dollar a ton on hay cut for sale, and the removal of dues on dry wood and fence rails." The second, not a new one with the Society, had added force with the presence of Henry Sayer, one of the Bresaylor Five, on the executive; it urged "the immediate settlement of the claims of the Bresaylor Half-breeds, payment to Mr. Charles Bremner for the furs taken by General Middleton, and the issue of scrip for the Battleford Volunteers."

The December resolution was followed by a petition of January 7, making definite charges against Middleton. Momentum was gathering again, in spite of the spring setback, and this time no one could claim that the supportive petitioners were outsiders, ignorant of affairs, newcomers, or dupes. Dogged pursuit of restitution for rebellion losses was spurred at the turn of the year 1889 when Xavier Batoche went to Ottawa, accompanied by Capt. Begin of the Mounted Police, "to explain that he did not participate in the late rebellion, being away from home at the time." He had an interview with Sir John A., Sir Hector Langevin, and Dewdney. Apparently the door on settlers' claims was not altogether closed. Batoche's claim was for $20,000. He was awarded that sum.

Possibly Batoche's action, together with the persistent petition from Battleford—after all, Charles Bremner and the rest of the captives had also been away from home—goaded Macdowell, M.P. for Saskatchewan, to reconsider Charles Bremner's claims, at least for the furs. There was a small flurry of exchanges between him and James

Clinkskill, M.L.A. for Battleford, both of them Conservatives. Macdowell brought the amount of the claim down to a sum that he thought
the government might consider and that the estimates could accommodate. He wired Clinkskill from Ottawa to offer Bremner $3,000, and
received in return a paper addressed to James Clinkskill, dated 24th
March, 1889: "Sir—I hereby authorize you to telegraph to D.H. Macdowell, M.P., to accept $3,000 in payment of my claim for furs lost dur-
ing the late rebellion," and it was signed by Charles Bremner, His Mark.
The winter had been a hard one, and Bremner was ready to accept anything. However, his other advisors (Liberal) urged him not to take the
offer. Instead, they insisted that suing Middleton for the original sum
was the only way in which Bremner or the others were likely to get
redress, if the whole matter came up in open court.

Clinkskill, however, was not confining his efforts to a single
approach. As a member of the Legislative Assembly, he was enjoying
the new sense of Territorial autonomy, and he introduced a resolution to
the Assembly "to open a simple way by which some unconsidered
claims of Half-breeds for compensation might be disposed of." Declaring that "some who were known to have been loyal have had their
claims rejected, while others well-known to have been directly implicated in the rising have had their claims recognised," his request was
that the resolution be forwarded to the new Governor General, asking
him to sponsor a new review. A reply came promptly from Ottawa, but
not from the Earl of Fife. It was from Dewdney saying that "no claim
otherwise valid was refused on the ground that the applicant was implicated, unless it was proved by evidence that the claimant was party to
his own loss. Evidence was taken and facilities were available at a time
when all the facts were fresh in the memory of the witnesses." Dewdney,
who had been firm in keeping the elected members of the Territories
Council in their place while he was lieutenant-governor, was not more
eager to entertain their proposals now that they constituted an elected
Assembly. Nor was he going to allow them to go over his head to the
Governor General. Another avenue was closed.

Before the summer was out, Lieutenant-Governor Royal presided
over a ceremony that would bring an important development to the people of Saskatchewan. It was the sod-turning for the extension of the railroad north from Regina to Prince Albert. The Regina and Long Lake
Railway was a venture that both Davin and Macdowell had worked for
in the House "indefatigably" and they rejoiced in their success in what
had been an otherwise disappointing Parliament for the members from

the Territories.

The plan was that the railway would be completed to Saskatoon by the end of the year, and to Prince Albert early in 1890. There was an immediate bonanza for settlers along the route and indeed as far as Bresaylor, when shortly notices went out that "Contractors for railway ties at Duck Lake and Prince Albert are paying good men $26 a month and board." In the longer view, the coming winter would be the last one for the long freighting haul from Swift Current to Battleford. By the next year the journey would be only ninety miles to Saskatoon instead of the present two hundred miles to Swift Current.

But for this year, through September and the rest of the fall, there was work for freighters bringing in goods for Alex Macdonald and for Mahaffey & Clinkskill, as well as for the police and the Indian agency. Charles Bremner and Louis Caplette started out in mid-September for Swift Current, and within days, according to the *Herald*, "all freighting teams are busy, greatly in demand."

While Bremner was off on the freighting trip, the Agricultural Society received a belated response from Ottawa to their petition of the previous January. A.M. Burgess, Deputy Minister of the Interior, arrived in Battleford on September 19, and met a deputation of settlers at the Land Office to discuss their submission. Together, they went through the litany of hay-dues, scrip for volunteers, and so forth. But on one matter Burgess was unyielding. Laurie wrote, "The claims of the Bresaylor Half-breeds for compensation for their losses in the rebellion, and a reconsideration of the cases of many of the settlers were brought up, but Mr. Burgess thought they had been finally disposed of by the Claims Commission."

Undaunted, the Battle River Agricultural Society made yet another effort. At the end of their annual meeting on Monday afternoon, December 27, "a public meeting was organised to take some steps towards pressing upon the Government the importance of re-opening the rebellion losses claims; and taking steps to establish the loyalty or otherwise of the Bresaylor settlers." This was an activity of the winter season in which Charles Bremner and his companions were busy. The meeting was held at the beginning of the New year, 1890. Yet another petition was drafted and sent forward to the Minister of the Interior, but with copies to James Lister, Liberal member for Lambton West, an Ontario attorney, elected to the House in the last election, who had been designated to spearhead the Liberal attack in the Bremner case.

This time, however, Charles Bremner was not prepared to await a leisurely response to the petition. This time he would make the furs work for his loyalty and for the loyalty of the whole group. Since no one could sue the Crown without the Crown's permission, neither could Bremner, but he could sue Middleton, and in that way, at last, bring the whole evidence—sworn evidence—into court and give the petitioners an open trial as they had requested. The *Herald* reported, "Charles Bremner of Bresaylor, about the matter of whose furs much has been said since the rebellion, has declined the offer of settlement made by the government, and is about to bring action in the courts against General Middleton, Warden Bedson, and Hayter Reed to recover the value of his property. He has been advised in this course as the proper one to assure all the facts of the case being put on record, and his legal advisers are confident of being able to secure substantial justice to Mr. Bremner."

The next session of Parliament began on February 5 with great ceremony in honor of the new Governor General. Among the Liberals, Edward Blake, returned from England, was back in his place at the right hand of Laurier. Bresaylor matters moved into the House in the opening days with a notice of motion from James Lister, and he presented the motion on March 3: "for the appointment of a committee to enquire into the claims of the Bresaylor Half-breeds for losses sustained during the rebellion in the North-West, and also in reference to furs taken from Charles Bremner, a Half-breed residing at Battleford. That the said committee have power to send for persons and papers, and employ a stenographer, and report from time to time to the House."[5]

Lister pointed out that the matter had been brought to the attention of the House at least twice, but only as information that the claims existed and had not been settled. His purpose was different. Then he issued his challenge:

"I am animated simply by a desire to have the claims of these people investigated, and if it turns out that they have not been properly dealt with by the Government, then it will be the duty of the Government to do what is right under the circumstances. In going over the facts connected with this matter, the names of eminent men are necessarily brought up. The name of General Middleton as officer of Her Majesty's army and Commander of the Canadian force must necessarily take a prominent place in the remarks which I have to make. The names of other officials of the Government—Mr. Hayter Reed, a Commissioner of Indian Affairs in the North-West, and Mr. Bedson, keeper of the Manitoba penitentiary—must also appear, and if I am able to establish that the conduct of these men had been unbecoming that of an officer, and unbecoming that of officials of the Government—in other words, that the conduct of the general in command amounting to nothing more and nothing less than a looting of the property of the Half-breeds, he can be no longer fit to occupy the position he occupies, and the other officials of the Government ought to be dismissed."

Lister read excerpts from the latest Battleford petition, which gave a new light on at least one aspect of Bresaylor movements: "From all that can be learned, it was the intention of all the settlers of that district to remain at their homes and protect their property, not anticipating so serious an outbreak, and it was only the pressure brought to bear on one of their number who happened to be in town on the day previous to the outbreak, that any of the Bresaylor people came to the barracks. . . . With the exception of three or four, the whole settlement took no part in the rebellion, but rendered assistance to most of the prisoners taken by the Indians; and in some cases saved their lives. We believe that it was through their persuasion that Poundmaker's men were prevented from following Colonel Otter's troops on their return march from Cut Knife to a large ravine, where in all probability a large number would have been massacred. . . . It is a fact that their cattle were taken and slaughtered by the Indians in common with all other cattle. . . . Some of their horses were taken by General Middleton's officers for scouting purposes and have never been returned, and they have had no indemnity for either horses or cattle."

Coming to the matter of Charles Bremner, the petitioners were forthright: "The taking of Bremner's furs by General Middleton and the refusal of the Government to give him redress in the matter is an injustice that is keenly felt by every right-thinking man in this district. We have proof that General Middleton took these furs under the pretense of keeping them safe for Bremner. We have proof that these furs were shipped by General Middleton's orders to himself and others, and when a deputation brought that matter before the Minister of the Interior [Thomas White] we were assured that Bremner would be paid for his furs, whether he would be paid for his other losses or not."

The Minister of Justice, now *Sir* John Thompson, rose: "By whom was that written?"

The credentials were impeccable. Lister replied, "It is signed by James Clinkskill, member of the North-West Assembly, chairman, and by J.M. Skelton, secretary."

Lister continued that as far as Bremner was concerned, rebel or not, the government had taken possession of his furs. "Having possession of the furs, they are bound in law, they are bound in equity, they are bound in everything that men cherish as good and right, to recompense that man for those furs if they were lost while in the custody of the Government by those officials in the North-West Territories." He ended by suggesting that Macdowell, member for Saskatchewan and living in Prince Albert, had been less than zealous in his pursuit of the interests of his constituents. Macdowell indignantly denied the charge and defended the loyalty of the claimants in his own way: "The hon. gentleman has appealed to our French *confrères* in this House for their sympathy because, he said, these were French Half-breeds, who resided a few miles from Battleford. I can correct him on that point, and I tell him that the settlement was called Bresaylor because it was founded by three families of Scotch Half-breeds, and I believe the House will agree with me when I say that, having the blood of Scotch forefathers, that was enough to protect them against improper influences or discouragements."

As for the furs, however, Macdowell, having been a temporary member of Middleton's force, repudiated the charge against the general, "a man for whom I have the very highest respect," and also the charge against Hayter Reed, "whom I believe to be a thoroughly good servant of the Government." He simply did not believe that Reed had taken the furs, although he knew that there had been wide-spread looting.

"I can remember well . . . after the troops returned from Battleford there was never such a large fur trade as was carried on in Prince Albert. There was scarcely a man from any part of Canada, who took part in the rebellion, who did not, when passing through Prince Albert, have a little bundle of furs to sell to the fur dealers there. . . . Probably they got them from Charles Bremner's stock."

So that, while Macdowell objected to accusations that Middleton and Reed had taken the furs, he conceded that they had been taken, a theft had occurred. He had got a copy of the list of furs and the claim for them from Bremner and had taken it to the Prince Albert fur dealers who had been raking in furs from soldiers, and they gave him a much lower estimate than Bremner's. On the basis of their estimate, a year earlier, he had offered Bremner $3,000, but nothing came of it. He said, "I think he could justly claim $3,500, and I hope that that sum will be put in the Estimates." Yet Macdowell was immediately in the awkward position of having to admit Bremner's current brusque rejection of his aid: "I telegraphed him when I came down this Session to ask him if I should continue to do the best I could for him, and I read the following reply:

Battleford, N.W.T. 24th February, 1890
D.H. Macdowell, M.P., Ottawa

Telegram received. Claim is now in my solicitor's hand for collection. Charles Bremner.

The Minister of Justice rose to speak, firm as ever. "The Bresaylor claims were investigated by the Commission. They had the same chance as everyone else. The Commission recommended that their claims not be paid because these people had been rebels, and therefore had contributed to their own losses as well as to the losses of others. There is no new evidence to justify re-opening the investigation." Rather lamely, he added, "Anyway, in the last few days Charles Bremner has decided to go to court against the officers. Therefore, the Government should not be required to undertake further investigation."

Laurier saw the chink there. "Mr. Lister should be satisfied with the result of his motion today in that the Government has at least been obliged to admit that Charles Bremner was despoiled of his furs. The investigation is asked as to whether a public offence has been committed, and that is why a committee should be granted."

But there was the other, more profound matter to be considered. Laurier continued, "The Half-breeds who have been stigmatised with the stigma of rebellion come before this Parliament and ask to disprove the charge made against them. They ask to begin another hearing . . . an act of grace which they ask of the Parliament of Canada. It may not be strict justice, but it is an act of grace when they ask to have the privilege of disproving the charge brought against them, and confirming their innocence."

Sir John A. Macdonald spoke for the first time in the Bremner debate. He supported his Minister of Justice and took the escape route. "The Commission was a fair one, they heard evidence and gave judgement. We are now asked to set aside their judgement in the case of Mr. Bremner. As regards that, the Government have no desire to protect any person who has injured Mr. Bremner. But he has taken his case to court, and if he establishes his case he will get judgement for his losses. There is no case or ground for this committee."

The Hon. David Mills rose in his place: "I brought this case to the attention of the House early in 1887, and the Government have had from that day to this to enquire into this claim." He urged that the officers named be given a chance to clear themselves, but "if their guilt should be established, let the Government take proceedings against them for the purpose of making them pay for what they have taken, and dismiss them from the public service. That would be a perfectly honest, straightforward, commonsense proceeding."

Mills's proposal touched some of the members of the House who had commanded troops during the conflict. For instance, William O'Brien, Conservative, Muskoka, Lieut-Colonel of the Volunteer Militia, who had commanded the York and Simcoe regiments in the rebellion, was deeply disturbed by the serious charge against Middleton, which, he thought, ought to be withdrawn or established: "I, as an officer of that force, feel bound to say that I cannot permit charges of this kind to be made in this House and allowed to pass without notice. The system of looting, which certainly did prevail to a very great extent in the North-West, is one disgraceful to either officers or privates as subjects, and also disgraceful to them as soldiers. Mr. Macdowell's charge argues a very great want of discipline in those commanding the force. . . . I should like our men distinctly to understand that the Government and the people of this country will, in the most strenuous and emphatic terms condemn—and if necessary punish—any practice similar to those which are alleged against gentlemen in high positions in the forces of Canada. I hope an expression will go forth condemning any such practice no matter by whom it is carried on."

Sir Richard Cartwright, Liberal, South Oxford, offered an amendment, limiting an enquiry to the furs only: "That a select committee be appointed to enquire into the statements made in this House in reference to the furs said to have been taken from Charles Bremner, a Half-breed, resident in Battleford."

Sir John A. objected that this was a new proposition, and it would not be fair to try Middleton twice—both in court and in the House. He proposed an adjournment of the debate "to give Mr. Bremner a chance to consider his position, and maybe he will drop his proceeding in court. He can consider the new position proposed and decide what the course should be."

Cartwright retorted, "Year after year these statements have been made. An investigation should be undertaken at once."

Laurier rose too. "Under a motion to adjourn, the question would be killed for this session."

Sir John A., obviously wanting time to consult with his cabinet, promised, "I will take care that the motion shall have every opportunity of coming up."

Laurier yielded. "Under those circumstances, we will agree to an adjournment of debate."

Three days later, Sir John A. Macdonald submitted names for a committee of seven; they had been carefully chosen. Three were from Quebec—Philippe Casgrain, Désiré Girouard, Edward Holton—two of them Liberals; two Conservatives from Ontario—Alexander McNeill, an Irishman educated at Trinity College, Dublin, a barrister at law of Middle Temple, London, and a farmer; and David Tisdale, vice-president of a lumber company, lieutenant colonel retired with rank— and two from the Maritimes, Richard Weldon, Conservative, Dean of Law at Dalhousie University; and Josiah Wood of New Brunswick, Conservative, ship-owner, farmer and stock raiser. All of them had been called to the bar, several were Q.C.'s. They ranged in age from Weldon at 51 to Casgrain at 75.

Edward Blake suggested that Lister, who had been so active in the matter, should be added as a non-voting member. Macdonald agreed, but added another non-voter, the Hon. George Kirkpatrick, Q.C., Conservative, former Speaker of the House, also a Trinity College, Dublin man, and a lieutenant colonel, commander of the 47th "Frontenac" Battalion and President of the Dominion Rifle Association. Middleton, as well as Bremner, would have a non-voting champion.

The Select Committee was constituted by vote in the House on March 10. Charles Bremner had won a victory.

The news came to Battleford by telegraph on the same day. Charles Bremner and a few of the Battleford petitioners had been waiting for it in Clinkskill's store, and as the word spread, others hurried in until there was a fine celebration, with cheers and congratulations spilling over each other. After all, Battleford had made the front news in Parliament and in the nation's headlines. Laurie came over too. Clinkskill was jubilant that the government—his party—had justified his faith and rewarded his efforts. If there was as yet no recognition of the justice of the Battleford petition, nevertheless there was a fair chance that the investigation by a Select Committee of Parliament, though it was restricted at present to the furs question, would reach further than that. The other signatories to the Battleford petition also felt that, though they had not received the reply that they had hoped for, yet they saw a possibility that their pleas would be answered.

As for Charles Bremner, it was a moment of great excitement and great hope. The nation's outstanding men were working for him. He was swept up in that heady excitement. Yet, as he drove home to take the news to Emily and the others, he reflected that his victory was a small one. He might get some money for the furs, in time—that was problematical—but his other great loss had not even been understood.

Even his Liberal champions were taking it for granted that he was a rebel—"it is not a question of loyalist or rebel," Lister had said. "Loyalty or not is irrelevant to the matter," Mills had said. They all still believed, or were willing to concede, that he was a liar; that he and his neighbors had perjured themselves in their sworn testimony. There was one bright spot: Lister had read out before the whole parliament and it had been entered in the records of *Hansard*, that he and his companions had helped to save lives; there was support for his claim that through their persuasion, Poundmaker's men were stopped from following Colonel Otter's retreating troops. And there was the fact that Laurier believed them.

He still had a choice—to pursue the suit against Middleton in the courts or to accede to the vote of Parliament. It wasn't really a choice. If the Parliament of Canada had decided to launch an enquiry into his affairs, he had no alternative. He would accede. As Sir John A. had said, Middleton could not be tried twice—in the courts and in Parliament. A Parliamentary investigation would be the more likely to bring all the evidence before the country. It would give the widest publicity. He would have to drop the court case. Once more it would be a matter of waiting, waiting for restitution of any kind. But if the judgement should go for him, there was a chance of restoring not only his own integrity but also that of his friends.

Bremner's victory and the high selling price of hay—$10 going to $20 a ton—were the only bright spots on the spring horizon at Bresaylor. The winter had been hard, trapping meagre, and the spring the latest on record. High winds and snow storms had stopped work on the Regina and Long Lake Railway at the end of December, with the end of track still 75 miles from Saskatoon. Freighting was difficult in the deep snow, eight feet in places near the Elbow, and the temperature went down to 43 below in Saskatoon on February 25. Influenza was prevalent all along the line, attacking young and old, priests, doctors, freighters, and housewives. The toll was heavy.

Chapter Thirteen

The General and His Aide

The Select Committee met on Friday morning, March 14, 1890, in the Committee Room of the House of Commons.[1] They ranged themselves along one side of the long table, with the short-hand writers Payne and Burrows at either end of it, and N. Robidoux, Clerk of the Committee, on the other side, the more easily to administer oaths.

The meeting proceeded with admirable alacrity. They chose as chairman the Irishman, Alexander McNeill, who then directed the clerk to read out the terms of reference, which included the specific directive, "To inquire into the statements made in the House in reference to furs taken from Charles Bremner, a Half-breed residing in Battleford." As the clerk sat down, Weldon, the Dalhousie Dean of Law, spoke: "Mr. Chairman, I think that in order to guard against our wandering off on tangents, it would be desirable to have before us a clear record of the statements made in the House that our Order of Reference alludes to."

This sensible suggestion was adopted, and Wood, the other member from the Maritimes, followed it up by proposing that Lister be delegated to draw up the record since he was in touch with the Battleford people, being the recipient of their petition, and he had presented the motion that brought the Select Committee into existence. Agreed to.

The next detail was the order of calling the witnesses, and again there was no difficulty. Casgrain said that obviously General Middleton must be called first as befitted his rank as well as his importance in the whole matter, and that Hayter Reed, his erstwhile aide, should come at the same time. Casgrain further said that these two witnesses should receive copies of Lister's document so that they could study it and prepare replies to the charges before they met with the Committee.

The chairman asked if there was anyone in Ottawa to speak for Bremner or present his case. Lister replied, "Not precisely. That is, there is the lawyer Mr. Henderson, who can speak in part, but he is not familiar with the background or the country; and there is Ronald Macdonald, now employed in Ottawa, who actually handled the furs and is acquainted with all the circumstances."

"Has he Bremner's confidence?"

"Yes. I believe he has a power-of-attorney for Bremner."

"Then will the clerk notify these three gentlemen to appear at our next meeting. And when should that be?"

After a little discussion, Lister agreed that he could draw up a statement over the week-end and distribute it by Tuesday. The Committee decided therefore to meet on Wednesday morning, five days hence. The stage was set.

But Wednesday March 19 proved to be only the prologue. When, at 10 o'clock, the clerk went to summon General Middleton and Hayter Reed, they came—not two but four, having brought their lawyers with them. After the statement of charges was read, including the text of Reed's letter already entered in *Hansard*, General Middleton's lawyer, J.J. Gormully, spoke: "We simply say the charge is not correct."

Taken aback, Lister asked, "Will the General make any explanation?"

Kirkpatrick, the other non-voter, interposed in the curious now-he's-here, now-he's-not convention, "He wants to hear some evidence taken on the letter; then he will make a statement." But Lister was not going to allow Middleton to manipulate the proceedings to his advantage: "It is the mere investigation, and if General Middleton has any explanation to give, I think in all fairness to the Committee, he should now give it on the charge made. If he says there is no truth in that charge, that is quite sufficient."

The General's lawyer grew more affable and more evasive. "Of course, the charge as made there we do not admit," but it was all a long time ago, the General had no clear recollection of it, there seem to have been some furs belonging to a man called Bremner, "I believe some one did come in and say to the General that they were taking furs . . . and if they were put in the barracks, there is no doubt they were put there by his order."

The chairman, wishing to see light through the vagueness, "That is the statement he makes through his counsel?"

Casgrain didn't like the drift of things either. "I think we ought to ask Mr. Gormully—what is your answer to the charge?"

Gormully waxed and waned in his reply. The General "had never seen the furs to this day," he had some recollection of being asked at Fort Pitt what was to be done with the furs in the police barracks "that were taken from this man Bremner, who was a rebel as they considered, and believing he had the power, he ordered them to be confiscated. Of course, he may have done wrong in that, or he may not. He does not recollect anything distinctly after that."

Casgrain was determined about two things. The General was going to make a declaration, and he was not going to be allowed to get away with the shifting account of his lawyer: "The point is, General, this declaration has to be made in your presence. Do you admit the truth of it?"

General Middleton materialized. "Yes; it is substantially correct—I think it is substantially the facts of the case; but of course, they are roughly put there. I do not know that I can make any alteration of it."

Gormully's statement was read over to the General, he acknowledged its correctness, he was sworn, and he signed it. So far, with some difficulty, the Committee had established that the furs had been taken and on authorization from Middleton.

Hayter Reed had been sitting silently through this deposition, not too happy with some of it. Now it was his turn. But he too was only a shadow. When Lister asked, "Does Mr. Reed desire to make any statement to this Committee?" Reed's lawyer, A. Ferguson, spoke, "I appear on behalf of Mr. Reed."

Ferguson, like his client, was less self-assured than the preceding pair had been: "While at Fort Pitt, I think, in temporary charge of the transportation, the General being out, I think, in pursuit of Big Bear, he took a flying trip to Battleford."

Reed saw the furs there, supposedly belonging to rebels, and reported that to the General at Fort Pitt: "The General said the furs should be confiscated, and that some portion of them might be put up for the General and his staff," and he wrote a letter under those orders to the Quartermaster of the Mounted Police in charge of the stores. "Mr. Reed was not present when any action was taken upon the letter."

Then came an attempt, as Inspector Morris had foreseen, to imply at least carelessness on the part of the police. On the other hand, Reed, himself, had never received any of the furs. "I do not wish to appear to be afraid to make a statement. I have nothing to keep from the Committee."

Ferguson's statement was read over to Hayter Reed, he declared it to be correct, he was sworn and he signed it. The two principals in the case were then excused. Their lawyers remained.

Charles Bremner now entered by proxy. Ronald C. Macdonald was ushered into the Committee Room and sworn. He had no lawyer with him; at last the Committee could examine a witness directly. Macdonald was a witness of the utmost value because of his direct involvement with the furs, because of his irreproachable standing with the police, the army and the citizens of Battleford, and because he was a reliable authority about the value and quality of furs. His was therefore important testimony not only to the events concerning the furs, but also to the justice and honesty of Charles Bremner's claim.

Lister began the examination, establishing that Macdonald lived in Battleford, that he had been quarter-master in the Home Guard during the rebellion, assisting with the rationing of food to civilians, that he knew Charles Bremner, that he had known Hayter Reed, though not intimately, for about five years before the rebellion, that he had gone over to Bremner's camp after Poundmaker's surrender, and had seen the furs, which he valued at from $5,000 to $7,000. He had also seen General Middleton and Colonel Otter at Bremner's camp in conversation with Bremner's clerk, Louis Caplette. He said that the furs had been brought in to the store room where he was, that he had laid them out, and that they had remained there intact until July 5.

Lister asked, "What became of them then?"

Macdonald said, "The day previous to this, a courier had arrived from Fort Pitt, where General Middleton, Hayter Reed and staff were camped, as far as we knew."

"Did he bring any information from Fort Pitt of any kind?"

"Nothing beyond this letter."

"When that letter was received, what did you do?"

"We complied with the request—or command, as it might be taken—of the letter to put up bundles of furs for the parties mentioned in the letter."

Macdonald had put up the requested bundles, three for Middleton, one for Reed and one for Bedson. He was not at the barracks when the boat arrived early the next morning from Pitt. "In connection with myself, to make my story intelligible, I may say that Warden was quarter-master for the North-West Mounted Police, and there was a storeman, Dorion, and I myself was in the capacity of quarter-master of the Home Guards. These furs were put up partly by myself, but chiefly by the storeman. He was there for that kind of work. The day following, I was not in the barracks at certain hours in the morning, but I was told—"

"Never mind what you were told. Tell me what you know."

"I know that when I went back, there were two boxes of furs put up and addressed to the boat for General Middleton."

"You were there in the afternoon and saw the boxes—two boxes?"

"Yes. Filled with furs."

"Additional?"

"Additional."

Kirkpatrick asked, "What proportion of those packed furs would they be of all the furs taken from Bremner?"

"I should say a little over half."

Girouard, "Would they be the best?"

"Yes."

Lister came in again, "What became of the rest of the furs?"

"I never heard. At least part of them, I can tell you, were given out on the orders of the commanding officers."

Gormully, sharply, protecting his client, "Is this hearsay?"

"No. I gave them out myself on orders from the commanding officers to young officers commanding the corps, who wanted one or two or three furs as souvenirs."

Kirkpatrick was quick to defend the military, "Written orders?"

"Yes."

"Where are they?"

"I presume Warden has them."

"You saw them?"

"I saw written orders."

"Who would these be signed by?"

"I think on several occasions, if my memory does not fail me, that they were signed by General Middleton himself. 'Please allow Mr. So-and-so to take so many furs.' These orders were filled by Warden."

"Were these officers commanders of the different corps?"

"Nobody besides General Middleton and Colonel Otter issued orders."

Kirkpatrick seized on this: "You swear that you saw an order signed by Colonel Otter?"

"No; but we received orders day after day to issue these furs to different parties, and as far as my recollection goes, they were signed by General Middleton or Colonel Otter."

"You said that orders came in every day, some signed by General Middleton?"

"No; I did not say anything of the kind." Macdonald was growning weary of Kirkpatrick. "If you will pardon me—if you want to facilitate this matter—I have no desire to keep anything back and I have no desire that you should twist any statement I should make. But if you wish to have those orders, you can easily have them by referring to the quarter-master of the North-West Mounted Police at Battleford, who I have no doubt, will bear out any statement I have made before this Committee."

Lister came to the rescue. "The main point is that orders did come to the men in charge of these furs to deliver furs to officers of certain of the troops, and those officers did take furs out of this pile of furs?"

"Yes."

Girouard wanted to know more about Macdonald himself, and why he was present. Macdonald told him that he had accompanied the January 1890 petition of Battleford Citizens for the re-consideration of claims for rebellion losses, and he had come in particular to represent Bremner and his fur claim.

"You came down here in Bremner's interest for nothing?"

"I expect my expenses will be paid if he gets his claim."

"That is all you expect to have?"

"Yes."

"What is your business in Battleford?"

"Contractor."

"Contractor for what?"

"Contractor for everything."

"Do you contract for the settlement of claims too?"

"No, not that altogether."

On further sceptical questioning from Kirkpatrick, Macdonald said that Bremner had offered him five percent of his claim, and he had refused it. "The man is starving. He offered to accept anything at all rather than not get anything. He said he would take $3,500 [Macdowell's offer] and he would give anybody what they could make over that, and I positively refused to accept it in that form."

Kirkpatrick, "How are you employed in Ottawa?"

"As a sessional clerk in the Buildings."

Lister was exasperated, "He is a perfectly respectable man."

Girouard and Kirkpatrick tried another tactic with a letter written by Macdonald, dated Battleford 1888, at the request of Inspector Morris. Casgrain had had enough of this. "I rise to a question of order. The witness is here, and as long as he gives his evidence he must be protected."

Kirkpatrick yielded to a degree. "This is the extract of the letter: 'Next day, Monday, Mr. Reed called at the store and asked Warden for the order authorising the packing of the furs. Warden professed not knowing where it was, keeping it, I suppose, for his own protection, as there was no other order either for receiving, storing or disposing of them, and it was generally understood that General Middleton had confiscated the furs.'"

Lister protested, "I put that letter in. He cannot read an extract and keep back the letter."

The chairman agreed, and Lister read out the letter, with the concluding sentence, "The General was not satisfied with the quality of the furs prepared for him and had the packages supplemented by a large saddle box fulled with choice furs, which with the packages were sent to the boat. There were a few remnants of furs left, but I am under the impression that they were given out on the order of the General. Next day, Monday, Mr. Reed called at the storeroom. . . . It was generally understood that General Middleton had confiscated the furs."

Middleton's lawyer took up the questioning. "You say about one-half of the furs were taken away?"

"Yes, I should judge that."

"What is the quantity of furs you saw in the camp first?"

"I can only judge."

"Did you count them?"

"No."

"Did you examine them one by one?"

"No."

"You cannot tell exactly their value?"

"No."

This was too important a point to let pass. Lieutenant Col. Tisdale came in. "How do you fix your value? You say you saw them packed in bales?"

"Yes."

"How do you account for their value?"

"After they were brought into the barracks, they were brought to me, and I placed them in rows. I should judge 50 to 100 beaver skins were packed together."

"What did beaver bring there by traders at that time?"

"Seven to eight dollars."

"They would pay that for them in bulk in Battleford."

"Yes. Seven to eight dollars."

Kirkpatrick picked up where Gormully had left off. "Were there any furs taken by persons before the General came down?"

"No."

"There were a great many people in and out of the stores?"

"Yes."

"You do not know whether any persons helped themselves?"

The Scot was firm. "I know they could not. The inner office was at one end and there were large doors that were not opened except when Warden, Dorion, or myself were in there."

"If Mr. Warden says he cannot be responsible for them and says some were taken, you do not agree with him?"

"I was not there all the time. I was in and out. I differ in my judgement from that."

Ronald Macdonald was excused.

Bremner's furs had been taken from the barracks. That was clear. And they had been taken under authorisation from General Middleton. That too was clear. But Middleton's recollection was hazy, Hayter Reed was evasive, and there had been activities in fur-packing in the barracks when Macdonald was not present. There was much vagueness—the quantity of the furs, the value of the furs, the furs taken at other times by other officers—and the military members of the Committee in particular wanted further evidence that might fill the gaps. After some discussion, the Committee agreed to summon to Ottawa to appear before them Charles Bremner, Louis Caplett, Stephens Warden, Arthur Dorion, Colonel William Morris, Major Sam Steele, and Father Pierre Boissonault.

Having given the clerk the order to transmit, the Select Committee adjourned soberly on this day of March 19, to the call of the Chair.

There was a great flurry in the Bremner and Caplette households when J.J. Skelton, the unofficial spokesman for the claimants, rode out to Bresaylor with the summoning telegram. None of them had ever been on such long journey nor to such a high place. The women washed, starched and ironed shirts, brought out the best suits, aired and brushed them, polished the best boots, and brought out the large grips to pack them all in. Then there was the planning of provisions, for there would not likely be many places to get food. It was something like providing for a winter's trapping. Charles Bremner was elated too. After all, it was less than two weeks since the Committee had been constituted. The summons suggested at least speedy action. As word got round, the large yard outside was filled once more with buggies and wagons, with people who were curious and those who wished him well. Bresaylor was in the national news. But the excitement and the anticipation faded when, on March 24, Skelton rode out again, carrying a cancelling telegram. The Committee had "for the present cancelled the order requiring the attendance of these persons, so as to save expenses."

In Ottawa, the call went out to Committee members to meet on April 1. The three main participants in the hearing so far—Middleton, Reed, and Macdonald—arrived at the Committee Room, this time all three with lawyers, a Stewart Henderson of Ottawa appearing as solicitor for Charles Bremner and hence as a buttress for Ronald Macdonald.

His replies to queries after he had been sworn, however, suggested that he would be of dubious value to Macdonald. No doubt since he had never met Bremner, his uneasy position of defender at second-hand accounted for some of the great wariness with which he answered Kirkpatrick's questions, but he began to sound like the comic relief of the proceedings.

"Have you, Mr. Henderson, in your possession, any document signed by Mr. Bremner relating to these furs?"

"I think I have; I have not looked at the papers. There are a number of papers in my office in connection with the North-West."

"Is there a power of attorney?"

"I think there is a power of attorney, from Bremner to Mr. Macdonald."

"Is there an agreement as to the amount he will take?"

"No.—At least, I am not sure. I have several papers from different parties in connection with this. I think I have some of them in my office."

"Will you produce any agreement, power of attorney, or papers?"

"I will produce any paper that does not reflect upon the interest of my client."

"This is not the interest of your client?"

"Yes. Mr. Bremner is my client, and I have papers at the office. I refuse distinctly to disclose, or I reserve that right distinctly. I might not show the papers, after I bring them."

Col. Tisdale intervened, "If you bring them to the Committee, the Committee will settle the question then. You bring the papers, and we will decide afterwards."

The chairman, McNeill, had a thought, "Is there anything to prevent your getting the papers now?"

"I won't present any papers without consulting my client. I am a solicitor, you know."

General Middleton was becoming restive at the legal chit-chat, and he asked to speak. Thereupon Henderson and Macdonald, Bremner's men, became auditors for the rest of the morning.

Middleton opened his testimony as the candid confession of a bluff old soldier who was yet the man of authority who had graciously consented to appear. Indeed, his first words implied, to the surprise of the Select Committee, that the Committee had been created at his request and for the purpose of giving him a public platform from which he could, with propriety, explain his actions. This time, Middleton's statement was prepared, and he read it, but his memory seemed not to have improved since the first statement, which he had signed.

"Gentlemen,—My object in asking the Government to grant this inquiry was that, in justice to myself and others, the real facts of the case will be made public officially, and with that object, with your permission, I beg to make the following statement:—I must premise by pointing out that owing to the lapse of time, nearly five years since the occurrence took place, I have experienced considerable difficulty in recalling all the circumstances connected with an affair which I confess, to me then, was considered of little importance; still, I think the following embraces the principal and most important points."

On May 26th, 1885, after Poundmaker's surrender, Middleton was told that people were carrying off furs belonging to Half-breeds from Poundmaker's camp, and he believed that he had had the furs sent to the barracks. "I may remark that, to the best of my belief, I never went near the half-breed camp, nor did I see nor speak to Bremner nor his clerk, though it is possible I may have done so."

At Fort Pitt he had been told that these Half-breeds were rebels—"a rifle belonging to one of the men killed at Cut Knife or Eagle Hills had been found in the possession of this very Bremner"—and he had ordered the whole of the Half-breeds to be sent to Regina. Reed had told him about the furs, he had ordered them to be confiscated, and authorised some for his staff and some for himself.

On July 5th he arrived in Battleford and attended a funeral but "I did not go to the Police stores at all, nor did I see nor select furs whilst at Battleford; and any statements that have been made to that effect are wholly untrue." He added that Ronald Macdonald's statement that numerous orders for furs for young officers had been signed "some by myself and some by Lieut. Col. Otter is, I believe, quite untrue." Otter had authorised him to say as much. "To the best of my belief, I have never at any time received any of the Bremner furs." If they had been put on board the steamer at Battleford, it was without his knowledge.

The General had finished, and Lister began the questioning, first establishing the presence and function of both Reed and Bedson on his staff, from Battleford to Pitt and back.

"You knew that Bremner was at the fort?"

"When I returned?"

"At the time the furs were stored."

"I knew he was there."

"What was the report made to you as to the furs?"

"Simply that these men had a lot of furs and they were being taken away."

"You ordered, what, to be done?"

"As far as I can remember, I suppose I must have ordered them to be taken to the Police barracks."

"Did you or did you not?"

"I do not remember, but I have not the slightest doubt, I ordered them to be taken into charge."

"Were these half-breeds arrested and taken to Regina?"

"I know as to that only by hearsay. I never saw them again."

"You ordered their arrest?"

"I believe I did. I must have done it, because I was the only person, I fancy, who could have done it."

"Do you know of your own knowledge that they were kept in prison in Regina?"

"I do not know anything about that."

Lister then moved on to establish responsibility for the confiscation order that had resulted from a conversation with Reed at Pitt. "What was the conversation?"

"Simply that after having talked about those men being rebels, he reminded me that the furs were there. They were, he said, in bales in the Police Barracks. He had been to Battleford, I think."

"And these men having been said to be rebels, you decided that they were rebels?"

"Yes."

"There was no proof about it?"

"No."

"Was the letter that was written by Reed written in your presence? It was in a tent, was it not?"

"I do not know. I was in a tent."

"Did you know that Reed had sent the letter off by a courier?"

"Well, I cannot certainly remember. In the first place, there was no other means of sending letters that were sent."

"Now if Reed did write a letter directing the man in charge, Warden, to put up these furs—two for General Middleton, one for Bedson and one for himself—you will not say that these were not instructions given by you?"

"No, I will not say that he was not justified in giving those instructions."

"I suppose you are satisfied now that you had no power to confiscate the furs?"

"Well, I suppose, virtually, really and legally, I had not."

"When did you acquire a knowledge of that?"

"Only recently. I do not think I ever considered the point at all."

"You give the Committee to understand that at the time you gave these directions, you believed you had the right to confiscate the furs—that is, to appropriate them to your own use?"

"Yes. I thought I was the ruling power up there, owing to the state of the country, owing to the state of war, that I could do pretty much as I liked, as long as it was within reason. I did not think it was unreasonable to allow a few of those furs to be taken, and the bulk left behind."

"Was the bulk left behind?"

"That I do not know."

"Did you authorise anybody to give a receipt for them?"

"I do not know. I think that when I told them they could take the furs—I rather think I said they would have to give a receipt."

"Did you, prior to leaving on the boat that day from Battleford, ever give any order for furs to any of the officers?"

"No."

"Did you ever authorise anybody to give orders?"

"No, to the best of my belief. I never did."

At this point, Casgrain wanted to be clear: "Did you know, as a matter of fact, whether any of your officers had any of these furs?"

"No, it was never told to me or brought to my notice."

Lister resumed, "Where were these furs to go, General?"

"I do not know. I never gave any orders for them to be taken anywhere. I supposed they would be put on board the steamer."

"Did you ever make any inquiries about these furs?"

"No, I did not."

"Never inquired of the captain of the boat, coming across the lake?"

"I never even saw them. My luggage was looked after by my aides-de-camp."

"You have no personal knowledge as to whether they were put on the boat or not?"

"None whatever."

"Did you sell any?"

"I had some sent to Devlin, here in Ottawa; I do not know what he did with them."

Casgrain was curious again. "What quantity of furs did you deliver to Mr. Devlin?"

"I do not know. I bought a lot of furs when I was up there, and had a great number given to me. There were some that I did not want to use—they were of no use—and the money I got from these was to pay for the dressing of the others."

"Were there any of the Bremner furs?"

"None whatever."

Lister was interested in the sudden acuteness of the General's memory, "Why are you so sure, General?"

"Because I know the exact number of the furs I bought, and I also know that the furs I got were most of them very bad and worth very little."

"You had 400 to 500 skunks?"

"Yes."

"350 to 400 minks?"

"I do not know exactly."

"500 to 600 muskrats?"

"I happen to know that I had forty-three and a half beaver."

Lister now ventured on another issue. "You said that the only furs you brought down were such as you had bought or which were given to you?"

"Yes."

"Do you state that you did not get a quantity of furs from Prince Albert?—the Batoche furs?"

"Part of the furs given to me were those taken at Batoche."

Col. Tisdale intervened, for this was not within the Committee's terms of reference. "If he asks the General about any other furs, in justice to himself the General ought to be allowed to make a full statement."

This was what Lister had hoped for. "I wish to ask the General about the Batoche furs. If the Committee say they do not desire it, why, that is an end to the matter. If General Middleton wants to make a statement regarding the Batoche furs, I am quite content he should do so."

Middleton said, "I would like very much to make a statement, merely with a view that this fact has been made public."

And so another box of furs entered the account. Behind Lister's question lay Father André's accusation of looting at Batoche. The General spoke at length. He readily admitted that after Batoche was taken there was looting, of furs and other things. He defended it on the grounds that, if the troops had not done the looting, camp-followers would have, and they would have destroyed everything. He insisted that the property of loyal people was not harmed, nor was that of women and children. "I would like to take this opportunity of saying that I am perfectly certain in a general way that the conduct of the force during the campaign was most creditable. They did nothing that would not have been done by the highest trained troops in the world, and they behaved in that way."

As for the Batoche box of furs, it had been on the steamer from Batoche to Prince Albert which was carrying some wounded men, and then it was sent by team to Qu'Appelle and thence to Ottawa. "That box held the furs that you have listed there on that paper."

Weldon became interested in the steamers and their cargoes: "Was that the same steamer that you afterwards went down from Battleford in?"

"The steamer I went in afterwards was the *Marquis*, I think."

Weldon persisted, "What steamer was it you came in from Fort Pitt to Battleford?"

"I think it was the *Marquis*."

The Maritimer was not satisfied. There were too many steamers, too many chances of a slip-up. The steamer from Pitt to Battleford and on to Prince Albert certainly carried the Bremner furs. But what happened at Prince Albert? Was it the same steamer that went from Prince Albert to Lake Winnipeg? When the chageover took place at Grand Rapids, were the furs put on the lake steamer? The General did not know. He didn't see any of his luggage till he got to Ottawa.

Kirkpatrick was interested in the venue of the General's furs: "Did you get any furs when you went to the Rocky Mountains?"

"Yes, I bought a lot of furs at the Stoney Reserve."

"Did you see Mr. McLean at Fort Pitt?"

"I got some from him."

"You say McLean and other people gave you a lot of furs?"

"I had innumerable furs given me."

"These were the furs that you sent to Devlin?"

"These were the furs, and the ones that I got which were sent to me from Batoche."

It began to seem as though the Commander-in-Chief of the Canadian Armed Forces was in a fair way to outdo the Hudson's Bay Company as a fur trader.

The Law Dean, Weldon, reflected that the Committee had been formed to enquire about the furs of Charles Bremner, a subject that had almost been lost sight of. He asked, "You never saw Bremner at all?"

"To the best of my belief, I never did."

"Do you recall seeing his clerk, Caplette?"

"I have no recollection whatsoever; he certainly never came to me, to complain about anything."

Lister took this up. "Did you see him in Winnipeg about his furs?"

"Bremner? I never saw the man in my life that I remember."

"He says he went to Sir Adolphe Caron, you, and somebody else about the furs, in Winnipeg."

"I am perfectly certain that had he come to see me, I should have remembered. . . . If Bremner had come to see me and spoken to me about the furs, I am perfectly certain I should have remembered it. Moreover, if he had come to me and appealed to me, I certainly should have listened to him."

Lister, "He says he did, General."

"I never saw him at all, to the best of my belief."

Fortunately for Charles Bremner, a lawyer had accompanied him at the meeting in Winnipeg.

The Committee now turned its attention from the General and his fitful memory to Hayter Reed who, like Middleton, had a prepared statement. It included the now familiar account of the General's confiscation order, Reed's letter about the furs, and his going to Battleford with the General on the steamer. It soon developed that Reed, too, had a leaky memory. Lister asked, "Did you know who the furs in Battleford belonged to?"

"I believed they all belonged to rebels."

"To what rebels?"

"To the rebels."

"Did you not hear they belonged to Bremner?"

"I did."

"Then it was to a rebel, not rebels. You heard they were Bremner's furs. That is what they were called at the fort?"

"Yes."

Casgrain queried, "Did you know Bremner at the time?"

But Hayter Reed, like an echo of the General, said, "I do not believe I ever saw Bremner before that time."

However, Reed had interesting news about the packages of furs put up for himself and for Bedson. Bedson had never received his. They had been stolen "on the way down, in the steamer." That was why he had never sent a receipt for them. Weldon's concern about the boats and their cargoes had been pertinent. Reed's package had been taken by police to Regina for him, and he did not see it for some months because he was away visiting reserves. But after he had been back in Regina for a couple of months, he returned the parcel, again through the police, to Battleford.

Lister asked, "Why did you not keep it altogether?"

The reason was more interesting still: "Because of a question of propriety. It was a question as to the confiscation, and I sent it back."

With some amazement, Lister asked, "You questioned the propriety of the confiscation?"

"The question was asked about the propriety of that confiscation."

"Who asked the question?"

"I heard it spoken of."

"They were sent to Regina for you, and, after two months, the question of propriety arose, the legality of the confiscation, and you returned them to Battleford?"

"Yes."

It would appear that the question of propriety had arisen some time after Bremner, released from the Regina prison, had made his visit to Winnipeg, which was so well publicised by the *Free Press*.

But much the most intriguing part of Reed's testimony concerned the career of his letter that he had written in the tent at Fort Pitt.

Lister asked, "Did you ever see Warden about the letter afterwards?"

"Yes."

"What for?"

"Because it had some private correspondence in it."

"Your letter is, that by General Middleton's order he was to put up so many packages of furs. . . . Was there anything more in the letter?"

"I think I told Warden not to make this public."

"That was in the letter?"

"Yes."

"Was that done at the General's request?"

"It was."

"What excuse did Warden give for not giving up the letter?"

Reed had another surprise. "He did give it to me."

"Where is the letter?"

"It is torn up."

"When was it torn up?"

"At that time. I want to say this—it was only the private part, and I gave the formal order back to Warden."

"Here is a copy of the letter upon which we based the charge. The letter reads thus:

> Dear Warden,—General Middleton has instructed me and authorised me to send you the present letter, desiring that you put up bales of fur for the undermentioned: two bales for General Middleton, one for S.L. Bedson, and one for myself. Please

select the best and pack them, as we will be down there tomorrow by boat.

Hayter Reed
Assistant Commissioner of Indians.

Do you undertake to swear, Mr. Reed, that that is not the letter?"

"It is substantially correct, but I put in the word 'confiscate'."

"Will you swear that in writing the letter you put in the word 'confiscate'? Be careful about your answer."

"It is my firm belief I put in that word."

Girouard was concerned. "And in the re-written one too?"

"Yes."

Lister held out a letter: "Look at that letter and say whether it is substantially a copy of the substituted letter."

"I would not express myself that way—'General Middleton has instructed and authorised me to send you the present letter.'"

"How would you express yourself?"

"I think it would be this way: 'General Middleton has decided to confiscate the Bremner furs, and desired that these packages be made up.'"

"And not make it public?"

"Yes."

The shifting letter was becoming remarkably interesting. If it ordered confiscation, then the property confiscated belonged to the Crown, not to individual soldiers. But if the copy in the Committee's possession was not the copy that Reed had given Warden, who had written the bogus substitute? Why had Reed—possibly the General—wanted the transaction kept secret? And what authority had been issued that permitted any officer who asked for furs to be given them?

The chairman sought clarification. "Do I understand you to say you commenced the letter with the statement that General Middleton had confiscated the furs?"

Reed was precise, "'Had decided to confiscate'."

Lister wanted further confirmation. "That letter was written by order of General Middleton?"

"Yes."

Girouard was puzzled. "Where is the second letter? Is that in the hands of Mr. Warden?"

"I do not know."

"Where did you see it later?"

"In the hands of the police."

Reed had not exhausted his surprises. He had seen the letter in Ottawa within the past two months at the North-West Mounted Police Department when he went there to ask questions about the present case. Weldon, too, had a surprise to offer. He produced the letter.

"This is the letter you wrote at Battleford, and which you saw in the Department?"

"Yes."

"You recognise it as your handwriting?"

"Yes." This turn of events, with its odd implications, brought a general stirring at the table. Wood, the other Maritimer, spoke, "I understand you, Mr. Reed, to say that the General knew the contents of the first letter written?"

"Yes."

"Did he give instructions that it should be kept private and that that should be inserted?"

"Yes."

"Did he know that you wrote the second letter?"

"No; he did not."

"That was issued without his authority?"

"Yes."

General Middleton had been growing more and more wary during Reed's testimony, and presently he entered the discussion: "I would like to say that I perfectly agree with all that Mr. Reed has said with the exception of that part where he intimated that I directed him to say it should be kept quiet. I certainly never directed him to put that in the letter, to the best of my belief, neither did I think it necessary. At any rate, there was no secret made at the time about these furs, and I certainly do not remember ever having suggested to keep things quiet. I did not hear nor see what he had written. I, merely having given the order, trusted the carrying of it out to him, and I never saw or heard what he had written. Had I seen the thing, I certainly would not have let it go."

Col. Tisdale wanted this point to be clear. "In other words, you gave him no authority to keep it secret?"

"Not to the best of my recollection."

Hayter Reed came in for further questioning. The letter or letters and his motives had acquired a very strange air. Kirkpatrick challenged him: "Identify that letter and say whether it is the letter referred to as the second letter."

"This is it."

"Read it."

"It reads as follows:

> Fort Pitt, July 1st, 1885. To the officer in charge of the property taken from Rebel: The General having decided to confiscate the furs now in your care and taken from the Rebel, desires that you should make up a select bundle of beaver and fisher for him and a selection also for those of his staff. Have them properly packed and addressed, and keep a memorandum of what is packed.
>
>   (Signed) Hayter Reed"

Girouard, "When did you write this?"

"After I went to Battleford the second time. Within a day or two after the General left on the steamer."

"Who told you to change this letter for the other one?"

"No one."

"You did that of your own motion?"

"Yes."

Lister, too, challenged him: "This is not the shape of the letter at all. Will you swear this is a copy of the letter you wrote at Fort Pitt in all respects, excepting that it is not to be kept quiet?"

"And those names."

"Did your letter from Fort Pitt commence 'Dear Warden'?"

"I think it did."

Lister, with some exasperation, "You do not pretend to say that this is a copy of your first letter?"

"No, that is not."

"In your original letter there were to be two bales put up for General Middleton?"

"Yes. It says so here."

"It does not." Lister was not going to allow further vagueness about this very slippery letter. "It says, 'Put up a select bundle of beaver and fisher.'"

"Then it means two."

The chairman, McNeill, intervened. "Do you recollect that that is not a correct copy of what you said, with regard to the letter in *Hansard*?"

"I believe that it is not a verbatim copy."

So somewhere there was yet another letter, a third letter, the original one that had started the whole train of events moving.

Weldon came back to the boats and their cargoes. "When you

applied for the receipt to Mr. Bedson, he told you that he had been plundered on the boat?"

"Yes."

If Bedson's furs had been stolen, the General's could have been stolen too. At any rate, there was no proof that they had not.

That ended the hearing for the day. The witnesses were dismissed and the Committee sat behind closed doors to contemplate the hodgepodge that the morning had brought to light—the General's flickering memory, mysteriously disappearing furs, shape-shifting letters, crisscrossing boxes and bundles, looted looters, steamship puzzles, and sparring between the General and his aide. What had all this to do with the matter they had started out to probe? After a time, they adjourned again to the call of the chair.

As for Charles Bremner, his men, Macdonald and Henderson, alert but silent auditors, would have a great deal to tell him. They had learned much about the kind of men that Middleton and Reed were, and something of the actions and attitudes of the military, but the concerns that had brought them to that place—Bremner's loss, his need, his claims— they were swept up in the dust storm.

The next meeting of the Committee was on Friday, April 18. Only three witnesses were called: Macdonald, Henderson, and A.M. Burgess, Deputy Minister of the Interior, who had visited Batttleford the previous September. He was ordered specifically to bring all papers relating to the inquiry filed with the Rebellion Claims Commission. The lawyers for Middleton and Reed were present. Macdonald was not.

Henderson, called first, was still canny and coy, and after an unenlightening exchange with him, in which Bremner's interests seemed to be as nebulous as ever, the chairman turned with some relief to Burgess. He had papers containing evidence under oath "taken before, and the report made by, the Commission appointed to inquire into the North-West rebellion losses." Girouard suggested that Bremner's evidence before the Claims Commission should be taken down for the Committee's record, and Robidoux, clerk of the Committee, read the documents aloud for that purpose. They consisted of Charles Bremner's statement of the events leading up to Cut Knife, the battle, his claim for stolen furs, and Father Cochin's testimony on behalf of the Bresaylor group.

There was still the mystery of the disappearing furs. Girouard moved, seconded by Casgrain: "That inasmuch as the Committee have no evidence of what became of the case of furs addressed to Colonel

Bedson, Colonel Bedson be summoned to appear and give evidence before this Committee." The motion was lost by two to three, the argument of the trio being that the Committee was ordered to inquire into Charles Bremner's loss, not to chase down the subsequent adventures of the furs.

The Committee did agree, however, that they wanted a further meeting with Bremner's representatives and Burgess about the claims that had been before the Royal Commission. They assembled for the last time on Wednesday, April 23, at 11 a.m. Burgess produced "a copy of the original list furnished by the Royal Commission to the Department" in which the total amount claimed for furs was $5,364.50. The Department also had the earlier list that Bremner had sent to White after his trip to Winnipeg. The sum there was $4,374.66.

It was clear that the essential information had lain with the government, contrary to what the Minister of Justice had said a couple of years before, since at least the beginning of 1886. The Committee's work was drawing to a close.

Lister, being asked, said, "I have no further evidence to offer. We accept the evidence given before the Royal Commission as evidence given before this Committee."

Gormully and Ferguson also said they had no more evidence on behalf of their clients.

At this point, Lister announced, "I, for Bremner, state to the Committee that Bremner will accept $4,500 in full of his claim for furs."

The inquiry was over. All that remained for the Committee to do was draw up its report and submit it to the House.

Macdonald immediately wired Skelton in Battleford with the good news for Bremner, and there was great joy in Bresaylor that night. The Valley papers reported, "The Bremner Furs Committee report is to the effect that charges against General Middleton have been proven. The confiscation of furs was illegal and improper, and Bremner is to be paid $4,500 with accrued interest."

Fittingly enough, all signs were fair. The spring was early, ice break-up was shorter than usual, poplar and willow buds were plumping out, and Bremner and his neighbors were seeding by April 2. Laurie published a special edition of eight pages, giving information about the Battleford section of the Saskatchewan country. Saskatoon reported that regular freight and construction trains were running daily between Regina and a point some 30 miles south of Saskatoon. Men were needed for construction work. The long, dangerous hauls from Swift Current were over.

Charles Bremner and his companions in captivity were encouraged that Father Cochin's testimony in their favor had been resurrected and read into the Committee's record. But they were still 'rebels' in the eye of the government.

Chapter Fourteen

The Highest Tribunal

The Committee had been authorised on March 10 and it reported, with exemplary dispatch, on May 12, the anniversary of the fall of Batoche five years before.[1] On this day, the affairs of Charles Bremner came before the highest tribunal in the land, and had the distinction of becoming henceforth an item in *Hansard*: "The Bremner Furs."

Alexander McNeill, chairman of the Committee, rose in his place to move adoption of the unanimous report. After reviewing events and circumstances leading up to the confiscation of the furs and the order to put up bundles for Middleton, Bedson, and Reed, the report concluded:

> 8. Your Committee consider the confiscation of the furs unwarrantable and illegal, and in his evidence General Middleton admits that he has recently become satisfied it was not legally justifiable. Your Committee further are of the opinion that, if the confiscation had been legal, the confiscated property vested in the Crown; and while your Committee believe that General Middleton acted under an unfortunate misconception as to his powers, they are of the opinion that the appropriation of any portion of the property, under such circumstances, by General Middleton to his own use, and to that of the members of his staff, was highly improper.
>
> 9. On behalf of Bremner it was stated to your Committee that he is willing to accept $4,500 inclusive of interest in compensation for his loss, and this your Committee consider a fair compensation.
>
> 10. For the information of the House your Committee submit herewith the minutes of the evidence taken by them in this enquiry, also the minutes of the proceedings of the Committee, which, with this Report, they recommend to be printed.
>
> All which is respectfully submitted,
>
> A. McNeill
Chairman

It was the Hon. Edward Blake, former leader of the Liberal party,

Chancellor of the University of Toronto, famous for his oratory and for his championing of minorities, who rose from his place beside Wilfrid Laurier to begin the debate. He said what Charles Bremner had said five years before, "There has been a grievous wrong done to a Canadian subject." He insisted that payment should be made "by those who have done the wrong and not by the Canadian people . . . and I believe that we ought not to indemnify, either in reputation or in purse, the man who did the wrong. . . . He has honors and rewards enough, and he should now pay for his misconduct, and should receive the censure which is his due."

Middleton had no excuse for his action, Blake continued, for the government had specifically and commendably declared that there would be no martial law in that country, but that the Queen's subjects, rebel or no, would be dealt with by the Queen's civil and criminal courts, and by them alone. "There was not the shadow of a claim to confiscate, and if there was even a shadow of a claim for confiscation . . . there was not the shade of the shadow of a claim to appropriate on the part of the confiscator, and that appropriation and that confiscation are each of them unlawful and criminal acts, the appropriation being only more improper than the confiscation."

Blake then began a survey of the articles of war in British military practice from the Monmouth rebellion of the 1680's through the Duke of Wellington's Despatches and General Orders, down to the general articles of war drawn up in 1872, about a dozen years before the North-West rebellion. Under that doctrine and practice, "a British subject can be deprived of his property only by judicial or legislative action"; a man could be convicted of treason and executed as a rebel "and yet his property is not alienated but it goes to his children."

Middleton had said, "'I thought I was the ruling power up there, owing to the state of war, that I could do pretty much as I liked as long as it was in reason.' He knew, however, that he had no power to try Bremner to determine his guilt. He determined, therefore, to send him on for trial, as to his person; but, at the same time, he determined to condemn and appropriate his property . . . and that he did without trial or proof or anything else. . . . I am glad the loss had been ascertained; and I hope the Government will see fit to take steps to see that the General makes good the loss and withdraws from our service."

Blake had spoken for about two hours when he sat down. From the government benches opposite, the Hon. Sir Adolphe Caron, Minister of Militia and Middleton's superior, rose in an attempt to restore some stature to the fallen hero.

He wished to state "in the most frank and open way possible that I consider the action of General Middleton is the result of a most unfortunate error of judgement on his part," which had come from his lack of information at that time, and which he now deeply regretted. There were other extenuating circumstances. The General had been "in the midst of preoccupations" which affected his sense of prudence—he had, after all, rendered services to Canada. Beyond that, after he had given the order to confiscate, he neither saw nor knew anything more of the furs. The tactic of Caron and Middleton was now revealed:

"I admit that this is an unfortunate matter, but the General has tried, so far as he is concerned, to make up for that want of judgement, or that error of judgement on his part, and has expressed his willingness to indemnify whoever is entitled to be indemnified. But, before this question is settled, I have no doubt that it will be admitted that it is important for the General to investigate the matter more fully in order to know the value of the furs which are known to have been removed by his order, and to ascertain whether those furs belonged to Mr. Bremner or not. . . . I repeat, from what the General has told me, that he is prepared, after a proper valuation of the furs is arrived at, to indemnify the persons who may be shown to be entitled to that portion of them which he is supposed to have removed, or which is supposed to have been removed on his order."

The Minister and Middleton were not conceding that the Committee had conducted a satisfactory investigation, and they were not agreeing to the recommendations in the report. Both of the Minister's proposals—leniency from the House for Middleton, and acceptance of Middleton's offer of conditional indemnification to persons unnamed of a limited and uncertain sum—outraged James Lister after his long and hard struggle on Bremner's behalf. This was the height of arrogance. From the Liberal benches he rose:

"My hon. friend tells us that General Middleton is now willing to settle. How is it that he has waited for five long years before saying he is willing to settle for any portion of the furs which were taken there? For five long years, General Middleton has denied over and over again that he ever took any furs, that he ever authorised the taking of any furs, or that he knew anything of their disposition. And it is only now, when the matter has been investigated, that he knows something about the matter of which he has denied all knowledge for five years past. . . .

"As for the report itself, it is the unanimous finding of the Committee; but I desire to say that, in that report, for the purpose of having it unanimous, General Middleton has been treated with the utmost consideration. The report is mildness and gentleness itself, and I have no hesitation in saying that the report might have been much more severe than it is. . . .

"It is absurd for the Minister of Militia to get up here and say that a gentleman who has served in the British army for over 40 years can be so ignorant of the regulations of that army as to pretend for one moment, that he did not know he was violating the army regulations when he appropriated any portion of the property. . . . General Middleton now admits, and he has only recently acquired the knowledge, that he had no right to confiscate, much less to appropriate, the property of this man Bremner. For five years Bremner has been pressing for the payment of this claim, for five years he has been asking the country, or some person, to pay for the property of which he was despoiled. His property was taken and he was sent to prison and kept there for two months; he was discharged without a trial, and he is now broken in health and living in poverty, and the Minister of Militia asks this House and the country to excuse General Middleton upon that ground."

Lister then went on to the letter that had contained the words "not to be made public," and said that the information had been forced out of Reed in cross-examination: "this fact, sworn to by Mr. Reed, an unwilling witness, one desirous of protecting himself as well as General Middleton, must be accepted as a fact; and if we so accept it, then General Middleton knew as well as Mr. Reed that what they were doing was an illegal act. . . . This transaction from beginning to end is a discreditable one in the extreme. . . . So far as General Middleton is concerned, his usefulness to this country is gone."

The Chairman of the Committee, Alexander McNeill, rose to remonstrate with Lister as to the terms of the report, which "I conceive to be very severe strictures in regard to his conduct, that his conduct is unwarrantable, illegal and highly improper. But I must say that I do not like to kick a man when he is down."

As for the "not to be made public" matter, there it was, Reed's word against the General's, who insisted that he had never made such a stipulation, and the Committee had felt that they could not decide as between the two. McNeill thought that the General should be given the benefit of the doubt, particularly since he had ordered that "receipts should be taken and a memorandum made of the furs which were so disposed of. . . . I think the action of the General on this occasion was just as we described it, to be highly improper and quite unjustifiable— but I do think we ought to endeavor not to strain too far the case which is brought against him."

In this defense of Middleton as a thief but not a sneak thief, Sir John A. entered. He reproved Lister for his remarks about the report of the Committee, "They were unanimous in their finding, and the report therefore comes before this House as a judgement given without regard to political considerations, by gentlemen sitting on both sides of this House, who were animated with the spirit of doing justice to the wronged party, Mr. Bremner, and the accused, Sir Frederick Middleton. . . .

"With respect to the case itself, I am inclined to think that the want of judgement as to the confiscation has more weight than would ordinarily be given it." In Middleton's experience in China and in India, "there was a good deal of practical confiscation." However, in this case "the General was decidedly in the wrong. My hon. friend from West Durham [Edward Blake] has proved beyond a doubt, that Sir Frederick Middleton's conduct deserves the verdict which has been passed upon it, and passed upon it, I think, in as strong a language as could well be used. It is quite clear that the General acted wrongly and illegally and that the strong language of the Committee was perfectly justified. Still, I would be charitable enough to believe that the confiscation of the goods was an error in judgement; but as to the appropriation of the goods, it seems to me, that was not an error of judgement. That was an illegal and improper act, and it cannot be defended.

"Upon these grounds, I think that the report ought to be unanimously adopted by this House. . . . I think it is very important, in order to give great weight to the judgement of the Committee, that it should be accepted by the House almost without debate."

But Sir John A. was overly sanguine if he thought the debate would end there. Casgrain was concerned lest, once more, the victim of the theft be lost sight of in the verbal jousting. "As a matter of equity, I think Bremner ought to be indemnified at once, without delay, and the General ought to find some means to reimburse him as soon as possible for the furs which he took for himself."

Peter Mitchell, Liberal from New Brunswick and, like Sir John A., one of the Fathers of Confederation, was not willing to let Middleton off so easily, and so, once more, in spite of Casgrain's efforts, Charles Bremner faded into the draperies: "The Right Hon. First Minister as well as the Minister of Militia have endeavored to palliate the conduct of General Middleton. . . . In this matter, I do not think we should make any difference between General Middleton and the meanest private, except in this respect: that if we admit any extenuating circumstances, they would apply rather to an uneducated, ignorant private in the army than to a General who ought to know the Articles of War, and who ought to know what his powers and duties are; who ought to know at any rate, what an honest man should do. . . . The General got those furs; they were put on the steamer by his orders. Whether they arrived in Ottawa and were put into the hands of a furrier here, as alleged, is not for us to inquire. . . . The Right Hon. the First Minister says that he adopts the report. Yes, that is an absolute necessity. But I go further, and I place upon the responsibility of the Government their positive duty to tell this House what action they are going to take. It is their duty to compel the General to refund the money and dismiss him from the command of the military force of Canada—to report him to the Horse Guards; and if the latter do not give him their dismissal, they will not be doing what is incumbent on them as the guardians of the honor and public faith of Canada."

Sir John A. Macdonald rose again to reply to his old colleague and political adversary. "The hon. gentleman wishes to hold the Government responsible for not stating what action will be taken in the matter. The Government could not take any action until the report was passed upon by the House of Commons, and when the House has passed upon it, it will then be the duty of the Government to consider what it is their duty to do."

This was the great loophole—a possibility of continuing inaction even after adoption of the report. Now Laurier rose. "I am quite prepared to believe that General Middleton acted on an error of judgement; but if he is going to do what is suggested by the Minister of Militia, it seems to me he is going to commit another error of judgement. He is answerable for the full measure of the wrong that has been inflicted on Charles Bremner. No other compensation than this will satisfy the end of justice; but I understand the Minister of Militia to state that General Middleton was to hold a sort of enquiry to ascertain what had been packed for him, and when he had found that out, he would tender the money to Bremner. This would be no palliation at all of the offense; it would be no compensation for the great wrong done. The only satisfaction that Bremner can and must have, is that he shall be restored all the furs taken from him, or compensated in money for those which are not returned. I do not intend to press this further, but I hope that full justice will be done; and if it be not, I intend to bring the matter up again in another session."

Others spoke. It didn't matter whether or not General Middleton got the furs; he had ordered them to be put on his steamer and he had appropriated them to himself. If General Middleton did not know the

Articles of War, "it is absurd that he should fill the position he does." The Government knew for the last four years that there was distress "in regard to the stealing of this property . . . and they are to blame for not taking action before this."

Alexander McNeill, who had presented the report, appropriately and briefly ended the debate: "On behalf of the Committee, I do not wish the House to suppose that any member of the Committee supposed that the accidental fact that the furs were not received by General Middleton made any difference at all. We found that the appropriation had been made and we condemned the appropriation."

Put to the question, the House concurred in the report. Sir John A. got his wish; the adoption was unanimous. Everyone felt good about it. Lister and the Liberals felt that they had won a long and hard-fought battle for justice. The Government were satisfied that they had demonstrated their integrity and fairness. Bremner's advisers were jubilant, and Charles Bremner saw the possibility of having $4,500 for a new start. The Edmonton *Bulletin* reported, "The Committee's report on the charge made against Middleton was unanimously adopted by the Commons. Middleton must pay for Bremner's furs or resign, or perhaps both."[2] In Battleford, Laurie reported, somewhat prematurely, in the *Herald*, "The Bremner fur claims have been settled by the payment to Bremner of $4,500." The Minister of Militia and Sir Frederick Middleton were pleased that they had made no commitment to pay anything to anyone. Parliament was prorogued four days later, at 4 p.m., Friday, May 16, 1890.

Middleton was not in Ottawa for the debate nor for the prorogation of Parliament. He had gone out on a routine spring inspection of brigade camps, intending to have his family join him and spend the summer on the Pacific coast. But when Gormully wired him of the result of the debate, with both Sir John A. and Caron concurring in the unanimous adoption of the report, Middleton cancelled his summer plans and started back to the capital. This time there was no luxurious private railway car and no crowds cheering at the station stops.

Middleton resigned in July, the resignation to take effect in October. In August he was interviewed by a Toronto *Globe* reporter: "Sir Fred's feeling is one of resentment and bitterness. He believes he has been badly and shabbily treated by the Government, politicians, and the press. 'They appear to forget that I risked my life for them. I am treated this way all because of politics. I don't mean party, for I have no preference, but it was because I am a British soldier. I was sacrificed to the French vote. That's the long and the short of it. The press of Canada will be sorry for what they have written.'"[3]

He wrote a letter in his own defense, "A Parting Address. General Middleton to the People of Canada," in which he tried to implicate Caron and, of course, the much less innocent Hayter Reed, who was made to look, not just two-faced, but a two-faced scoundrel. There were a few voices that gave him some support, among them Frank Oliver's: "The *Bulletin* does not defend General Middleton against the charge of stealing, but his advisors, Bedson and Reed, appointed by the Canadian Government, were no better." But in Ottawa, "Another officer" delivered a kind of valediction: "A prominent feature of the General's career in Canada was lack of discretion."

On August 19, the Middletons left for England. A number of Ottawa's elite, including high-ranking officers, were at the station to see them off. It was not a happy occasion, but it was further depressed by a sorry little incident. A man accompanied by a detective waving a warrant for Middleton's arrest pushed through the company of notables just before the train was to pull out. It was an auctioneer demanding his commission of $36.30 on the sale of Middleton's household furniture. The manager of the Bank of Montreal was hastily called; he arrived and marked Middleton's cheque good for payment. The warrant for arrest was not executed.

Chapter Fifteen

Waiting

Poundmaker and Middleton had each had his time of triumph, and Charles Bremner had witnessed them. Each had had his time of defeat, and Charles Bremner had witnessed them too. Both men had marred his life. But in May, 1890, the chain of events had brought him his own triumph. The man who had cavalierly dismissed him in Winnipeg, denying all knowledge of him, had paid a high price for his arrogance—and for the furs. Charles Bremner had been the instrument of his downfall, and he took pride in that.

As soon as Ronald Macdonald returned from Ottawa to his contracting business, Charles Bremner drove in to Battleford. There was another meeting in Mahaffey & Clinkskill's store, and Macdonald told them of all that had happened, the recital of great deeds. Charles Bremner was the hero of the hour; he had slain the dragon. There were other reasons for jubilation. In the closing hours of the session, Parliament had passed a Bill authorising the building of a railroad to Hudson Bay—a long-held dream of the Territories and Manitoba. More than that, closer to home, a great steel arm now stretched north from Regina to beyond Saskatoon, where the first locomotive had arrived on May 15, to a torchlight parade, a band, and dancing in the streets. Eighteen Ninety was a good year.

Privately, Bremner talked to Ronald Macdonald about plans for a new house—a frame house with two stories and a shingle roof; and he talked to Clinkskill about furniture for the house, and about clothing for Emily and the girls—shoes, coats, ready-made dresses. But all that would have to wait until he got the money.

He waited. Days passed, weeks passed, months passed, and no money came. Emily stopped talking about the new house; the children stopped asking about new dresses. Bremner went doggedly about his daily work. He put in a crop, helped Emily to seed her garden, and went freighting whenever Clinkskill had a job for him. He tried to join in the evenings of the Literary Society, in which Emily and the girls sang and people came out from Battleford to take part, but the pleasure was gone. The glow of excitement and anticipation faded and only weariness was left. His triumph was short-lived. Some hero.

The government, with Parliament no longer in session, showed no great zeal to carry out the recommendations about Bremner's furs that they had so warmly endorsed. An awkward hiatus—and a convenient excuse for inaction—had developed as a result of the failure to specify who should pay. Bremner's lawyer, Henderson, paid fruitless visits to Cabinet ministers in Ottawa. In August, Caron looked grave and said the government did not hold itself responsible, but that the claim of course ought to be paid and he would bring the matter up before Cabinet. In November, the Battle River Agricultural Society got a cool reply from Sir John Thompson, Minister of Justice, to their annual petition for a re-opening of Bresaylor claims: "I think it would not be proper for me to advise claimants for rebellion losses, or for any other, as to how they should present their cases; nor am I prepared to say what evidence the Government would consider sufficient to authorise the re-opening of claims of the kind." Middleton had implied in his farewell message that no legal charge for reimbursement for the furs could be made to stick, and he followed that up from London in December by thumbing his nose across the Atlantic and declaring that he would not pay a penny towards compensation for them. Charles Bremner felt that he was the butt of another cruel joke, like the one when he was arrested as a rebel.

In the New Year of 1891, Sir John A. created an unexpected diversion. Shortly after January 11, his 77th birthday, he dissolved Parliament and called an election for March 5. There was a gamble in an election, of course, but the odds were with him. Quebec would be a close race, but Ontario and the Maritimes could be counted on, and so could B.C. As for the Territories, the Assembly might be dissatisfied at unfulfilled promises of responsible government, but they were pleased with the decision on language, which left the power to determine language use within the Assembly itself, and they were gratified with railway developments. The second branch line, going north from Calgary, was nearing Edmonton. The gamble was worth it.

The game of electioneering began. Public meetings were held, speakers praised and blamed and promised. In Saskatchewan, Macdowell came from Prince Albert in mid-February to a meeting in Battleford where J.M. Skelton, president of the Liberal Club, secretary of the Agricultural Society, and liaison man for the Bremner fur case, charged him with having neglected the interests of his constituents, particularly in failing to secure payment for the furs. Bremner and several of his neighbors who had driven in to hear Macdowell applauded Skelton's challenge.

Macdowell angrily denied the charge of neglect. He had obtained railroad work at good pay for any in the constituency who wanted it, and for some that had been a real windfall. He had had a large part, together with Davin of Regina, in bringing the railroad so near in the first place, with all of its advantages to farmers in shipping their produce out and to businesses and settlers in getting supplies in quickly and handily. Besides that, when the Hudson Bay railroad was built, they would be that much closer to European markets.

As for the Bremner furs, "I had practically obtained a settlement of this claim two years ago, and a more favorable one than Mr. Bremner had agreed to, and the money was not paid over because of the interference of some of Mr. Bremner's pretended friends. Mr. Bremner had been unwilling to take $3,000; I got that raised to $3,500, which the Government agreed to pay. But Mr. Bremner's lawyer intervened, on the urging of certain Battleford politicians, more interested in politics than in the welfare of the people of this constituency, than in Mr. Bremner's welfare, with a suit against General Middleton. It was due to the injudicious conduct of Mr. Bremner's friends that the claim was not paid, not to the neglect by the Government or myself." Macdowell, indignant in his virtue as he had been rebuffed in his good intention, would not raise his voice again for Charles Bremner. "Bremner's Furs" would not be an issue in this election.

When the results of the election came out, Sir John A. had won by an overall majority in the House of 29, though he had lost Quebec, as he thought he might—the Liberals won there by five seats. All four of the sitting Tory members from the Territories were returned, including, of course, Macdowell. Frank Oliver, in Edmonton, was dismayed at the Tory sweep. But Macdowell and the Tories did not win in Bresaylor, where the vote went to the Liberals 32 to 10. Macdowell had little occasion to visit them. On April 30, 1891, Sir John A. Macdonald was again Prime Minister of Canada when, at 3 p.m., the Governor General opened the first session of the Seventh Parliament of Canada.

It was the last triumph for the great artificer. Five weeks later, on Saturday, June 6, Sir John A. died and the nation mourned. The devoted Liberal Frank Oliver headed his piece, "THE END. Bells in every town, city, and village in Canada were tolled. Sunday was a day of national mourning. . . . In Ottawa, there was a cortege of 8,000 people, 50,000 in the streets. The funeral was the largest and most impressive ever seen in Canada. . . . In the United States and Britain, he is acknowledged to be one of the foremost men of the time. . . . Sir John's death was more than an event, it was the close of an era in Canadian history."

Eight days after John Abbott, the ailing and reluctant Government leader in the Senate, had been sworn in as Prime Minister, James Lister rose in the House and asked, "Has an application been made by or on behalf of Charles Bremner for payment of the furs taken by General Middleton? Is it the intention of the Government to pay for such furs?"

Sir John Thompson, still Minister of Justice, answered, "An application has been made on behalf of Charles Bremner, but it only came to the Privy Council at the close of last week, and it is too soon for me to state what the intention of the Government is."

Bremner and Skelton had been busy in the spring trying to open an avenue for another hearing of Bresaylor claims. After all, Xavier Batoche had got his $20,000 only two years ago, so it was not impossible. There was no point in pursuing the furs question again; that had been decided by a unanimous vote of Parliament. It was just the payment that was lacking. But the vote had suggested at least that Bremner was no longer considered a rebel. Therefore, an approach for rebellion losses might work. This time, Bremner would apply for $20,000 to cover the furs, crop loss and "imprisonment during the rebellion." It was not until October that word came that the claim was before the Department of Justice. By the end of that month, there was a further report that Thompson was considering it.

During the waiting time of November, wild geese flew over by the hundred, threshing was finished and both settlers and Indians had good crops, and there was also the excitement of elections for the Territories Assembly. In the Battleford constituency, two of Bremner's friends faced each other, Clinkskill and Skelton, the president and secretary of the Agricultural Society. Clinkskill won, but—it was becoming a refrain—not in Bresaylor, though it was close: Conservative Clinkskill 18, Liberal Skelton 23.

The waiting ended for that year with a despatch of December 11 from Ottawa. Thompson's report argued that recognition of the Bremner claim would involve recognition of other claims not reported on by the Commission (which, of course, was what Bresaylor had hoped for). He could not recommend such a course of action. It could lead to great expense. Moreover, "the Government was prejudiced by the great lapse of time and the lack of witnesses lost through death or other causes." One of those involved in the furs affair, S.L. Bedson, had recently died of a stroke, but the "great lapse of time" had been the government's doing. Thompson concluded by saying, "Bremner does not ask redress as a matter of right, but only as a matter of grace, and therefore it is not necessary to deal with the Crown's liability." In the

Herald Laurie commented, "The report no doubt will be voted on and adopted and will set aside forever Bremner's claim for recompense." For the Bremners, as for the other Bresaylor claimants, the New Year of 1892 was not auspicious.

Neither was it for the Tory party. The unhappy prime minister, in this "year of scandals," found himself deep in disclosures of bribery, corruption, fraud, and plain incompetence. One Tory member was expelled from the House on a motion by Thompson; Caron was among those suspected of corruption, and Dewdney was removed from his important and sensitive position as Minister of the Interior to become lieutenant-governor of British Columbia. He was replaced by Senator Daly of Selkirk, Manitoba. Utterly wretched, Sir John Abbott (the Queen having knighted him) resigned on November 24. Four days later, Canada had another prime minister, the sturdy, young—only 48—handsome Sir John Thompson. His installation gave neither aid nor comfort to Bresaylor petitioners in a winter of bitter cold.

Still undaunted, when Daly toured the Territories as Minister of the Interior at the end of August, 1893, the people of the Battleford district presented him with a twelve-point petition. The first six points dealt with the land rights of settlers, including once more the abolition of hay and wood dues, which Daly agreed would receive serious consideration. The seventh asked for a reopening of rebellion claims, but he said he could not hold out any hope of that. The twelfth item asked that legalised roads be established between Saskatoon and Battleford, and from Battleford west to Bresaylor and other points of settlement. Daly agreed that the first part of that proposal was reasonable, and shortly P.G. Laurie's son was on the survey team for the road to Saskatoon. But the second step Daly thought premature; there was not enough traffic now to justify the expenditure. The two branches of the railroad were taking care of most of the needs of settled areas. Bresaylor folk would have to put up with the gumbo and pot-holes of the old Edmonton trail a while longer.

On the other hand, the freighting haul was now only ninety miles to Saskatoon and there was plenty of hauling to do. And there were other ways of making money. Women and girls were getting $5 to $6 a pound for Seneca root, and in the wide-spread collection of buffalo bones along the railroads, Laurie reported that in Saskatoon the railway was paying $100 a carload. Then there was always trapping in the winter. Anything that brought cash was vital to most settlers.

In the fall of 1894 the woods were golden again with turning leaves, in some of the fields the grain was still in stook, in others there was only gleaming stubble left, the harvest done. Crops had been good this year, both for settlers and for Indians. The Sweet Grass reserve had done well and so had Poundmaker's people. They had gone into cattle raising (farm instructors had been reinstated on reserves), and they were selling beef to the Indian Department and getting cheques of $700 and $800 for it. They had sent 150 head of cattle to winter quarters. Perhaps by some miracle, the buffalo had re-appeared though in another guise, and would again provide food, hides, footwear, sinews, tallow, and above all in this new world, solid cash.

Settlers were filling up the countryside. Because of that, Hugh Cinnamon and his sons were preparing to leave Bresaylor with some 500 head of cattle to move about 100 miles west to the Vermilion district in Alberta, where they could get the amount of range land that they needed for their herds. The Cinnamons were one of the big success stories of Bresaylor; their cattle had been winning prizes at the Winnipeg Exhibition for several years now. But they were not the only ones. Peter Taylor was importing thoroughbred pigs, and Roderick Spence was producing prize wheat. A Regina *Leader* reporter, up visiting Bresaylor, wrote, "The people now settled there are mostly French and English Half-Breeds, but they are a very industrious lot. This is one of the best districts in the Saskatchewan country for wheat and cattle."

But in the Bremner home, things were different. The big man lay inert. A terrible surprise had come while he was working in the fields stooking the wheat to be ready for the threshing machine. He had been struck as with a mighty paw, and he fell. Carried home, he was silent, his left side motionless. Some of the paralysis would wear off, the doctor said, but there would be no more freighting, the winter mainstay. Nor would he play his violin again.

Before the year was out, the nation, too, was stricken. Again, columns of newspapers were bordered in black, this time for the sudden death, in England, of the young prime minister. Sir John Thompson died on December 12, 1894, at Windsor Castle. That morning he had been sworn in as a member of the Queen's Privy Council, and he had just finished lunch with the Queen when he had a heart attack, collapsed, and died.

Once more, the government and the Conservative party were in a shambles. Once more they turned to the Senate, and they called on the Hon. Mackenzie Bowell, aged 71, former Grand Master of the Orange Lodge, latterly Thompson's Minister of Trade and Commerce, and looking a little like the Emperor Franz Joseph of Austria. Lord

Aberdeen, who had succeeded Stanley as Governor General, swore him in on December 21, and he was quickly knighted in the Queen's New Year's honors, possibly because of the high mortality rate among Canadian prime ministers (Abbott had died on October 30, less than a year after he resigned). Bowell spent a year of friction and frustration, enmeshed in the Manitoba Schools Act.

Then pure farce took over. With the New Year of 1896, Davin reported to the *Leader*: "Confusion reigns. Conservative Ministry Split into Factions. Seven Ministers Resign. Bowell vs. Tupper. Present Condition Unprecedented in the History of Canada." Bowell's resignation was demanded, he tendered it, the Governor General refused it "inasmuch as the Speech from the Throne was not passed." Bowell had to continue, he shuffled the cabinet, six of the ministers who had resigned agreed to return, a peace was patched up, a Remedial Bill was fashioned to restore separate schools in Manitoba, Tupper moved second reading on March 3, Laurier, resenting the bishops' interference in the whole matter, moved a six months hoist of the Bill by way of amendment, the amendment was lost, the Bill carried by a majority of 10 on March 20—the last sitting a continuous one of thirty hours—it was sent to committee on April 2, dropped on April 15, Parliament was prorogued on Thursday April 23, dissolution was declared April 24, and elections were called for June 23. Bowell resigned and Sir Charles Tupper became Prime Minister of Canada for 69 days, from May 1 to July 8, 1896.

In these frenzied years, politicians had no interest and no time to spare for things like Bremner's furs. Nevertheless, with the coming election a new vista opened both for Bremner and for the other Bresaylor petitioners. There was no doubt that the Liberals would win, and the Liberals had been their champions. Hope quickened, even in Charles Bremner, almost in spite of himself.

He was recovering slowly, very slowly, from the debilitating blow of the stroke. Speech was still difficult for him. But he could do small things for Emily around the house and the barnyard. The sons-in-law had looked after the crops and the animals, and they had cut and hauled wood for Emily. There were now four of them. Clara, like her eldest sister, had married a Taylor—George Taylor—and Mary had married George Pichette. Like Louis Caplette, they had farms nearby, and Emily was looked after.

As for the election, Saskatchewan had a moment of unusual excitement. Among the three candidates for the seat was Wilfrid Laurier himself, leader of the Liberal party. If he was elected, he said, he would sit for Saskatchewan. He won in Saskatchewan as the party won in the country, and this time Bresaylor was on the side of the winner, 53 to 34. The joy was dimmed slightly when, after the Governor General had called upon Laurier to form a new administration on July 9, he announced that he would not sit for Saskatchewan after all, but instead would take a seat in Quebec. A bye-election would be held for Saskatchewan. Bresaylor would not be represented by the Prime Minister of Canada. However, J.M. Skelton, returning from a visit to Ottawa to celebrate the victory of his party and to witness the opening of the new Parliament on August 19, declared, "The Bremner fur claims are to be paid in full!"

But the new government, like any other new government, had left-over problems. The main left-over problem for the Laurier government was the Manitoba school question. Laurier had his hands full with settling that problem on the one side and fending off the attacks of the bishops on the other. The Saskatchewan bye-election was delayed until December. Thomas Davis, general store-keeper of Prince Albert, endorsed by Laurier, won easily. In Bresaylor, the school house was the polling booth, Alex Bremner enumerator, and the vote for Davis was unanimous.

A cautious budget was brought down in April 1897, and it was not until the House sat in Committee of Supply that Davis thought the moment had come for Bremner's furs.[1] He had been warned that, to gain a reconsideration, he should present some new evidence about the affair, and so he brought along a letter from Warden, the erst-while quartermaster of the Police stores. It was dated Battleford, April 26, 1897.

On May 5, Davis rose in his place to make his plea for Charles Bremner, and he read the letter:

"In the summer of 1885, just after the rebellion, Mr. Hayter Reed and the late Mr. Bedson came to my room at the Quarter-Master's store, Battleford, about four o'clock in the morning, saying they wanted to get some of the furs lying in the store, as the General had confiscated them. They wanted a parcel put up for the General, and one each for themselves. I said that as soon as the storeman, Constable Dorion, came in, he would attend to their wants. Dorion came in about 6 a.m., and I told him to give these gentlemen what furs they required, and that he could pack them in some of the empty saddle boxes. Dorion, Reed, and Bedson then went to the storehouse and packed the furs. Some time in the forenoon, a team came from the steamboat landing, and took three cases away to the steamboat."

This statement varied considerably from the sworn testimony on both sides received by the Select Committee, and it left the odd picture of two thieves in the night skulking around for two hours until the storeman came in to help them to the loot. It did confirm the confiscation, the men involved, and the carting of the furs to the steamboat.

The case that Davis made was that the so-called confiscation was simple theft by government employees, that Bremner was a loyal citizen and did not have the rebel status presupposed by Blake and others, and that the government was "morally and legally bound to pay the claim for the furs." Lister rose to support him: "General Middleton resigned, he left the country; but poor Bremner, the Half-breed of the North-West, never could get the hon. gentlemen opposite to extend to him one atom of simple justice. The man since then has been afflicted, paralyzed; he is ruined, he is a pauper today, and what my hon. friend asks is that a measure of common justice should be meted out to this man."

Davis's motion for all papers relating to the claim to be brought up was passed; there was evident goodwill in the Committee of Supply. Yet nothing happened. There was no item in the supplementary estimates. No money was appropriated.

In the Valley, the *Herald* of May 31 carried a long piece on "Bremner's Furs" on the front page: "Davis the new member for Saskatchewan is making a mark by gross exaggeration and falsification . . . for the sake of throwing dirt on the late Government. . . . All of the facts stated have long been on record in the Department and might have been obtained there. . . . Mr. Davis goes into heroics over Mr. Bremner's loyalty and honesty. These subjects were threshed out and disposed of when Sir John Macdonald agreed to pay Mr. Bremner the appraised value of the furs alleged to have been stolen . . . which he would have long since received but for the advice of advisors who had influence over him at the time, who thought they could do better by suing General Middleton. . . . On hearing of their decision, Sir John said that they could not look to both Middleton and the Government, and stopped all further negotiations in the case. . . . The long delay in settling this claim is not due to the negligence of the Conservatives, but to the cupidity of Mr. Bremner's agents."

Laurie could mis-remember things too, and his latent antagonism towards the Bresaylor claimants heightened his indignation, but he made a strong point against the sincerity of Davis and the new government: "If the Government is in earnest in its desire to compensate Mr. Bremner and to give him the full benefit of his claim, they should see that the cheque is placed in his own hands, for then, and only then, will he get the justice they profess themselves so anxious to render."

Charles Bremner, 46 when the furs were stolen, was now 58, and, as Lister said, paralyzed, disabled.

He sat in the sun on the stone-boat by the river, resting before he started back to Emily with the barrelful of water. The hills around, once richly clothed with timber, were stripped, black and dreary, after a great prairie fire of last fall. He felt akin to them.

Fifteen years ago—almost exactly fifteen years ago—he had come here, a settler. He had brought his skills, the power of his body, his wealth, to work, to achieve, to build something that had not existed before. The land had yielded to him, the animals had increased his wealth, even the Indians had contributed, and the family had prospered. In the midst of dangers his confidence had grown. He was special, he was protected. He was the master.

And now? His wealth was gone—where, nobody knew. To the Indians, a settler had been only another exploiter, and where he had built, they had destroyed. As for his body, some strength had returned, he had seeded the fields himself this year, but he was crippled. His skills. He still had the skills he came with, but they were no longer enough. This had become a reading-and-writing world, and he was crippled in that too. He couldn't even be a postmaster.

The business of the furs was a millstone around his neck. Year after year, promises; year after year, nothing. He had been to blame in raising the hopes of Emily and the girls, that they would have pretty dresses, comfortable furniture, a pleasant home. But when the whole Parliament of Canada declared that he should be paid, surely he had had a right to expect that the money would come. That was seven years ago. Then when the new government was elected—the men who had been his champions—surely it wasn't wrong for him to hope then. But nothing came. He had become an object of resentment to people like Laurie, of embarrassment to Davis and Skelton, and of pity in Bresaylor. Nothing would ever come to him here, and the waiting was intolerable.

But in the world outside? The gold rush was on. Dawson City had begun. Edmonton was now the point of supply for the overland route, and the trail north was busy with fortune-hunters. More than that, there had already been hints of other riches—black gold—in the tar sands of Athabasca; and Indians, whose reports had been brushed aside, told of similar wealth not far from Edmonton. And there was the known treasure of grain to be reaped from the Peace River country.

Charles Bremner began to dream of the west. He could not go to the gold-fields nor bring oil out of the tar-sands, but he could still homestead, his skills were adequate for that, and he would be part of the new life, the new excitement, the new land. And Emily was a good cook. There was a way out. He would wait no longer. He would leave. He stood up on the stone-boat, gathered the reins, slapped them lightly on the horses' backs, and started to return to Emily.

Chapter Sixteen

Delayed Justice

This time it was a solitary prairie schooner that set out for the west. There was no company of neighbors as there had been fifteen years before, but only the four of them: Emily, the two youngest girls— Gertrude, fifteen and Mabel, twelve—and himself. It was lonely, but they were leaving behind unhappiness, discouragement, and embarrassed faces. If it was lonely, it was also independent.

After the first day or so, settlement was sparse. Further along they found the Cinnamon ranch flourishing and rested there. Then there was a long stretch of unsettled land to Vegreville, but after Vegreville, settlements of French Canadians, Belgians, Germans—half of Europe, it seemed—led the way to Edmonton. There they saw some of the new immigrants they had heard about, who were a puzzle. They had arrived about six months before from Galicia, Austria, but no one could talk with them for they spoke only Russian or Polish; and they were peculiarly clad, with shirts gathered at the neck, sheepskin coats, and leather leggings. They were part of the great settlement scheme of Clifford Sifton, who had been appointed Minister of the Interior the year before. Charles Bremner and his little family were scarcely noticed. He was only one more settler in the concourse of people.

A day's driving, thirty miles or so north of Edmonton, on the trail to Peace River, Athabasca, and the Yukon, the little caravan ended its journey. It was here that Charles and Emily set up a stopping-house, and became part of the ebb and flow of the new life.

They heard tales from the gold-seekers; Twelve-foot Davis, famous in the Yukon, stopped over with them on a visit south. Men from Athabasca told of their visions. Homesteaders from the Peace River boasted of virgin, uncharted forests and of the incomparable yields of grain in that valley. Charles Bremner worked his own farm—the effects of the stroke gradually wore off—and he pronounced the benediction on Sundays. They were alive once more.

The other world became remote. Word came of Middleton's death in London at the beginning of 1898; two years earlier he had been appointed Keeper of the Royal Regalia in the Tower of London, and

Charles Bremner had smiled at the news. Middleton had been keeper of his valuables at one time. He hoped that the Queen had had better luck.

In the spring of 1899 word came of yet another discussion in Parliament of the Bremner fur case, now become historical. The voices seemed far away, echoing in an empty dome. They were telling each other stories, weaving legends. They said that Charles Bremner had been a wealthy man, a fur-trader employing trader agents who had brought their furs to him to be stored, and when the rebellion broke out he had sent all the furs to Battleford to be stored.

Thomas Davis was eloquent in his mixture of myth and history when he addressed the House on May 15:[1] "This Bremner was a comparatively wealthy man. He had been all his life gathering this bit of money, and so, probably, had his forefathers before him. . . . What did Bremner do with his furs when the rebellion broke out? He did what any law abiding citizen would have done— he sent the furs to the representative of the government. . . . He wanted the guardians of the law to look after [his property]. They looked after it so well that the man never saw any of his property again. And then, to make matters worse, in the hope of justifying themselves, for stealing his property, they trumped up a charge against him and tried to make out that he was a rebel. . . . I say it is a crying shame that this old man is living in the constituency of my hon. friend from Alberta in poverty."

Frank Oliver, M.P. for Alberta, added his word on behalf of the Bremner claim, "inasmuch as Mr. Bremner is now a resident of my constituency. . . . There is no question whatever in regard to the legality, the circumstances, or the amount of Mr. Bremner's claims. These points have all been settled and the only point that has not been settled is that Mr. Bremner has not been paid. I am at a loss to understand why this payment has not been made. . . . By reason of this occurrence, Mr. Bremner is practically a pauper. He is past the age when he can help himself. This old man has a just claim against the government of the country; he is today a pauper because the money owing to him by the country has not been paid."

Then a friend of General Middleton, who was new to the House, spoke up to say that the general never got the furs, knew nothing about them, and Bremner was a rebel. One who had been a member of the Select Committee replied that the general had admitted taking them and that the evidence was that Bremner was not a rebel.

The Prime Minister rose: "I recollect the facts very well. This man Bremner had been trading in the north in the winter of 1885. He was arrested with Poundmaker's band. But he gave the explanation that he was coming from the north and was not a rebel. The furs were taken from him and sent to Battleford. . . . The result was that Bremner lost his furs—there was no doubt about that. I think the result also was to show that Bremner was not a rebel."

Thus encouraged, Davis resumed his urging. "I hope the Government will see not only that Mr. Bremner is paid his just claim, but that they will investigate all the other claims and find out what is just and pay them."

It being six o'clock, the Speaker left the Chair. No cheque was issued.

Three months later, the voices were even fainter and more ghostly. An item appeared before the House in Committee of Supply: "Amount required to pay Mr. Charles Bremner, of Bresaylor, for value of furs entrusted by him to Dominion Government authorities at Battleford on the 26th May, 1885, and never returned to him—$5,364.50."[2]

One member asked, "Why is this being paid?" Another, "Who is going to reimburse the Government for that money?" Another, "Where is the report?"

Laurier said, "I believe a report was made in 1889 or 1890 . . . to the effect that this man had been illegally deprived of his furs and that the furs had been taken by officers of the Government."

Another member, a Conservative, "I have recollections of the causes which led the late Government to resist the payment of this claim. The chief reason was that this man, having participated in the rebellion . . . was not entitled to any compensation. However, as the members of the present Government sympathised with the late rebellion, I am not astonished at their paying this claim."

The Committee of Supply moved on to the next item.

The next day, August 10, the Bremner item was read again. This time the Prime Minister had the Select Committee's report with him, and he read aloud its resumé, with the concluding paragraph:

"On behalf of Bremner it was stated to your Committee that he was willing to accept $4,500, inclusive of interest, in compensation for his loss, and this your Committee consider a fair compensation."

Laurier said, "This is the basis of the vote we now ask from Parliament."

A member grumbled, "It is unfortunate that this comes at a time when we cannot look into it."

In the Auditor-General's report for 1899-1900, under expenditures for the Interior Department, there appeared an entry:

MISCELLANEOUS: CHARLES BREMNER VALUE OF FURS LOST IN 1885. Chas. Bremner, Bresaylor, value of furs entrusted by him to Dominion Government authorities at Battleford, on May 26, 1885, and never returned to him........$5,364.50.[3]

On September 6, 1899, the *Saskatchewan Herald* had an item: "Charles Bremner having received payment for his furs has decided to return to Bresaylor and re-establish his home there."

But that was not Charles Bremner's idea. The next week, Laurie had another item: "We were misinformed when told that Charles Bremner would return to Bresaylor. So far from that being the case, he has sent an invitation to Louis Caplette to throw up his place there and remove to Edmonton where Mr. Bremner will establish him on a farm. The invitation has been accepted." On October 11, "Mrs. Louis Caplette and family, of Bresaylor, have removed to Edmonton."

Nineteen hundred. A new life in a new land at the beginning of a new century. Charles Bremner, patriarch and provider, celebrated this New Year with his children and grand-children in the stopping-house on the road to the north. The money for the furs had helped to bring them together. Emily and the girls had the pretty dresses. They were once more living comfortably. They had a firm basis. After nearly fifteen years, he had won back what was his own. What he gave to his family was theirs by right—and his.

More than that, those ghostly voices in far-off Ottawa had declared that he was not a rebel. The gray cloud of "not proven" was gone forever. In this new life, he could match adventure stories that travellers told with stories of his own: stories of rebellion, of Poundmaker, and of Middleton. Yet those stories seemed almost dreamlike: stories of another time in another world, a world that had passed away. He was again his own man.[4]

Appendix

Depositions and Petitions

I (a) Charles Bremner's deposition before the Royal Commission on Rebellion Losses.

NORTH-WEST REBELLION CLAIMS, 1885.

Before J. Alphonse Ouimet, Esq., of Montreal: Henry Muma, Esq., of Drumbo; Thomas McKay, Esq., of Prince Albert, Commissioners, duly appointed and sitting as a Royal Commission at Battleford, District of Saskatchewan, North-West Territories, to investigate the said rebellion losses.

Personally came and appeared Mr.Charles Bremner, of Battleford, farmer and merchant, forty-seven years of age; married—Claimant. And the said Charles Bremner, said Claimant, being duly sworn, deposes and says as follows:

I live at Bresaylor Settlement, between the two rivers, about twenty-two miles from town. I lived there at outbreak of rebellion, and was there on the 14th and 15th April, 1885. We sent a letter down here in April to the Chief of the Police, begged for an answer, but got none. I have no copy of this letter. We were ready to leave our property if he had said so, and we got the priest, Father Cochin, to write for us, and he told us that, perhaps, they were about through with the affair, and it might be that we would be all right if we did not leave the place. The letter was an application for assistance or advice. We got no reply, so we remained at my place. On the evening of the 13th April about 200 Indians came and said they had come for us, we refused to go; and that night they broke into my stable and took all my horses, and what I had in the pack [?] as well. The next day they went into my store alongside my house, and took my goods, and told us to get ready and go with them. So we had to go; they hitched up for me, and started to shoot the dogs, pigs and hens, and they took us away, driving with them at the same time about 300 head of cattle at least, mine among the rest. There were about 15 families taken then; they had all camped about my place, and we

were all taken over Battle River to Poundmaker's Reserve. We remained
there until the fight of Cut Knife Hill took place, when just before sun-
rise we heard the attack. Our little camp was about one-quarter of a mile
from the Indian camp; the troops were about three-quarters of a mile
His   across a big bridge from us, and I put up a big white flag; before
C + B   this we had sent down Tom Dennison as a messenger to let the
Mark   police know to come for us, and to say to them to not
shoot at the square tents, but at the Teepees only. The second
cannon ball came near our camp. While with the Indians we were treated
badly. I then hitched up the horse and sent my family away to hide
themselves in a deep creek, and we went up into a high hill on horseback, intending to go to the police, and they fired at us twice with the
cannon, and I saw some of our party of Half-breeds get ready to fight the
police, and I said to them: "The first Half-breed I see shooting at the police, I will blow his brains out;" and we went back, found our families,
and had breakfast at our old camp of that night about 1 p.m. The police
just then gave in, and a lot of Indians then got ready to follow them,
when I told Poundmaker to stop his men, and he said he would. I came
in then on the day Poundmaker came in and surrendered; we were kept
with them until then, and were not able to leave; we had to follow the
dancing tent like the rest. At this time I was a prisoner against my will
and held by force. The food we got we had to buy from the Indians. The
Indians had 21 Canadians, prisoners captured when the bull team was
taken, and they were sent on ahead by Poundmaker with me and three or
four others. I wanted him to come along, but he was scared, and I was
told by Colonel Otter and Colonel Herchmer that if the Indians would let
the horses and captured property go and give up their arms it would be
all right. This was put in a letter and taken by Father Cochin and myself
back to the camp, and read to the Indians, and they were glad. We asked
the chief to leave with our families; he said to leave myself and five men
with him and he let the others go. We did so and that evening he got
news and let us all go, and we came to our families who were on the way
here. I was arrested here by order of Colonel Herchmer, because I had a
rifle which I had bought from a Half-breed. It was a Government rifle, a
Winchester, but I did not know it. I bought it from John Wells to keep it
from the Indians. He is one of my neighbors. I was held here almost a
month and was then sent to Regina for trial, and was held there, but no
charge was made against me and we were let go to appear if called upon.
I got home here about 18th September; came here the same evening as
released.—I took no part in the Rebellion one way or the other, except
as stated as to capture by the Indians. On my return I found my home

and store barely standing—windows, stoves, furniture smashed, flooring gone and ceilings torn down. I saw a lot of new hats and clothing on the Indians when they came out of my store. They shot some of our cattle along the road to camp. I do not read, but I recognise the accounts now shown to me of goods that were in the store. I now file the original invoices from Winnipeg of goods sent to me in fall and summer before Rebellion, and were all in my store on 14th April, except such as were sold. My books were lost. I find these invoices afterwards. I had them in a tin box. The goods from W. Macdonald were bought here, and I paid as shown on these invoices. I paid $150.00 freight on these goods to the Canadian Pacific Railway to Swift Current, and $400 land freight to Bresaylor. Almost one-half of this stock remained unsold in my store on 14th April. The furs were at my place in the carts, and went with us to the Indian camp, but the Indians did not take possession of them. Middleton gave orders to put the furs in a safe place. I have not seen it since. I enquired for it, but have not recovered it. The list now read over to me is a correct list of my furs as list Exhibit 'B'. The list now read to me is a true and correct statement of my losses in house and on farm separate from the store (Exhibit 'C'.) And Exhibit 'D' is the general statement *Reply* of my claim as at present put before the Commission. My *to* residence is about 22 or 25 miles from town. I have a farm, and *Chair-* had a store and house there; had been there four years last July. *man* Was there at out break of Rebellion. There are in that settlement almost twenty or thirty families altogether. I never heard word of the Rebellion until shortly or at the beginning of 1st April, 1885. When I heard of the Rebellion the settlers there in Bresaylor were all on their farms; some of them came to barracks here, about ten or twelve families, for protection at once. I did not come here to barracks but remained on my farm with about ten or twelve families—John Wells, Andrew Pozer, Alexander Pozer, Cornelius Pruden, one Breland [name illegible], David Poitras, Narcisse Ducharme, Andre Ducharme, Louis Caplette, Lusette Genoux, and my own family and James Bremner and their families, who remained in camp with me, and went to the Indian camp on Poundmaker's Reserve. We were notified by Edward Payton at midnight that they were hitching up, and that if we wanted to get away to come then. But my horses were away eighteen miles, and my own mother, 95 years of age, was with me, so I asked him to wait until the next night, when I could get my horses in; but he said he could not wait, there is quite a stir, and the Indians are coming and will kill us all. I sent for the horses, but they were lost and could not be found the next day; and this is the reason we did not come in with the others; the horses were

afterwards found. I packed my furs as I bought them, and they were
His   near the store; we did not leave to join Poundmaker for a while
C + B after this. Almost ten days, at least, had elapsed before I saw the
Mark   200 Indians. We could not come in when the horses were found
the   because of Indians. I had no reasons not to come at once, instead
next   of sending the letter to the fort. Father Cochin, already referred
day   to, advised us to send the letter by the Brother. We
remained there then until the store was pillaged, when we were forced to
go with them. The priest was there and went with us, and I remained
there until about the time of Poundmaker's surrender. I was in my house
on the 14th April; when the pillage was commenced my store was
locked. I had no reason to try and prevent the pillage; the Indians were
too wicked; they were all armed and broke open the store. The furs were
there in the carts that day, but I am positive the Indians left in the morning, and I and all the people there as named went with them, and they
took my goods along. The furs were in my carts, and I brought them
with me along with the Indians. I can't say what became of the goods,
but my furs were brought in here at the time of Poundmaker's surrender,
and were delivered to the police here then. It was on the 2nd of May, at
Cut Knife fight that I saw some Half-breeds preparing to fire on the police, and while I was in the Indian camp, I and all my party were armed;
we refused several times to give up arms to the Indians. We had just a
little bit of ammunition with us. I had a breech-loading gun. On my
arrival here I was arrested and sent to Regina, but I am sure no charge
was made against me there. I do not remember having pleaded guilty to
any charge made against me here. No sentence was passed on us there.
We were released on bail on our security of $400. I was brought with the
others before Judge Richardson in the court room; the clerk read nothing
to us; I can't recollect if the judge read anything to us, but I never
pleaded guilty—I am positive of this.

The furs in Exhibit 'B' are the furs I lost. I can't say if I had
counted them all; I had counted what was packed. I made out my lists
from memory as soon as released, when I went to Winnipeg, and I have
not received any of them. Personally I can't say who took them. The
prices mentioned for the goods are prices in Winnipeg and freight
added. I sent my first claim about end of November last. I did not send
my list of cattle at same time as other claim, as I wished to be paid for
furs and goods first. I had hoped to find some horses and cattle after. I
have made a statutory declaration in Winnipeg before James Fisher on
November 9, 1885.—

Reply to Mr. McKay I swear that I never took part in the Rebellion in any way, never aided or assisted them in any way while I was with them. I never took part in any of their movements, never acted as scout or went away with any party whatever of Half-breeds or Indians. I was coming [illegible] when Lafontains, a Police scout, was captured, and my nephew, Alex B. Sayers was with me, and the Half-breeds came and caught us when we were crossing the Battle River, and we crossed first, Sayers and I, and galloped off pretty lively when over, and came 7 or 8 miles this side of the river, and they caught us and we came with them a piece, until we saw the Police scouts, and then went at once straight after the Scouts and I saw Fontaine then ahead. This party overtook me at the river; I did not know then that they were after the scouts; they had started after the cattle only. When Fontaine went into the woods, it was not me who told him if he came out he would not be hurt. I could have escaped at any time with the men on horseback, but we could not leave our families. When we sent our families away at Cut Knife, the Indians sent a guard of 50 men after them and a lot of Indians came and watched us. It was Louis Sayers asked for Henry Sayers' rifle to shoot the Police; he is a young man; he was the only one I heard, but if he had begun all would have begun. I know a party of Indians and Half-breeds, so

His C + B Mark the day before I heard, came down here. Otter arrived when Rouleau's house was burnt, but I can't say who they were. I do not know anything about the raid on the teamsters. I do not know if any of our party had any Government or private property. I had traded my fur from all around, some from Turtle Lake, Cold Lake, other side of Frog lake, from Chippeway Indians, from the Big Mountains south of Fort Pitt. I had three men and myself trapping. I had six carts and two waggons when I went to the Indian camp and the same number when I came in here and was arrested. I can't say how many

Reply to Mr. Muma bales I had; I can't at all remember. I had over ten packs—pretty near twenty packs, I suppose. I had been with the Indians seven or eight days before Cut Knife fight. There were about twenty men of Half-breeds, and between 200 and 300 Indians in camp when it was fought.

In re JAMES BREMNER

I know the claimant. I know he has a claim. And I know he had and lost the articles mentioned in his claim as read to me. I saw the wages paid to the Men. I paid him out of my store; he was one of the settlers at the Bresaylor, but he was away from home.

And further deponent sayeth not.

The present deposition having been read to the witness, he declared it contains the truth, nothing but the truth, persists therein, and—has declared he cannot sign.

Taken, sworn and acknowledged before us, Commissioners duly appointed by Royal Commission as aforesaid at Battleford, District of Saskatchewan, North-West Territories, on the seventh day of June, in the year of Our Lord one thousand eight hundred and eighty-six.

His
(Signed) CHARLES + BREMNER
Mark

(Signed) J. ALPHONSE OUIMET
    "   THOS. McKAY
    "   H. MUMA

              Commissioners

I(b) Louis Cochin's deposition before the Royal Commission

NORTH-WEST REBELLION CLAIMS, 1885.

Before J. Alphonse Ouimet, etc.

Personally came and appeared Mr. Charles Bremner of Battleford, merchant and farmer—Claimant. And the said Rev. Father Louis Cochin, of Poundmaker's Reserve, Missionary Priest, on behalf of the said Claimant, being duly sworn, deposes and says as follows:

At the time of outbreak I was at Bresaylor Settlement. I know all the circumstances attending the capture of Charles Bremner and party by the Indians; I was in the camp at Charles Bremner's place with 10 or 12 Half-breed families, and I say they were not rebels. They did not come here because they did not believe that the Indians would rob or injure them at all, and they had no certain news, they were separate from the others who came in here from the English Half-breed settlement by the river. Charles Bremner, I would say, was not a rebel at all. And those people acted on my advice. I told them that probably the best thing to do was to remain and work on their farms. A portion of them were willing to come here, and the rest thought it best to remain there. Some of them were very poor and had no horses, and while they were discussing what to do, the Indians came. Before this, I had written a letter to the Police captain signed by C. Bremner and H. Sayer, asking what we had to do, and we received no reply to this. The Indians forced us to go along with them. I was kept as a prisoner under guard, but not in a tent, but the camp was all guarded around and we could not excape; we were not close prisoners but our camp was visited frequently to see if we were there. The Brother sent with the letter was kept at barracks, and not allowed to return. These people have all lost property. James Bremner was the same, and was very quiet all through the trouble, and was with the party. Louis Caplette and the others, and John Wells, and all the party, lost their animals and property. Chas. Bremner had a large band of cattle and lost many, and he had a large quantity of fine furs, I should say I saw from $2,000 to $3,000 worth. He had about 80 head of cattle, he had also a good stock of boots in his store, and had merchandise in his buildings as well. It was not a very large store, but can't say as to the amount, and I think it was all pillaged, and he has found some animals, but no goods, I think. Many of the animals I saw killed by the Indians.

I was with Poundmaker during the entire time of the captivity of these people, and I did not see any disloyal act on his part.

And further deponent sayeth not.

The present deposition having been read to the witness, he declares it contains the truth, nothing but the truth, persists therein, and has signed.

Taken, sworn and acknowledged before us, Commissioners duly appointed by Royal Commission as aforesaid, at Battleford, District of Saskatchewan, North-West Territories, on the seventh day of June, in the year of Our Lord one thousand eight hundred and eighty-six.

(Signed) L. COCHIN, O.M.I.

(Signed) J. ALPHONSE OUIMET
    "   THOS. McKAY
    "   H. MUMA

Commissioners

II. Commons Debates, May 17, 1888, p. 1516

Charles Bremner's letter to James Edgar, dated March 10, 1888, read into *Hansard* by James Edgar May 17.

"In connection with my claim for losses and my petition to the Hon. Thos. White, I beg to submit the following:—In the winter of 1884 and 1885, I was trading with the Indians and had accumulated a lot of furs, the amount claimed by me was about $7,500. After the surrender of Poundmaker, I was sent with all the Half-breeds of our settlement to camp, near the barracks, having the fur in my possession, was arrested and placed in guardroom. In the evening General Middleton came to our camp in company with Colonel Otter. The soldiers had for some little time had been trying to take furs from us by force and had succeeded in carrying off a few. Caplette here asked General Middleton if his soldiers had authority to take the furs. General Middleton said no, and asked to whom the furs belonged; being told he said he would send two or three men to protect them; a short time after three men came with a team and removed all the fur to the barracks without our permission. We were taken to Regina, tried for treason, not proven guilty, and let off on our own recognisances. On returning to Battleford, I at once went to Col. Morris, of the N.W.M.P., and asked for my fur. He replied that he had had a telegram from General Middleton telling him to give the balance of the furs he had left to certain parties mentioned in his telegram, and that most of the fur was gone. I afterwards went to Winnipeg and engaged a lawyer, of Archibald, Howell & Co. We went to see the Hon. Caron about my fur, but he did not give any satisfaction, saying it was outside his department. Mr. Howell asked to whom would we go for information and the Minister replied to go to General Middleton. We went to see Middleton but he said he knew nothing about the fur and said that he had never commanded that Bremner or his party should be arrested, and in reply to a reference to his telegram to Col. Morris, he denied having ever sent him a telegram the subject. We left Middleton in that manner without any satisfaction.

"On returning from Winnipeg I went again to Morris and asked for the balance of my fur, he said it was all gone, and on my referring to Middleton's denial of having sent a telegram to Morris *re* furs, Morris again asserted that Middleton had sent the telegram and he could prove it. This was said in the presence of Louis Caplette.

"I put in a claim for the furs but have not received any compensation for them so far nor for any other losses."

III(a). Commons Debates, March 3, 1890, p. 1362

Petition from Bresaylor dated August 25, 1887

"To the Hon. Thomas White, Minister of the Interior

"Sir,—We, the undersigned, by this our petition, humbly represent—

"That we settled in the neighborhood of Battleford, at a place known as the Bresaylor Settlement, in the year 1883-4. That having sold our property in Manitoba at the time when property was very high, we brought with us here considerable horses, cattle and cash, and were in a very prosperous condition until the rebellion broke out.

"That at the beginning of said rebellion we were made prisoners to the Indians, left destitute, and forced into their camp.

"That since the rebellion the Government has paid or indemnified all the settlers for the losses they sustained on account of said rebellion.

"That on the supposition that we joined the Indians of our own free will, and that we acted as rebels in connection with them during said rebellion, payment for our losses has so far been withheld unjustly, without enquiry of any kind, and on mere suppositions which have no foundation whatever.

"Your petitioners strongly protest against such a course. We are British subjects, and as such we should be considered innocent until we are proven guilty; and we consider it arbitrary and unfair to be condemned without a trial.

"Although the *onus probandi* does not or should not rest on us, we have always been ready, and are still ready to appear before Government Commissioners or a jury of our fellow citizens and prove to their satisfaction that we were forced to follow the rebel Indians as their prisoners, and never ceased to be loyal to Her Majesty's Goverment.

"To better satisfy you as to the genuineness of our pretensions, your petitioners take the liberty of herein stating a few of the leading facts relating to doings and movements during the late rebellion which will help you to form some idea of the circumstances of the case.

"As our settlement is twenty-five miles from Battleford, with no other settlements between us, we were not made aware of the movements of the Indians until a large number of them were assembled at Battleford on the south side of the Battle River, and when Payne and Tremont had already been murdered.

"That as two Indians reserves between us and Battleford at a spot where the Battle and Saskatchewan rivers are only about three miles apart, we could not avoid passing through these reserves without considerable risk to our lives. As soon as informed about the movement and warlike attitude of the Indians, we sent for our horses, which were herded twenty-five miles west of our place, and made ourselves ready to start for the barracks, when the Indians appearing to be friendly came to us declaring that we were watched by the Indians, and that if we attempted to move towards Battleford, we would all be killed, but would not be troubled or interfered with if we remained at our home.

"On this information we wrote a letter and sent couriers to Capt. Morris, the commanding officer at Battleford, explaining our position, our desire to reach the barracks, and asking assistance to help us to make our way to Battleford. No answer came, and as we learned later, our communication was looked at with distrust and our messenger put in jail.

"About one week after the sending of our letter to Capt. Morris, one Angus Miller and Edward Spence obtained a pass from Morris and came to our settlement to look after their property. On being asked why the help asked for had not been sent out, Miller replied that they could not have spared any of their men, and that some were suspicious about our designs. Miller and Spence did not know if we could follow the road safely with our families, as they themselves had not thought it safe to follow; yet after some discussion we decided to attempt going to Battleford with them. We had our horses hitched up ready to go when seven or eight Indians suddenly broke upon us, followed by about two hundred and fifty others. Miller and Spence left at once full speed for the barracks.

"The Indians surrounded us, took possession of our cattle, and ordered us to follow them or be shot. We were also ordered to deliver up our arms, but as we persistently refused, and declared that we would fight before doing so, were finally allowed to keep them. We followed them surrounded all the way to their general camp at Poundmaker's Reserve.

"Towards the 18th of April, a few days before the battle at Cut Knife Creek, we sent during the night one Samuel Dennison, with instructions to proceed to the barracks and inform Capt. Morris that we were prisoners of the Indians; that if they were to come to fight, not to shoot at us; that our camp would be at one side and could be easily recognized by our square canvas tents while the Indians had teepees; that if a favorable occasion offered during the battle we would join the troops and fight the Indians.

"On the following day the Indians, taking notice of Dennison's disappearance, became suspicious about our intentions. They held a council and decided that we should remove our tents to the centre of the camp. On our refusing to comply with this order they rode around in a threatening attitude, yelling and firing, Indian fashion. We showed that we were determined to fight them rather than comply and seeing that we could not be intimidated we were finally allowed to remain where we were encamped.

"On hearing the firing of the cannon on the morning of the battle, Charles Bremner put up a white flag to indicate to the troops the position of our camp. The Indians wanted to pull it down, but we resisted, and to avoid a possible conflict we had to assure them that it meant nothing.

"Notwithstanding our message to Capt. Morris through the messenger Dennison, firing was kept up at our camp by the troops during the battle. Incensed at what we considered a breach of faith or an unpardonable distrust, a few amongst us—two or three—decided to take part in the fight against the troops, saying: 'Since the police do not take any notice of our letters and messages, we are not to remain exposed to be killed by both the Indians and the Police.'

"Your petitioners are ready to substantiate these facts before a court of inquiry and we feel that if such an opportunity is offered to us we will be able to dispell all doubts about the loyalty of our intentions; and prove besides that our firm attitude and our influence over the Indians has been instrumental in saving lives, and in preventing cruelties of any kind on prisoners and on the bodies of soldiers left on the battlefield.

"Wherefore your petitioners pray that an investigation be opened, and, if practicable, before men acquainted with the country and our circumstances, to hear any evidence for or against our pretensions, with the ultimate object of being paid and indemnified for our losses on account of the rebellion, if we succeed in proving our allegations and our loyalty to the satisfaction of your Government.

"And your petitioners will never cease to pray.

"Battleford, 25th August, 1887

"Charles Bremner, Henry Sayers, David Pointras, Baptiste Pointras, L. Cochin, O.M.I., J. Wills, Alexander H. Sayers, James Bremner, S. Mills, C. Sayers, W. Todd, J. Pointras, L. Caplette, G. Pichette, Louis Sayers, G. Pruden, William Villebrun."

III (b). Petition of Battleford citizens in support of Bresaylor petition, August 25, 1887.

Introduced in the House by James Edgar, *Commons Debates*, May 17, 1888, p. 1516.

"To the Hon. Thomas White, Minister of the Interior,—

"We, the inhabitants of Battleford, take the liberty of recommending to your favorable consideration the within petition of the Bresaylor Settlement.

"Though we looked with some distrust at the doings of the petitioners during the rebellion we firmly believe them to have been led astray owing to the intense excitement and general distrust then prevailing, and we do not hesitate to admit that subsequent developments and a better understanding have dispelled the erroneous impressions we had formed on their loyalty. Though some still retain the belief that a few amongst them took part and acted as rebels, we are fully convinced that the greatest number never ceased to be loyal in mind and in action.

"That the facts as stated in the petition are in substance true, and that the granting of the conclusion of their petition would be an act of justice to which they are entitled, and your petitioners will never cease to pray."

(Signed by some thirty of the resident settlers of the town of Battleford.)

Sources

1. Newspapers

The Edmonton *Bulletin* (weekly), editor Frank Oliver.

The *Saskatchewan Herald* (weekly), editor P.G. Laurie.

The Regina *Leader* (weekly), editor N.F. Davin.

The *Manitoba Free Press* (daily), editor W.F. Luxton.

2. Government Records

The Canadian Parliamentary Companion (Ottawa: J. Durie & Son), edited by J.A. Gemmill, Barrister-at-law.

Debates and Sessional Papers of the House of Commons (Hansard) (Ottawa: Queen's Printer, 1885-1900). Specific dates noted in text.

A. 1886 *Report of Royal Commission on Rebellion Losses*, April 20.

A. 1887 Sessional Papers: Rebellion Losses (claims received and amounts allowed.)

A. 1887 Sessional Papers (No. 9) Dept. of Militia and Defence: Appendix no. 4 to Report of May, 1886. *Final Report of War Claims Commission* by Adolphe P. Caron, Minister of Militia and Defence, Ottawa, Jan. 1, 1887.

A. 1890 (No. 1) *Report of the Select Committee in re CHARLES BREMNER'S FURS* (Printed by order of Parliament).

A. 1900 Sessional Papers (No. 1) *Auditor General's Report, 1899-1900;* Department of Interior; Expenses, Miscellaneous: Charles Bremner, value of furs lost in 1885.

Royal Commission on Rebellion Losses 1886-97; 62 pp. Letters of appointment and instructions; list of claims and awards;

reports of the Commission 1886-88; sample of forms used. (A bound volume which belonged to Capt. Geo. H. Young, secretary of the Commission. Provincial Archives of Manitoba.)

3. General

Neil Brodie, *Twelve Days with the Indians, May 14 - May 25, 1885* (printed at the office of the *Saskatchewan Herald*, Battleford, March 1932, 9 pp.) From the Archives of the University of Saskatchewan, Saskatoon.

William Bleasdell Cameron, *On the War Trail of Big Bear* (Calgary: Kenney Press Co., 1926; rpt. Ryerson, n.d.; rev. and retitled *Blood Red the Sun*, Vancouver: Wrigley Printing Co., 1950).

Louis Cochin, *Reminiscences of Father Cochin in Translation* (Battleford: Canadian North-West Society Publications, Vol. I, No. 2, 1927), 75pp. Rare Book Room, Winnipeg Centennial Library.

Robert Jefferson, *Fifty Years on the Saskatchewan* (Battleford: Canadian North-West Society Publications, Vol. I, No. 5, 1921), 160pp. Rare Book Room, Winnipeg Centennial Library.

Samuel Benfield Steele, *Forty Years in Canada: Reminiscences of the Great North-West* (New York: Dodd, Mead and Co., 1915; fasc. rpt. Toronto: Coles Publishing Co., 1973), 428 pp.

Notes

CHAPTER ONE

1. Carlton. At this time and until the end of 1882, Carlton House was the Headquarters of the Saskatchewan District of the Hudson's Bay Company. Communications and commerce went from Carlton directly to Fort Garry in the south. "There does not appear to be any significant connection between Carlton and Fort Edmonton during this period." This information was provided me by Shirlee Anne Smith, Keeper of the Hudson's Bay Company Archives, and by Michael Mooseberger of the Manitoba Provincial Archives.

2. "Off to the Plains," *Saskatchewan Herald*, May 23, 1881.

3. "Gabriel Dumont," Edmonton *Bulletin*, June 20, 1885.

4. Alexander Morris, *The Treaties of Canada with the Indians* (Toronto: Belfords, Clarke & Co., 1880; fasc. rpt. Toronto: Coles Publishing Co., 1971), p. 181.

5. William Francis Butler, *The Great Lone Land* (London: Sampson, Low & Searle, 1872; rpt. Edmonton: Hurtig, 1968), p. 228.

6. *Saskatchewan Herald*, May 1903. Obituary issue of several columns, including one title "Biographical", containing information about Laurie's experiences in the Red River Settlement in 1870. Also a biographical sketch of P.G. Laurie by his son, Major Richard Laurie, North Battleford *News*, March 9, 1933.

7. "Battleford and Vicinity, A Fine Field of Settlement," *Saskatchewan Herald*, Sept. 19, 1881.

8. Ibid., Aug. 1, 1881. This and other accounts of Poundmaker's movements and speech at this time are taken from Laurie's reports of local news.

9. Ibid., May 9, 1881.

10. Ibid., Sept. 9, 1881.

11. Ibid., May 24, 1919. From Charles Bremner's obituary.

CHAPTER TWO

1. Lewis Herbert Thomas, *The Struggle for Responsible Government in the North-West Territories, 1870-97* (Toronto: University of Toronto Press, 1956), p. 97.

2. Ibid., p. 99.

3. Edmonton *Bulletin*, October 21, 1882.

4. *Saskatchewan Herald*, July 22, 1882.

5. William Bleasdell Cameron, *On the War Path of Big Bear* (Calgary: Kenny Press Co., 1926), pp. 42, 222; rpt. Ryerson, n.d.; rev. and retitled *Blood Red the Sun*, (Vancouver: Wrigley Printing Co., 1950), pp. 26-27, 197.

6. Ibid., Wandering Spirit; *War Path*, 53; *Blood Red the Sun*, 34.

7. Edmonton *Bulletin*, Feb. 3, 1883.

8. Ibid., Jan. 27, 1883. Father Leduc was on his way to Ottawa about the Homestead and Pre-emption situation in and around St. Albert, when the public meeting at Edmonton appointed him as the Edmonton delegate also. Father Leduc "returned thanks to the meeting for the confidence placed in him, and assured the people of Edmonton that he would work to forward the interests which they had committed to his care, to the best of his ability."

9. Winnipeg *Daily Times*, Friday, June 29, 1883, p. 8.

10. *Saskatchewan Herald*, April 19, 1884.

CHAPTER THREE

1. *Saskatchewan Herald*, March 8, 1884.

2. Robert Jefferson, *Fifty Years on the Saskatchewan* (Battleford: Canadian North-West Society Publications, Vol. 1, No. V, 1929), pp. 106-7. Jefferson's account of the Thirst Dance and its sequel is contained in pp. 108-16.

3. Edmonton *Bulletin*, June 7, 1884.

4. Ibid., January 19, 1884.

5. Louis Cochin, *Reminiscences of Father Cochin in Translation* (Battleford: Canadian North-West Society Publication, Vol. I, 1927). Father Cochin's account of the events surrounding the Thirst Dance is contained in pp. 26-29.

6. Edmonton *Bulletin*, June 14, 1884, "The Thirst Dance."

7. Jefferson, *Fifty Years*, pp. 108-9.

8. Charles Bremner's deposition, see Appendix I (a).

9. Jefferson, op. cit., p. 123.

CHAPTER FOUR

1. Jefferson, *Fifty Years*, p. 125.

2. Cochin, *Reminiscences*, p. 30.

3. *Saskatchewan Herald*, April 23 entry for March 30.

4. Bremner's deposition, see Appendix I (a). All quotations from Bremner in this chapter are from the same source.

5. Cochin, *Reminiscences*, p. 31.

6. Ibid., pp. 31-32.

7. See Appendix I (b): Cochin's deposition before the Royal Commission.

8. Cochin, *Reminiscences*, pp. 44-45. Cochin's evidence at Poundmaker's trial.

9. Cochin, Appendix I (b). Deposition.

10. Jefferson, *Fifty Years*, pp. 140-41.

11. Ibid., p. 138-39.

12. Ibid., p. 136.

CHAPTER FIVE

1. Jefferson, *Fifty Years*, p. 141.

2. Cochin, *Reminiscences*, pp. 32-33. The posts that the Indians referred to were telegraph posts along the main road. All telegraph wires had been cut. The only news from anywhere came by courier.

3. Jefferson, *Fifty Years*, p. 144.

4. Cochin, *Reminiscences*, p. 34.

5. See Appendix I (a), Bremner's deposition. All quotations from Bremner in this chapter are from this source, pp. 298-299.

6. Cochin, *Reminiscences*, p. 34.

7. Jefferson, *Fifty Years*, p. 145.

8. Ibid., pp. 141-143.

9. Cochin, *Reminiscences*, pp. 34-35.

10. Jefferson, *Fifty Years*, p. 146.

11. Ibid., pp. 148-49.

12. Neil Brodie, *Twelve Days with the Indians, May 14 - May 25, 1885*, (printed at the *Saskatchewan Herald*, Battleford, March 1932), p. 6.

13. Jefferson, *Fifty Years*, p. 149.

14. *Saskatchewan Herald*, Monday, March 22, 1886. "IN THE PENITENTI-ARY." Laurie reprints the interview with Poundmaker with the dateline, "Cor. Toronto *Mail*, Winnipeg, Feb. 22."

15. Jefferson, *Fifty Years*, p. 149.

CHAPTER SIX

1. Cochin, *Reminiscences*, p. 37. Interestingly, though it was Jefferson who received the letter from Middleton and who read it aloud to the Indian camp, it was Cochin who published the text.

2. Ibid. Cochin's account of the collapse is contained in his *Reminiscences*, pp. 36-38.

3. Jefferson's account of the collapse is contained in his *Fifty Years*, pp. 151-53.

4. *Saskatchewan Herald*, May 11, "Battle of Cut Knife Hill by an Eye Witness."

5. Ibid., June 1, "The Rebel Half-Breeds."

6. Brodie, *Twelve Days with the Indians*, p. 7.

7. All quotations from Middleton and Macdonald are taken from their statements to the Select Committee *in re* Bremner's furs.

8. Cochin, *Reminiscences*; see Appendix I (b), p. 306.

9. Edmonton *Bulletin*, July 11.

CHAPTER SEVEN

1. Notes on the jail, the Court, the town of Regina, and so forth, are taken from accounts in N.F. Davin's Regina *Leader*.

2. Sandra Elizabeth Bingaman, "The North-West Rebellion Trials, 1885," esp. the section on the Bresaylor Half-Breeds, (unpub. M.A. thesis, University of Regina, 1971), p. 184. The Regina attorney, T.C. Johnstone, "had informed the Crown Counsel that he wished thirty-two witnesses summoned for the defence of his clients, a request with which Osler had declined to comply although he had agreed to give Johnstone whatever time was necessary to assemble them."

3. Edmonton *Bulletin*, August 29, 1885.

4. Ibid., June 20, 1885.

5. Jefferson, *Fifty Years*, p. 156.

6. Brodie, *Twelve Days*, p. 7.

7. *North-West Trials: Epitome of Documents, North-West Rebellion, 1885* (Ottawa, 1886), p. 347 (Man. Legis. Library, RBR).

CHAPTER EIGHT

1. Ronald Macdonald's account is taken from the verbatim record of his testimony before the Select Committee enquiring into Bremner's furs, pp. 3ff.

2. Charles Bremner's deposition before the Royal Commission on Rebellion Losses. See Appendix I (a).

CHAPTER NINE

1. Charles Bremner's deposition, Appendix I (a); see also *Hansard* March 7, 1888, p. 97, Report of Royal Commission by the Hon. Thomas White.

2. Charles Bremner's letter to James Edgar, March 10, 1888, see Appendix II; see also Canada, *House of Commons Debates*, May 12, 1888, p. 1516.

3. See Bremner's Deposition, Appendix I (a).

CHAPTER TEN

1. W.B. Cameron, pp. 207-8.

2. Steele, *Reminiscences*, p. 230.

3. Bremner's Deposition, Appendix I (a).

4. *Saskatchewan Herald*, March 8, "At Large Again" (by telegraph) Winnipeg, March 5, "Poundmaker and Eleven Others Were Released Yesterday."

5. Regina *Leader*, July 6, 1886.

CHAPTER ELEVEN

1. Canada, *House of Commons Debate*, 1886, Vol. II, June 2, pp. 1764ff.

2. Bresaylor Petition to the Hon. Thomas White, App. III (a).

3. Petition of Battleford citizens, App. III (b).

CHAPTER TWELVE

1. Canada, *House of Commons Debates*, May 17, 1888, pp. 1515-1522.

2. See Appendix III (a) and III (b). See also Canada, *House of Commons Debates*, March 3, 1890, p. 1362.

3. Joseph Ouimet, Speaker of the House, Lieut. Col. 65 Batt. Volunteer Rifles (Mount Royal). Commanded the Battalion throughout the North-West Rebellion, 1885.—This and other biographical notes on M.P.'s and M.L.A.'s are

taken from the *Canadian Parliamentary Companion*, 1885 ff. (Ottawa; J. Durie & Son), ed. J.A. Gemmill, Barrister-at-Law.

4. Edmonton *Bulletin*, Aug. 4, 1888.

5. Canada, *House of Commons Debates*, 1890, Vol. 1: 1358-1401; 1508-10; 1517-19.

CHAPTER THIRTEEN

1. This chapter is based on the *Report of the Select Committee in re CHARLES BREMNER'S FURS* (Ottawa, Brown Chamberlin, Printer to the Queen's Most Excellent Majesty), printed by order of Parliament, 1890 (No. 1).

CHAPTER FOURTEEN

1. The speeches in this chapter are from the verbatim reports of the *House of Commons Debates*, 1890, Vol II: 'Bremner's Furs,' 3810; 4449; 4732-62; 4931-35.

2. Edmonton *Bulletin*, May 17, 1890 (by telegraph from Ottawa).

3. Ibid., Aug. 23, 1890.

CHAPTER FIFTEEN

1. Canada, *House of Commons Debates*, May 15, 1899, pp. 3084-3106.

CHAPTER SIXTEEN

1. Canada, *House of Commons Debates*, May 5, 1897: pp. 1744-1747.

2. Ibid., August 9, 1899, p. 10113 (revised edition): August 10, 1899, pp. 10169-70.

3. Auditor General's report, 1899-1900; Sessional Paper No. 1; Interior Department, Misc., "Charles Bremner, loss of furs."

4. See *Saskatchewan Herald*, May 24, 1919, Charles Bremner's obituary. Charles Bremner died at the home of his daughter, Ellen Caplette, at the age of eighty. His wife, Emily, had died the year before.

Margaret R. Stobie was born in Vermillion, Alberta. She received degrees from the universities of Alberta and London and a Ph.D from Toronto. She taught at the University of Toronto and at Cornell. On retirement from the University of Manitoba, she was appointed Professor Emeritus of English. Margaret Stobie is the author of *Frederick Philip Grove* and of articles and reviews for journals that include *The Beaver, Canadian Literature, Queen's Quarterly, and Tamarack Review.*